A Garland Series

OUTSTANDING DISSERTATIONS IN THE

FINE ARTS

Dedication

For my parents

Studies
on Vasari's Architecture

Leon George Satkowski

Garland Publishing, Inc., New York & London

1979

Library of Congress Cataloging in Publication Data

Satkowski, Leon George, 1947–
    Studies on Vasari's architecture.

    (Outstanding dissertations in the fine arts)
    Based on the author's thesis, Harvard, 1977.
    Bibliography: p.
    1. Vasari, Giorgio, 1511-1574. 2. Architecture,
Renaissance--Italy. I. Title. II. Series.
NA1123.V5S27   720'.92'4   78-74377
ISBN 0-8240-3964-5

Printed in the United States of America

TABLE OF CONTENTS

i

LIST OF ABBREVIATIONS

A. Archival

ACV	Archivio della curia vescovile, Arezzo
ASA	Archivio di Stato, Arezzo
ASF	Archivio di Stato, Florence
ASM	Archivio di Stato, Mantua
ASP	Archivio di Stato, Pistoia
BNCF	Biblioteca nazionale centrale, Florence
FDL	Archive of the Fraternità dei Laici, Arezzo
LSP	Library of San Paolo fuori le mure, Rome
MKIF	Mitteilungen des Kunsthistoriches Institut in Florence
UA	Architectural drawing in Gabinetto dei disegni, Uffizi, Florence

B. Editions of Vasari's Lives

IV, 167
(example)   Vasari, Giorgio, Le vite de' più eccellenti pittori, scultori, ed architetti, ed. G. Milanesi, 9 vols., Florence, 1909, (photo-reprinted Florence, 1973).

Vasari-
Barocchi   Giorgio Vasari. Le vite de più eccellenti pittori, scultori, ed architetti nelle redazioni del 1550 e 1568, ed. P. Barocchi and R. Bettarini, 5 vols., Florence, 1966.

Vasari-
Ricci   Le vite del Vasari nell' edizione del 1550, ed. C. Ricci, Milan, 1927.

iii

C. Authors and Publications

Ackerman, 1964   J. S. Ackerman, The Architecture of Michelangelo, vol. II, catalogue, London, 1964.

Ackerman, 1970   J. S. Ackerman, The Architecture of Michelangelo, rev. ed., Baltimore and Harmondsworth, 1970.

Bargiacchi, 1890   L. Bargiacchi, Tempio e Opera dell' Umiltà in Pistoia, Pistoia, 1890.

Barocchi, 1956-1957   P. Barocchi, "Il Vasari architetto," Atti della Accademia Pontaniana (Naples), VI, 1956-1957, 113-136.

Barocchi, 1964   Vasari pittore. Milan, 1964.

Beani, 1890   G. Beani, Santa Maria dell' Umiltà, Pistoia, 1890.

Cochrane, 1973   E. Cochrane, Florence in the Forgotten Centuries, Chicago, 1973.

del Badia, 1902   J. del Badia, "Il corridore dal Palazzo Vecchio al Palazzo Pitti," Miscellanea florentina, I, 1902, 3-11.

Fanelli, 1973   G. Fanelli, firenze: architettura e città. 2 vols., Florence, 1973.

Fossi, 1967   M. Fossi. Bartolomeo Ammannati, architetto. Naples, 1967.

Fossi, 1973   M. Fossi, "La Basilica della Modonna dell' Umiltà in Pistoia. I lavori di Bartolomeo Ammannati." Atti e memorie della accademia Toscana di scienze e lettere 'La Colombaria' n.s. XXIV, 1973, 83-136.

Fossi, 1977   M. Fossi, "Il Vasari e la basilica dell' Umiltà in Pistoria," Il Vasari: Storiografo e artista. Atti del congresso internazionale nel IV centenario della morte, Florence, 1977, 127-142.

Frey I   K. Frey, Der literarisches Nachlass Giorgio Vasari's, vol. I, Munich, 1923.

Frey II   K. Frey, Der literarisches Nachlass
                           Giorgio Vasari's, vol. II, Munich,
                           1930.

Frey III   H. W. Frey, Neue Briefe, Burg b. M.,
                           1950.

Frommel, 1973   C. L. Frommel, Der Römische Palastbau
                           der Hochrenaissance (Römische
                           Forschungen der Biblioteca Hertziana,
                           XXI), 3 vols., Tubingen, 1973.

Gaye   J. Gaye, Carteggio inedito d'artisti
                           dei secoli, XIV, XV, XVI. Florence,
                           3 vols., 1839-1840.

Hartt, 1949   F. Hartt, Florentine Art Under Fire.

Heydenreich-Lotz,   L. Heydenreich and W. Lotz. Archi-
1974   tecture in Italy, 1400-1600.
                           Baltimore and Harmondsworth, 1974.

Howard, 1975   D. Howard. Jacopo Sansovino:
                           Architecture and Patronage in Re-
                           naissance Venice. New Haven and
                           London, 1975.

JSAH   Journal of the Society of Architec-
                           tural Historians.

Lessmann, 1975   J. Lessmann, Studien zu einer
                           Baumonographie der Uffizien Giorgio
                           Vasari's in Florenz, Ph.D. disserta-
                           tion, Bonn, 1975.

Sanpaolesi, 1939   P. Sanpaolesi, "Venturo Vitoni,
                           architetto pistoiese." Palladio,
                           III, 1939, 248-269.

Thieme-Becker   Allgemeines Lexicon der Bildenden
                           Kunstler. ed. U. Thieme and F.
                           Becker, 37 vols., Leipzig, 1908-1950.

Venturi, 1938-1940   A. Venturi. Storia dell' arte
                           italiana, Milan, 1938-1940, XII, ii.

Viviani-Fiorini,   D. Viviani-Fiorini, "La Badia di
1941   Arezzo e G. Vasari," Il Vasari, XII,
                           1941, 74-83.

Viviani-Fiorini,   D. Viviani-Fiorini, "La constuzione
1941-1942   delle Loggie Vasariane di Arezzo,"
                          Il Vasari, XII, 1941, 109-117, and
                          XIII, 1942, 49-36.

PREFACE

Almost any historical investigation has a complex history, and this is no exception. My interest in Vasari was first whetted during my study in the College of Architecture at Cornell University. This was mainly due to the interest and teaching of Colin Rowe whose belief that the Uffizi was an example of Urban Design of the highest order provided an introduction to Vasari. Over the course of several years my own interests and perceptions about Vasari's work changed as I became more familiar with the architectural and political background of 16th Century Florence, and if I do not discuss "Mannerism" in the body of the text, I can hope that he will not be disappointed.

In Italy, Professor Henry A. Millon, formerly Director of the American Academy in Rome, was unending in his tactical help in starting this study. With his aid I obtained access to the archives of the Fraternità dei Laici and of the Curia vescoville, both in Arezzo and necessary for any study of the Loggia and Badia respectively. Professor Millon also suggested that I give a talk on the Loggia at Convention of the Society of Architectural Historians in Los Angeles during February, 1977, and this experience led to many helpful revisions on that

chapter. His friend and colleague, Professor Craig Hugh
Smyth, Director of the Harvard Center for Renaissance
Studies at Villa I Tatti provided useful criticism and in-
formation on Vasari the painter.

Numerous residents of Tuscany provided useful help
for a stranger delving into the mysteries of archives and
buildings. Professor Luigi Borgia, formerly Director of
the Archivio di Stato in Arezzo, introduced me to the
archive of the Fraternità de Laici in Arezzo, which then
was closed for reorganization. The archive is located
within the offices of the Fraternità, and the staff of
that organization went to the extraordinary length of
actually giving me my own office for study during my entire stay in Italy. The free access to the documents
meant that immense amounts of time were saved during my
daily trips to Arezzo. Similarly, Don Salvatore Pieri,
the keeper of the Archivio della Curia vescovile, allowed
me an equal amount of freedom in my work. In Florence,
Arch. Francesco Gurrieri of the Soprintendenza degli
Monumenti arranged for numerous visits to the cupola in
Pistoia. Professor Ugo Procacci also arranged for several
visits to the Corridoio. Gino Corti transcribed the letters
in Chapter IV, and Professor Anthony Molho of Brown University provided additional help with some difficult
documents.

Helpful colleagues make any study more enjoyable and

worthwhile, not to say more rich through their insights.
It has been a particular pleasure to work with Johanna
Lessmann, whose dissertation on the Uffizi for Bonn is a
model of scholarship. I shall remain eternally grateful
for numerous conversations on Vasari architetto which took
place in Florence and Braunschweig, and her generosity included an important document on the Loggia for which she
had no need. In fact, her assistance included finding me
a livable apartment in Florence, coincidentally the same
one in which she lived for several years.

Numerous colleagues provided help on several occasions, and their lively discussions became fora for ideas.
Particularly important in this respect is Professor Edmund
Pillsbury, now the Director of the Yale Center for British
Art. His introduction to Vasari drawings was an initiation
into a field once foreign to my interests, and we freely
shared the results of our forays into archives in Arezzo
and Florence. Others who listened to my often ill-formed
ideas were Professors Caroline Elam, Marcia Hall, Nicholas
Adams, John Pinto, Richard Tuttle, and Mr. Andrew Morrogh.
I can only hope that my study provides adequate compensation for their efforts and patience.

Any useful study in the field of Architectural History
requires graphic documentation of the highest order. The
draftsmanship of Mr. Lee Jablin has made aspects of the
Loggia in Arezzo and the cupola in Pistoia more interesting

than I had ever hoped, and Joseph Marra's drawing of the
Corridoio was executed with considerable precision and
care. Jeffrey Stark turned my cloudy and scratched nega-
tives into clear photographic prints.

Professor John Coolidge has maintained an interest
in Vasari ever since his own pioneering work on the Villa
Giulia, and he provided wise counsel as well as numerous
ideas on several occasions. If the ideas in this study
are interesting, lively, new, and written in a clear and
readable prose, then it is due to the teaching and counsel
of Professor James S. Ackerman. I cannot think of all of
the ways in which he has encouraged my research on Vasari;
suffice it to say his example has forced me not only to
rethink my ideas but also to revise my own style of writing.
If the ideas contained within are incoherent, or even incorrect, then the fault is mine. If the ideas are written
down at all, then it is due to the generosity of the Fine
Arts Department and the Graduate School of Harvard University who allowed me two years of research in Italy. The
fact that my graduate study was begun is due to the generosity of the late Isaac and Edith Kingsbury, whose fund
has supported the education of numerous art history students at Harvard, including myself.

This study is a slightly revised and corrected version of the dissertation which I presented to Harvard University in June, 1977. This was necessitated by two factors.

First, additional information on Vasari's architecture has
appeared in the last two years (namely the publication of
the Acts of the 1974 Vasari Congress and an entire issue
of Studi e documenti d'architettura devoted to Vasari),
and this has been acknowledged in the text and notes.
Second, some errors of typography and grammar had to be
corrected, and this provided the opportunity to clarify
some of my arguments. Some paragraphs have been re-written,
and the order of presentation of material in the first two
chapters has been changed, but the real substance of the
dissertation has not been altered. Professor Howard
Saalman read Chapter I, and his suggestions have been in-
corporated into the text. In any case, the information
and interpretations presented in this study correspond
almost exactly to the thesis, and hence it conforms fully
to the spirit of Garland Publications' Outstanding Dis-
sertations in the History of Art.

Finally, I wish to extend my thanks to Syracuse University for aid in the preparation of this study. The
typing of the manuscript, so admirably executed by Mrs.
Joyce Bell, was made possible by a grant-in-aid from Dr.
Volker Weiss, our Vice President for Research and Graduate
Affairs. I am also obliged to Werner Seligmann, Dean of
the School of Architecture, for his continuing interest and
support of this and other projects.

Syracuse, New York
17 May 1979

INTRODUCTION

The name of Giorgio Vasari (1511-1574) is known to all
art historians. The Uffizi, certainly one of the most important museums in the world, is housed in a building designed by him. Vasari's Le vite de' più eccellenti scultori,
pittori, ed architetti, first published in 1550 and then re-
issued in a revised and amplified form in 1568, is a standard
reference work for Italian Renaissance Art. Italian writers
consider it one of the most important documents of their
literary heritage, surely to Vasari's countrymen almost as
famous as the works of Dante or Boccaccio. As a painter,
Vasari completed commissions throughout Italy, and in his
later years, he was in the dual service of the Pope and the
Duke of Tuscany. It is for these reasons why Vasari's fame
as a writer and painter has eclipsed his reputation as an
architect.

Vasari's career as a painter is well known and adequately served by scholarly study.[1] His eclectic education
combined training in the Florentine shops with study under
diverse artists like Michelangelo, Bandinelli, Sarto, Rosso,
and Salviati. Vasari's study took him to Pisa, Bologna,
and Rome even before his emergence as an independent artist
in the early 1530's. During the next two decades he was

1

one of the most active personalities in Italian Art, for his artistic career took him to such relatively distant places as Venice and Naples. After the mid 1550's, Vasari spent more time in his native Tuscany than outside of it. This coincided with the commissions to renovate the Palazzo Vecchio in Florence and to decorate the Sala Grande. Although Vasari had already completed several large scale decorations (particularly the Sala dei Cento Giorni in the Cancelleria, Rome), the sheer bulk of art which Vasari had to execute meant that he had to develop an almost formula-like style which could be easily executed by numerous assistants. While some of Vasari's large painted decorations are uninspiring, his contribution to history as artistic entrepreneur disarms further criticism by paving the way for the development of 17th Century court artists like Bernini.

Vasari's architectural career is directly related to political fortunes of the new Tuscan State under Duke Cosimo I de' Medici. In 1527, the Florentine Republic had been restored as a consequence of the loss of Medici fortunes during the Sack of Rome. Its base, however, was feeble and weak, and by 1530 the Medici had control of Florence once again. Shortly after the Siege of Florence in 1530, Allessandro de' Medici was named Duke of the Florentine Republic. Internecine feuds precluded any possibility of a firm and just rule, and in 1537 the Duke was assassinated. His cousin, Cosimo, ascended to the position of Duke at the rather young age of

17. Cosimo's fortune was somewhat better, but he still had
to fight off the personal ambitions of his advisors. In
terms of construction, this meant that the borders of the
State had to be secure before any large-scale commissions
could be undertaken in the cities. Cosimo wisely realized
that stability was a prerequisite to political survival, and
consequently funds were spent for fortifications at the edge
of his Duchy rather than on civic architecture inside his
domain.[2]

True consolidation was finally achieved in 1556 when
Cosimo   triumphed in the Sienese War. The last threat
to his rule was removed by military action, additional
wealth was to be gained from the subject territory, and
perhaps most important of all, Cosimo was now a mature and
experienced ruler and administrator. The consequences of
this victory are easily apparent--Cosimo's fate was now secure enough to embellish the cities which he ruled. In
Florence, there had been some renewal and construction before the victory over the Sienese, most notably Tasso's
Mercato Nuovo (1547-1551), but all of the major projects
were still to come. Cosimo indeed needed a new set of architectural symbols for a new kind of political state. Had not
Cosimo vanquished the Sienese forces under the command of
Piero Strozzi, the Uffizi might never have been built, nor
would have Cosimo been able to afford a residence as large
and luxurious as Ammannati's addition to the Palazzo Pitti.
Most of all, Giorgio Vasari, who had built little before the

mid 1550's, might not have had the opportunity to become an architect of distinction.

Vasari's fame as an architect was not confined to Tuscany. In the Quattro Libri, Andrea Palladio called Vasari "un architetto rarissimo," but this was done in gratitude for the Vicentine's inclusion in the Lives and possibly without first-hand knowledge of Vasari's buildings in Tuscany.[3] After Michelangelo's death in 1564, Vasari was called upon to render judgement on the completion of St. Peter's, but his response was only that the master's design should be followed.[4] By 1570, Martino Bassi chose Vasari (along with Vignola, Palladio, and the Mantauan architect Giovanni Bertrani) to render criticism in a dispute with Pellegrino Tibaldi on the perspective of a relief of the Annunciation which was to be placed over the North Door of the Duomo in Milan.[5] Another issue was the design of the "Tempietto" (actually a crypt-like space under the proposed choir) but Vasari's hastily written reply concentrated on the pictorial aspects of the former while all but ignoring the architecture of the latter.[6]

Vasari's architectural star seems to have fallen in the centuries immediately after his death. Baglione mentions that Vasari worked in architecture as well as painting, but he failed to name the buildings which were completed.[7] Apparently, Baldinucci never even included a biography of Vasari in his Notizie de' professori del disegno. In the 18th Century, Francesco Milizia's avowed intention to cure the

the faulty use of classical orders in architectural design
led to an uneven appraisal of Vasari's completed projects.
In the Lives of the Celebrated Architects, Milizia showed
his classical bias when he compared the Villa Giulia (which
he thought was designed totally by Vasari) to Rome after the
invasion of the barbarians.[8] In contrast, the Uffizi fared
somewhat better, being a building which, to Milizia's mind,
was one of the most handsome structures in Florence.

The foundations for a critical study of Vasari's
architecture were laid in the 19th Century. Gaye's
Cartegio inedito d'artisti dei secoli XIV-XVI included more
than one hundred forty letters from Vasari's correspondence
which were of use to scholars. His buildings found a
sympathetic critic in Jacob Burckhardt, whose description
of the Uffizi in the Cicerone combined a feeling for the
architect's expressive language with an appreciation of
the functions which the building originally contained.[9]
While Burckhardt discussed only one other structure by
Vasari (the Arezzo Badia, which, at that time, was only a
traditional attribution), Amico Ricci added the Loggia to
the architect's list of completed projects. In other
matters, Ricci was less perceptive than his illustrious predecessor, referring to Vasari's style as one which was not
to be imitated.[10]

The graphic documentation of Vasari's architecture
was not ignored. In the late 19th Century several valuable
collections of plans, sections, and elevations of buildings

throughout Italy were published. Grandjean de Montigny and
Famin, the Tuscan equivalents to Letarouilly, provided the
first published measured drawings of the Uffizi, but scarcely
little else.[11] Laspeyres was somewhat better.[12] His drawings of the Badia are correct and still useful, unlike
Grandjean's illustration of the Madonna dell' Umilità in
Pistoia which failed to show Vasari's dome! Their historical
information usually repeated whatever was available in the
guidebooks, but this was not the case with the greatest
publication of this kind, Steegman and Geymuller's Die
Architektur der Renaissance in Toskana.[12] At the time,
their effort must have been monumental--they collected all
of the known factual information on Vasari's buildings,
assembled an ouevre of works, and illustrated them with
what are often still the only published drawings on these
structures. The visual strength of this publication was
also its shortcoming, for its format dictated little space
to the analysis and history of the buildings themselves.
Like all of its predecessors, it failed to place Vasari's
architecture in the matrix of history, for value judgments
were always scrupulously avoided. Nevertheless, their publication remained for many years the only introduction to
Florentine Renaissance architecture.

Twentieth Century writers faced a critical dilemma in
their approach to Vasari. A comprehensive stylistic study
of Vasari's buildings could have been undertaken--surely
enough material was available to scholars--but for many

years Cinquecento architecture in Florence remained out of
vogue, and no really serious studies were begun in this field.
Yet Vasari's letters were known to exist in numerous locations in Tuscany, and access to documents in the Florentine
archives was relatively easy. It was truly a resource to
be mined, and this was done under the direction of Karl
Frey, resulting in the monumental, three volume _Literarische_
Nachlass.[13] Sometime incorrect or incomplete, often frus-
trating, but always necessary, the publication of _Nachlass_
is a _sine qua non_ of Vasari studies, since it collects most
basic information on all of Vasari's artistic projects from
which all other studies must start. Yet this publication
never brought about any cross-fertilization between history,
the buildings, and style--all later studies deal only with
single aspects of Vasari's architecture. Dorini[14] and
Viviani-Fiorini[15] resolved some difficult problems of attribution and documentation on the Uffizi, the Badia, and the
Loggia in Arezzo. Two major monographic articles dealt with
the buildings. Venturi's chapter on Vasari in the _Storia_
dell' arte italiana includes much of Frey's research and
includes a useful chronological table of Vasari's architectural activities, but its comments on style and development
were perfunctory, and the tendency to be inclusive in attribution often led to misinformation.[16] More correct but
less accessible than Venturi is a study written by Paola
Barocchi in an obscure Neapolitan scholarly journal which was
the first attempt to renew interest in Vasari's architecture.[17]

Its strengths reflect Barocchi's concerns for art theory and precise documentation, while its judgements on style and significance are scarcely an advance on Venturi.

In contrast to these studies, writers who were concerned with Mannerism dealt exclusively with Vasari's architectural style. On the whole, the literature on Mannerist architecture can be both misleading and helpful. Most studies which relied on the excessive periodization of style isolated superficial characteristics of Vasari's buildings. In almost every case, the Uffizi is cited as an example of raumflucht. To make their theories credible, critics were preoccupied with abstract concepts of form and space, and sometimes this created an undesirable separation of the building from its historical context. At its worst, this lead to incorrect characterizations which saw the Uffizi as a narrow courtyard like a giardino segreto![18]

On the other hand, any critique of Mannerist architecture should not ignore the observations of individual authors; the baby must not be thrown out with the bath. The most successful writers avoided dogmatic and watertight definitions of style, and often their insights bridged several disciplines. For example, several critics have rightly recognized the "painterly" aspects of Vasari's buildings. Hager provided a flexible definition of Mannerism which stressed the variety of possible solutions during the mid-16th Century, accepting the works of Michelangelo as one extreme and those of Palladio as the other.[19] Dealing with

the political background of Mannerism, Berti was among the
first scholars to note that Florentine buildings often em-
bodied the values of the Tuscan State, and this lead to
the discovery of convincing formal and typological parallels
with projects in Venice.[20]

Two additional studies deserve consideration. Erwin
Panofsky's magisterial "The First Page of Vasari's Libro"
does not specifically deal with Vasari's architecture, but
in the author's consideration of the Gothic as seen by
Renaissance artists, Vasari's opinions on stylistic con-
sistency are clearly articulated.[21] This question often
became important in the designs of his buildings. Ugo
Procacci's article on Cinquecento architecture in and near
Arezzo provided a broad background to Vasari's projects
in his home city.[22]

Most recently, a German dissertation written by
Johanna Lessmann under the direction of Herbert von Einem
and Christoph Frommel is in many ways a landmark in Vasari
studies.[23] It is a monograph on the Uffizi, and its sections on the urban planning of that famous building and on
the typology of the office structure provide new insights
into Vasari's position in Italian architecture. It is the
result of more than five years of research in Florentine
archives, and its documentary appendix provides much useful
information on building administration in Tuscany. Given
the immense amount of effort which was expended on the Uffizi,
the section on Vasari's other buildings is summary though it

contains other new perceptions on the complex web of sources
in Vasari's architecture.

Despite these achievements, no study has ever done full
justice to the wide range of Vasari's architectural interests.
His projects included building renovations, theatrical design,
temporary civic decorations, engineering works, and fortifications. To these must be added an impressive number of
paintings and decorations with significant architectural
backgrounds. Unfortunately, many of these commissions were
never executed, and we know of them only through Vasari's
letters or his autobiography in the Lives. Documentation
of several projects is still fragmentary at best, and this
is complicated by the almost total lack of original architectural drawings from Vasari's shop. Furthermore, Vasari
was peripherally involved in some projects (the Villa Giulia,
the renovation of the Pitti Palace) which were designed and
executed by others, and in these cases it would be hopeless
to define his role in their conception and execution without
further evidence. For these reasons a complete monograph
on Vasari architetto seemed neither desirable nor feasible.

Given the complex nature of Vasari's career, a study
of his four most important completed architectural commissions
other than the Uffizi provided the vehicle for contributing
to this relatively unstudied area. Each of the buildings
under consideration--the cupola of the Madonna dell' Umilità
in Pistoia, the Badia in Arezzo, the Corridoio in Florence,
and the Loggia in Arezzo--is studied in terms of building

type, urban design, and patronage. A final chapter concludes
with an assessment of Vasari's architectural style relative
to his theory, criticism, and completed buildings. Documents and other materials relative to the history of the
projects are found in the Appendix. While new documents
were uncovered during the preparation of this study, they
have not narrowly circumscribed my investigation. On the
other hand, I hope to suggest some of the social and political forces which brought these buildings into creation,
affected their designs, and supported their continued use.

The historical setting of Vasari's practice has already been mentioned, and much of it has come to light in
recent years, particularly in the lively writings of historians like Cochrane and Spini.[24] Vasari himself was aware
how these forces could affect the form of buildings, for he
stated in the Lives that an architect must respond to the
needs of the patron and to the sites where projects are
located (I, 145). While many other Renaissance artists pro-
fessed the same goals, Vasari's buildings responded directly
to the problems of patronage and urban design--they are
creative solutions to the pragmatic issues faced by an
architect for the Tuscan State. In other words, Vasari's
buildings are more complex and rich than just a homage to
Michelangelo's Florentine buildings.[25]

I

THE CUPOLA OF THE MADONNA DELL' UMILITÀ IN PISTOIA

> E stata similemente mia cura . . . la tribuna, o
> vero cupola, della Madonna dell' Umilità in Pistoia,
> che e opera importantissima.
>> Giorgio Vasari (VII, 704)

The cupola of the Madonna dell' Umilità dominates the skyline of Pistoia (Figs. 1-3). It was one of the largest domes built in 16th Century Italy, but it is also one of the least known.[1] It was technically the most difficult of Vasari's architectural projects, and it is certainly the least appreciated.[2] Vasari's solution--a double shell dome with a complex system of internal ribs--was placed over the octagonal drum of an existing church built largely by the Pistoiese architect Ventura Vitoni, and soon Vasari's patrons feared for its collapse. It elicited criticism from Bartolomeo Ammannati, who later made substantial repairs to its fabric. In the 19th Century, local architects continued to denounce it as structurally incompetent and visually offensive, and recently it has been called "a confusion of spatial values."[3]

The subsequent fate of the cupola's fabric has obscured any discussion of the history and significance of

Vasari's design. The dome was by no means structurally perfect, and its problems were shared by other architects as well. Nor was it a separate event in the development of domed structures during the Renaissance, for the sources form of its structural system are easily found in Florence. Its visual effects, unusual construction, and unique insights into Vasari's architectural style have never been discussed together. Since the cupola is neither well known nor readily accessible in the literature of architectural history, it first requires an adequate description.

The church of the Madonna dell' Umilità was begun in 1495 to house a miracle working image of the Virgin, and the design provided by Giuliano da Sangallo between 1492-94 was executed by the Pistoiese architect Ventura Vitoni.[4] The plan of the church (Fig. 4), in fact, pays homage to one of Giuliano's most successful designs, the Sacristy of Santo Spirito in Florence (1492-94). In concept, both designs are nearly identical--a domed, octagonal space entered through a disproportionately large vestibule. The Pistoiese church, however, is nearly twice the size of its Florentine counterpart (the diameters of their octagonal spaces are 12.3 meters and 21.0 meters respectively). Since the church was a public commission, Vitoni certainly felt that it should exert a powerful in-fluence on the skyline of Pistoia. Consequently it was

given a more prominent profile, making the proportion of
its height to diameter closer to 5:4 than the simple 1:1
ratio used in the Florentine sacristy.

The construction of the church was hindered by frequent interruptions.[5] The bitter political feuds between
local families common throughout Pistoia's history stopped
construction in 1496-1497 and in 1499-1502. Work was renewed again on a full scale in 1509 when the octagon was
begun. By 1522, the year of Vitoni's death, the vestibule
had been completed and the octagonal drum had been built
up to the entablature of the third level, twenty-five
meters above the level of the floor. No work was done
after this date; it even lacked a temporary wooden roof
to keep out the rain.[6] An interesting hypothesis accounts
for the unusual plan of the church. The over-sized vestibule was probably built on the foundations of the earlier
church which housed the miraculous frescoed image of the
Virgin, and religious services continued to be held there
until the consecration of the high altar in December,
1582.[7] In 1561, the project was renewed again, but now
under the patronage of Duke Cosimo I.[8] By 1568, the cupola
was substantially complete,[9] and in the following year
Vasari was paid for the completion of the structure.[10]

Vasari's own account in the Lives (IV, 166-167) corresponds to these facts. Vasari places the blame for the
difficulties on Vitoni alone. Calling the Pistoiese
architect a "falegname," Vasari claimed that Vitoni was

inexperienced in the construction of large buildings, thus
having contributed to the insecurity of the church in
Pistoia by not providing enough building mass to receive
the weight of the dome. To prepare the octagonal drum
for the construction of the dome Vasari reinforced the
six chapels with supporting arches 30 cm. in thickness
underneath the openings left by Vitoni. The arches join-
ing the octagon to the choir and to the vestibule were
left unaltered; any construction in these locations would
have compromised the size of the chancel and the view
towards the main altar. To compensate for any outward
movement by the walls of the drum, Vasari added pairs of
tie-rods at East and West corners of the second and third
levels of the octagon. This is precisely where Vitoni's
structure would have been weakest due to the lack of any
kind of buttressing; the mass of the vestibule and of the
choir contributed to the equilibrium of the building on
the North and the South.

Vasari's visible contributions began at a level
25m. above the floor (Fig. 5). Eight braccia (approximately 4.5m) were added to the drum, thus creating a
fourth story in elevation. This corresponds to a change
in material of the building's fabric from rubble masonry
to brick wall construction. The exterior faces (Fig. 6)
were designed as three panels equal in size and defined
by one of Vasari's favorite motifs, strapwork modling
with triglyphs assuming a function similar to column

capitals. Interest in the otherwise blank side panels is heightened by small recesses in the brick-work. The interior faces (Fig. 7) were designed in a similar three-part system, but here the strapwork dividers are capped by consoles. Originally, this zone included circular windows in the central panels of both exterior and interior walls, but these openings were later closed during Ammannati's renovations to the building.[11]

The structural means which Vasari employed are complex (Fig. 8). The dome is built with two brick shells roughly 95 cm. apart, the outer one 90 cm. thick, the inner one 80 cm.[12] Their semi-circular profiles were determined from a single center of curvature for all eight vaults, and the shells were constructed with bricks set parallel to the radius of curvature, all 43 mm. high and set in mortar courses 12 mm. thick. In the upper part of the dome, the 95 cm. dimension is often reduced by a few centimeters due to the uneven settling of the outer shell. Inside the dome, two ledges rise against the inner and outer shells to points respectively 4.3 m. and 3.5 m. above the entablature of the fourth level. The function of the ledges as possible buttresses can be seen in relation to location of the spring point of the dome which is 31.7 m. above floor level and 2.7 m. above the height of the fourth entablature. The spring point is clearly visible on the intrados of the dome, but on the extrados it is masked by a projecting cornice. Since both ledges rise above the spring line, the ledge of the outer shell stiffens its vault at the base while the ledge of the inner shell counteracts the forces of the inner dome by providing additional mass where the horizontal thrust of the dome would be greatest.

Three separate systems of ribs are located between the shells of the dome. A primary group of eight radial ribs run from the base of the vaults to the lantern (Rib A, Fig. 8). A secondary set of eight pairs of ribs rise from the ledges of the inner shell and run to points roughly two-thirds along the distance of the curvature (Rib B, Fig. 8). The secondary ribs do not converge at the axial center of the vaults, and if they were to be extended any further, they would collide with the radial ribs. A third set begins on the central axis of each vault where the secondary ribs stop, and they continue to the octagonal ring of the oculus (Rib C, Fig. 8).

Vasari's cupola stood, if at some times just barely, to judge by the vehemence of the criticism which was heaped upon it.

Its defects became visible shortly after its completion. In 1575, the Deputies of the Opera of the Madonna dell' Umilità passed a resolution to begin repairs on their new cupola, and shortly thereafter Bartolomeo Ammannati was named as the architect to superintend the new work.[13] Although the exact extent of the damage is not known, the problems of the dome were complicated by the fact that it

had been struck by lightning only a year earlier.[14] The
crack was repaired, but other difficulties appeared three
more times during Ammannati's tenure as architect to the
Madonna. In July, 1577, a crack was described as beginning at the architrave of the central panel of Vasari's
fourth level and travelling upwards as far as the pyramid
of the lantern. Its width at some points was the thickness of a large book, and from other documents it was
most likely on the inner shell.[15] In July, 1578, new
cracks were discovered in the cupola,[16] and in June, 1584,
they reappeared after several years of apparent stability.[17] Although a book of payments and a voluminous correspondence exist for the repairs made to Vasari's cupola,
they do not always give a clear indication of what
Ammannati actually did. The following points are the
known alterations to the fabric of the cupola:

A. The addition of four iron chains (cerchi
   di ferro) around the exterior of the dome
   near its base, each approximately 4.5 cm.
   square in section.[18] A fifth chain was
   added by Jacopo Lafri in 1617.

B. The walling-up of the tondo windows which
   Vasari built in the exterior and interior
   walls of the fourth level.[19]

C. Repairs were made to the lantern.[20] Several
   letters indicate that Ammannati had to
   "rasettare" the lantern, but, unfortunately,

there is not indication of what this involved. In 1581, a "pilastro" (lantern
pier) was rebuilt.[21]

D. The exterior surface of the dome was substantially rebuilt. The payment book
shows that there were numerous payments
for "mezzane" (roof tiles) throughout the
entire period of construction.

The long and costly process of reconstruction brought
adverse criticism to Vasari's design. It is important to
note, however, that Ammannati never blamed Vasari directly
for the damage to the cupola, and only on one occasion did
he make an assessment of the cause of all the difficulties.
In a letter of 1577, he spoke about the cupola in general
terms.[22]

> Le cose (sono) mal fatte, e pesi (sono) mal
> posati in aria: il tenervegli a più per la
> Gratia di Dio che saper degli huomini.

His successor, Jacopo Lafri, placed all blame squarely
on the shoulders of the cupola's designer. He first chastised Vasari for not having read Book IX of Alberti's De
re aedificatoria where architects are advised not to change
designs already set by their predecessors.[23] In his opinion,
Vasari's design was faulty: the dome was too large, ex-
ceeding the capacity of the drum to support its weight.
Lafri noticed Vasari's free use of architectural orders
(the placement of the Doric above the Corinthian). Invoking
Vitruvian terminology, Lafri claimed that the designer had

destroyed all commodious elements and had left the un-
commodious in their place. His criticism was, to a large
degree, an attempt to vindicate Vitoni's bad reputation
as seen by Vasari, and consequently he often attempted
to stretch points to his advantage. He explained Vasari's
opprobious designation of Vitone as merely a "fallegname"
as an honorable term for anyone who presented a "modello"
for a building, and his failure to complete the dome is
ascribed to a lack of funds and not Vitoni's lack of technical expertise.[24] While noticing important factors like
the inferior quality of the bricks and brickwork in the
cupola, Lafri stubbornly asserted that the extraordinary
weights of the lantern and the cupola were the major
causes of all damage.

However, it must be said that some of Vasari's problems were inherited from Vitoni. The numerous students
and critics of Vasari's cupola have never drawn attention
to the fact that the shape of the drum is far from a
perfect octagon. In the construction of any polygonal
building there is always the chance of error--even the
octagonal drum of Florence Cathedral is not perfect in
its geometry--but the differences are miniscule and without any effect on the structure of the building. Not so
in the case of the Madonna dell' Umilità; all sides of
the octagonal drum are different in length, running from
8.37 to 8.91 meters.[25] Of these, the longest is the South
side adjacent to the vestibule. Under these conditions,

it is impossible to achieve static equilibrium. The
effect of the weight of the dome on an unequally bisected
angle can be easily visualized; the mass of the dome
would move in the direction of least resistance. The
tendency of the dome to rotate would be evident even during
construction, and this was enhanced by the liberal application of mortar for the masonry joints, thus leading to
the slow setting of the entire fabric. The rotation is
most visible at the level of the lantern where the octagonal
oculus is in an eccentric relationship with the geometry
of the drum (Fig. 9). On the exterior, the clockwise
rotation of the ribs is clearly apparent from the base of
the lantern, whose vertical supports, too, are spaced in
an irregular manner (Fig. 10).

No Renaissance dome was satisfactory in all technical respects, since other architects did not avoid the
structural difficulties similar to those which Vasari
faced in the design of the cupola in Pistoia. There is
no way of knowing the exact nature of all repairs made
on Italian domes over the last four centuries, but it is
indeed fortunate that Giovanni Poleni, a Paduan mathema-
tician and scholar in the service of Pope Benedict XIV,
made a survey of corrective measures which were applied
to several domed churches prior to the massive repairs
on St. Peter's begun in 1743. Unlike Lafri, who could
see structural deformation only in terms of mass and
weight, Poleni observed that a number of complex factors

caused the widespread cracking on the Roman dome.[26] Disregarding external causes like lightning and earthquakes, he noted five factors which could be applicable to Vasari's cupola--imperfection in workmanship, uneven quality of materials, settling of foundations, and the effects of weather and gravity. Of these, the first two had already been noted by Lafri, and the remaining three played important roles in the ensuing problems of the cupola. It would have been difficult for Vasari to gauge the strength of foundations which had been built more than half a century earlier. Moreover, the ground into which they had been placed was susceptible to periodic inundations from the Apennines, often trapping water between layers of clay and thus weakening the bearing capacity of the soil.[27] Any major change in strength of the subsoil would cause movement in the foundations, thereby causing radial cracking on the surface of the cupola and on the drum. Though the foundations of the Madonna dell' Umilità have not been subjected to scientific study, it is not impossible to think that they were a contributing factor to the church's decay. The cracking in Brunelleschi's cupola in Florence was attributed to similar causes in the late 17th Century.[28]

Cracking is also caused by the expansion and contraction of the dome due to changes in temperature and humidity. Like everything else, construction materials expand and contract according to changes in the temperature of the environment around them, and this would be exaggerated in Pistoia due to its position at the foot of the Apennine Mountains. This type of cracking would occur most easily in masonry buildings where there would be no device such as changes in material along which breaks could occur; in the case of a masonry dome they would occur radially and in an irregular pattern. The lack of an effective "expansion joint" hindered the designers of domes, and it is no small surprise that all later cracks in Vasari's cupola were discovered in the Summer when it would be at its greatest state of expansion.

The problem of gravity, however, was unavoidable. Recent analyses confirm the fact that Vasari's dome was indeed too heavy for its base, yet it was probably statically secure after its initial deformation, thus rendering Ammannati's iron chains unnecessary.[29] To assign Vasari the entire blame for the structural difficulties of the cupola in Pistoia would be unjustified in terms of 16th Century dome design since Renaissance architects lacked both a theory of dome design[30] and the scientific ability to mathematically compute the statics of the buildings which they designed.[31] The former meant that there could be no consensus on how a dome would be designed and supported; the latter meant that they could not be sure if the dome would stand at all.

Renaissance architects approached structural problems in a non-scientific manner, and two methods were employed:

analogy and visualization. The analogous method meant
that architects could adapt the structure of a model which
spans and enclosed roughly the same space--e.g., the dome
of St. Peter's is approximately the same in span and structure as Brunelleschi's Cupola in Florence; similarly the
Pistoia church resembles the Florentine Baptistry, and
so on. In smaller domes the structural problems were
minimized because a relatively small amount of mass could
withstand lateral thrusts. The analogy to the Florentine
Cathedral cupola was good policy for larger domes since
the notable success of Brunelleschi could insure a modicum
of safety. It must be noted that this was the exception
and not the rule in Renaissance dome design. Relatively
few large domes were built in the Cinquecento; major examples such as S. Maria della Consolazione in Todi and
Sangallo the Younger's and Michelangelo's schemes for S.
Giovanni dei Fiorentini in Rome were either completed
much later or not built at all.

The ability to visualize structural forces at work
was a necessary tool for all architects. Michelangelo's
conception of the structure of the cupola of St. Peter's
was mainly poetic and evocative; his internal ribs seemed
to emphasize their muscular function in relation to the
colossal pilasters on the side of the church.[32] Though
Michelangelo (and della Porta, too) had a coherent vision
of the forces at work, they lacked a sufficient grasp on
the technical devices which could make their vision a

reality. The gravest defect at St. Peter's was the role
of the buttress on the exterior of the drum, since it
offered little strength to withstand the lateral forces
exerted by the dome. Vasari, on the other hand, reacted
to the structure of the Madonna dell' Umilità with visual
acuity but without a coherent set of principles to guide
him. The addition of tie-rods to the exposed corners of
the third and fourth levels of the drum and the construction of the supporting arches were clear reactions which
show how he thought the building would deform. The makeshift character of the internal structure of the Pistoia
cupola can be found in other churches, most notably in
Alessi's S. Maria del Carignano in Genoa were transverse
arches connecting the two shells of the main dome are
placed in an irregular pattern.[33] Though employing the
visual and analogous methods could not necessarily guarantee the stability of any dome, a consistent application
of their principles might have avoided much structural
difficulty.

Vasari and his contemporaries ignored the simple
geometric formulae with which Medieval and Renaissance
architects could erect a logically structured building.
The inability of Renaissance theorists to give a practical
exposition of structural principles is understandable
since the human figure, often the basis for the design
in Renaissance architectural theory, is inapplicable to
the principles of dome and vault construction. The

failure of the dome, in reality, a failure of method where the intuitive judgement used by Renaissance designers failed to indicate that a structural system lacked the necessary mass to withstand both weight and outward thrust. The repairs and difficulties encountered after the completion of the cupola in Pistoia should be considered not the exception but the norm in 16th Century dome design.

In designing the structure of cupola in Pistoia, Vasari faced a wide range of possible solutions. Renaissance architects never reached a consensus on the structural design of double shell domes, and in general, each design was conditioned by two factors: traditional examples and the size of the span which it had to cover. No architect outside of the Veneto seized upon the tradition of a masonry cupola surmounted by a trussed, wooden structure effectively creating a second shell. On the other hand, Brunelleschi's cupola (Fig. 11) exerted considerable influence on other designers, most notably on Michelangelo's and della Porta's designs for St. Peter's (Fig. 12).[34] In both cases their double shells are separated by a series of radial ribs traversing the distance from the lantern to the drum. The shaping of the ribs varies with each example: Brunelleschi's supports gradually taper inward as they approach the oculus, while della Porta's decrease their size in two stages in the manner of a Gothic buttress. Moreover, the horizontal ribs introduced by Brunelleschi kept the outer shell

self-supporting during construction while the spina pesce
method of bricklaying made centering unnecessary.[35] None
of his technical devices were required in later domes,
and in comparison they appear to be less structurally
sophisticated. The presence of monolithic Antique domes
encouraged their design in Rome (Santa Maria della Pace),
while Florentine domes were often smaller and built with
two shells (Santo Spirito).

Despite the numerous Renaissance examples available
to Vasari, Medieval examples suggested the structural
design of the dome in Pistoia. The span which he had to
vault was only half the diameter of Brunelleschi's
Florentine cupola, and common sense told Vasari that his
dome did not have to be structurally complex to cover a
comparatively short distance.[36] In terms of both its
size and structural principles, the true prototype for
Vasari's design was the dome of the Florentine Baptistry
(Figs. 13, 14). It was the only domed structure which
enclosed roughly the same volume, and its interior span
(25 m.) was comparable to Pistoia (21 m.) Moreover,
Vitoni's octagonal drum, too, recalled Medieval structural
principles. It is a massive double shell structure in its
own right, and its inner and outer walls function to a
great degree independently of each other. The only structural bonds between the two surfaces are the horizontal
floor levels; the remaining floor space is used for

circulation.[37]   In principle this reflects earlier
Florentine buildings like the Baptistry or the Campanile
of the Duomo.[38]   The Baptistry also suggested to Vasari
that the walls of the drum should be continued into a
double shell dome, since any attempt to build a single
shell dome on the cupola's broad, hollow base would have
created an awkward structure between the parts of the
structure, thereby endangering the stability of the entire fabric.   Although it is possible that Vitoni could
have planned a Pantheon-like dome for the Madonna dell'
Umiltà (Fig. 15), Vasari's solution avoided the addition
of any unnecessary solid mass at the spring point.[39]

It is easy to understand why Vasari's design recalls the structure of the Florentine Baptistry. Vasari
had praised the predecessor of Brunelleschi's cupola for
its double vault, and, in the second edition of the Lives,
he noted that many of his contemporaries agreed with him
(I, 332). His use of a combination of radial and per-
pendicular ribs clearly derived from the Florentine example, but the specific conditions of the Pistoia design
forced Vasari to diverge significantly from his Medieval
model.   In contrast to the Baptistry dome where the coni-
cal marble roof and inner shell verge well before the
lantern, the semi-circular curvature of the Pistoia dome
required the insertion of an additional rib in the upper
part of the dome near the lantern. Also, the shells of

Vasari's dome are of a standard thickness throughout their
curvature. The advantages to this were twofold. Like the
Baptistry, it offered greater continuity with Vitoni's
thicker outer shell, and it was also easier to build than
a shell of diminishing thickness. In applying the Baptistry's principles to his structure, Vasari limited the
function of the secondary ribs to merely separating the
inner and outer shells while the primary radial ribs bore
the weight of the lantern and parts of both shells as well.
The result was a curious, hybrid dome which combined the
external appearance of Brunelleschi's cupola with the
substructure of the Florentine Baptistry. It was still
conservative by Renaissance standards, lacking the technical devices (wooden chains, stone chains, herringbone
brick pattern) which had made Brunelleschi's solution so
notable.[40] Not surprisingly, this was consistent with
Vasari's approach to architectural form which emphasized
the overall appearance of a building and minimized the
expressive characteristics of its structural supports.

The architectural revolution begun by Bramante
brought about a major change in the exterior Italian domes.[41]
Quattrocento domes, whether raised on a tambour (Florence
Cathedral) or structurally integrated to the body of the
church (S. Maria della Pace, Rome) were distinguished for
their surface and volume, and their designers emphasized
contour and outline at the expense of mass. Both in

structure and visual function they were little more than neutral envelops enclosing architectural space. In comparison to these examples, it is easy to understand why Bramante's dome made a great impression on other architects. Its stepped, semi-circular profile indicated a return to ancient models with its reference to the Pantheon, and its colonnaded drum offered a solution for treating the base in a sculptural manner. Though Bramante's structure for supporting such a heavy dome was defective in its statics, his design was not without its imitators. Antonio da Sangallo the Younger's accepted Bramante's solution in his project for St. Peter's, but he also added an additional story to his design for the dome. Michelangelo, too, was profoundly affected by Bramante; but his solution modifies the forms of the earlier design to suit more expressive ends. Like Bramante, his use of paired columns articulated the drum as an architectural element almost independent of the body of the church, but their combination with the exterior ribs creates a powerful vertical thrust unknown to the earlier master. It must be pointed out, however, that other domes constructed in the space of time beween the St. Peter's domes of Bramante and Michelangelo-della Porta were more conventional in design. That formal innovation in dome design was confined to St. Peter's is explained by the nature of the commission--the dome of the most important church in the Christian West demanded

an exposition of grandeur and majesty befitting the aspirations of the Church itself.

Vasari could scarcely adapt the innovations of St.
Peter's to his own cupola. Because of the unfeasibility
of placing massive architectural membering on Vitoni's
base, Vasari had to resort to other domes for architectural
inspiration. Once again, Vasari returned to the Florentine
Baptistry for the idea of dividing the upper level into
equally-sized framed panels. His enthusiasm for the design of the medieval building was clearly stated in the
second edition of the Lives--to him its proportions were
perfect (I, 332). Moreover, Vasari was not the only
Cinquecento architect to use the Baptistry for inspiration. Antonio da Sangallo the Younger faced the same
design problem of convincingly articulating the base or
an octagonal cupola of S. Maria di Loreto in Rome, and
a drawing for the dome which he never executed (Fig. 16)
anticipated Vasari's own design in the complex use of
panels on the exterior of the drum.

While the uppermost level of the drum derives from
the Florentine Baptistry, other details reflect the innovative spirit of Michelangelo's architecture. Vasari's
admiration for Michelangelo is legendary, but the exact
nature of his indebtedness to the master is less clear.
Vasari emphasized the planar and decorative character
of architectural members in every detail. While Vasari's

motif of a large tondo framed by rectangular panels derives from the exterior of the cupola of Florence Cathedral,
the layering of the wall into distinct, razor-sharp planes
is similar to Michelangelo's treatment of the drum in an
early sketch[42] for St. Peter's (Fig. 17), and the similarity would have been even more apparent if Ammannati had
not walled up the oculi of the central panel. Moreover,
Michelangelo created different and ingenious combinations
of architectural vocabulary for each commission; Vasari
eschewed the use of architectural orders and preferred to
employ only a very few elements in any design. Though
Vasari used Michelangelesque motifs over and over again,
he placed them in a much more orthodox context. Among
these, the most common are consoles from the ricetto of
the Laurentian Library and the triglyphs from numerous
door and window frames in Michelangelo's ouevre. In
Michelangelo's designs, such elements are employed as
visual and expressive accents; in Vasari's hands, they
are used as substitutes for the standard elements of
Vitruvian grammar. Michelangelo's own modifications of
the classical vocabulary were not architectural solecisms;
they were the results of his experiments which "broke the
bonds and chain of a way of working which had become
habitual by common usage" (VII, 193). Any perusal of
the Lives reveals Vasari's urgent demand for rules of
artistic order. It is precisely this desire for ingenious

expression within the framework of Vitruvian grammar which characterizes Vasari's approach to architectural design.

The lantern of the cupola (Fig. 18) is another example of Vasari's indebtedness to Michelangelo. It is hybrid in style, combining the upper portion of Brunelleschi's Cathedral lantern with Michelangelo's lantern for the New Sacristy at San Lorenzo (Figs. 19, 20). Again Vasari derived characteristic features from Michelangelo's design. The reverse scrolls supporting the pyramid of the lantern are direct quotes from the San Lorenzo lantern, while Vasari's blind oval windows correspond to the circular windows in the main shaft of the same model. In contrast to the highly sculptural quality of Brunelleschi's lantern, the greater planarity of Vasari's forms is apparent in every detail. Powerful scrolls are now little more than three dimensional pen strokes, deep niches have become flat panels, a malleable mass has become a brittle surface. Vasari developed a variant of Michelangelo's lantern but his characteristic decorative features are no more than a different kind of cladding around an architectural skeleton which had been invented almost 50 years earlier.[43] While Brunelleschi and Michelangelo saw their lanterns as the continuation and climax of the vertical thrust of the exterior ribs, Vasari designed his lantern to stand visually independent of the dome. Any upward force is effectively halted by the projecting cornices of the lantern's

buttresses, and beyond that point it becomes an explosion
of detail. Vasari chose architectural elements weak in
their ability to convey movement at a point where strength
was required. His conception of the lantern is basically
an exercise in planar architecture, and his refusal to design in three dimensions reveals Vasari's two dimensional
training as a painter. This was an incalculable aid in
the design of facades (the Uffizi, for instance), but it
became a hindrance to the design of an object isolated
in space. One way to measure the success of any design
is by the number of copies made from it; Vasari's lantern
had no progeny.

The decoration of the cupola's intrados reveals
another aspect of Vasari's architectural sources (Fig. 21).
When the lack of painted decoration permitted Cinquecento
architects to use architectural elements on the interior
surface of a dome, they normally adapted the system of
the Pantheon with its grid of diminishing coffers following the model of Michelangelo's New Sacristy cupola. In
his solution, Vasari reversed the structural implications
of the coffering by treating the intrados as a series of
connected geometric shapes projecting from the surface of
the cupola. In concept, this is similar to the Uffizi
loggia vault, and taken together, both examples constitute
novel variations on traditional coffering design. While
Lotz has suggested that Vasari's model for the cupola's

coffering was Michelangelo's design for San Giovanni de
Fiorentini in Rome, the history of this motif has never
been adequately explained.[44] A comparison between the
two designs (Figs. 21, 22) reveals the different solutions
achieved by both designers. Michelangelo's emphasis on
the structural continuity of the ribs contrasts radically
with the lack of support in Vasari's design. When seen
from below, not the pilasters but the void between them
continues toward the oculus in the Pistoia cupola. Moreover, the geometric shapes between the ribs are integrally
connected and thus form a decorative lattice across the
surface of the entire dome. What differentiates Vasari's
design from its Michelangelesque parallel is its direct
lineage from ancient fresco borders found in antique vault
decoration. As a painter, Vasari saw the efficacy of
decorative forms as elements of architectural design, and
consequently he transformed the ancient union between
stucco and painting into a source of the cupola's details.

Vasari certainly must have studied remains of ancient
stuccowork like the Volta degli Stucchi in the Golden
House of Nero.[45] He thought that grottesques were "dilitte-
vole" (I, 116), and their whimsical and fantastic monsters
were justified in terms of the artist's liberty for invention.[46] In some of his early fresco decorations Vasari
included grottesque elements recalling ancient painting,[47]
but his architectural vault decoration is closer to ancient

stuccowork. The transformation of ancient stucco design
into architectural details first occurred in painting at
the end of the 15th Century, and one of the earliest examples is Aeneas Piccolomini Called to Eugene IV (Siena,
Piccolomini Library) by Pinturrichio (Fig. 23), a painter
towards whom Vasari was otherwise antagonistic (III, 493-
511).[48] The coffered ceiling of the audience hall uses
the same architectural system which Vasari later employed
in Pistoia. Deriving from the stuccoes in the Golden
House, Pinturrichio's coffers have no structural function,
and a finely applied shadow line around their perimeter
emphasizes their role as applied decoration. Another example of this kind is the barrel vault painted by
Rafaellino del Garbo adjacent to the Caraffa Chapel in
Santa Maria del Popolo (Fig. 24). Never admired in the
modern literature, it was highly esteemed by Vasari and
his contemporaries (IV, 235). The reason for its favor
was probably functional and not aesthetic: it was a simple
and rationale means of dividing a surface into smaller
decorative units.

Both Vasari's personal views and his artistic practice directed him towards a more decorative solution for
architectural detail. The rectangular, oval, and tri-
angular "frames" which Vasari employed in Pistoia were
part of his artistic repertoire and reappear constantly
throughout his career, most notably in the unexecuted

designs for the del Monte chapel in San Pietro in Montorio, Rome.[49] Yet Vasari was not unique among Renaissance architects in his adoption of these forms. While the availability of ancient monuments imposed upon Roman architects a conservative attitude towards coffer design, the lack of authentic Roman buildings elsewhere freed North Italian designers from the constraints of archeological correctness. The most fanciful adaptations generally occurred in Venice: the wooden vault of S. Maria dei Miracoli and the exterior of the campanile of S. Giovanni Crisostomo are two examples of this approach to architectural detail. The greatest similarity to Vasari, however, is found in Jacopo Sansovino's Library in Venice, a building which, in the judgment of Vasari and his contemporaries, had no peer (VII, 503). Sansovino applied a similar system of raised coffers to the vault of the Loggia facing the Doges' Palace,[50] anticipating Vasari's own Uffizi (Figs. 25, 26) by more than twenty years.[51] Sansovino also developed a similar system for the courtyard vault of the Venetian Mint (Figs. 27, 28), and he even employed a circle and triangle system for a small dome at the foot of the stair-case leading to the Library's reception room (Fig. 29). To both Sansovino and Vasari, coffering was more than an element of the classical tradition in architecture--it offered an opportunity for free and innovative design.

Vasari's solution was more classical in inspiration

than in fact. What was classical was the radial disposi-
tion of framing elements; the planarity and severity of
the unornamented geometric shapes were not. Furthermore,
Sansovino was influenced in his design of the arcade vaults
by a conscious desire to treat the Piazetta as an ancient
forum and the Library as a basilica flanking it,[52] while
Vasari's cupola was designed without reference to a specific
ancient prototype. On the other hand, Vasari probably
knew classical dome decorations which distributed illusionistic scenes in a radial manner, and this significantly
affected the design of the interior of the cupola in Pistoia.
A gradual diminution of the height of each story was already begun in Vitoni's drum, and thus it was easy for
Vasari to continue it by employing a sequence of shapes
which also diminished in size, thus heightening the effect
of an illisionistic perspective. If the triangle, oval,
and rectangle seem excessive in size when isolated on the
intrados of the cupola, it is only because they are not
seen together with the scale of the window openings of the
drum. The effect should be compared with Michelangelo's
Pantheon-coffered dome of the New Sacristy in San Lorenzo;
Vasari's vertical exaggeration of the interior is equally
striking, but the rhythms which lead the observer's eye to
the oculus are slower and broader. Unfortunately, Vasari's
achievement was only partially successful despite its links
to Antiquity and Renaissance decorative traditions. Critics

like Lafri were correct when they observed that he ignored
Vitoni's cupola, particularly since there is scarcely no
connection between the elements of both parts of the structure, and the number of disparate elements contributes to
a lack of artistic unity throughout the interior. The importance of the cupola lies in another realm--its symbolism for the Tuscan State.

Why did Vasari think that his cupola for the Madonna
dell' Umilità was *importantissima*? Undoubtedly he knew
that he was building one of the largest domes in Italy,
but he was also aware that his design could have served
as a model for other projects commemorating the name and
achievements of the Medici family. Before his death
Vasari was involved in two projects involving the design
of an architectural monument with dynastic pretentions--
the Capella dei Principi at San Lorenzo (1566?)[53] and the
Temple of Victory at Foiano della Chiana (finished 1572).[54]
In different ways both projects bear witness to Vasari's
cupola in Pistoia. The adaptability of the features of
the Madonna dell' Umilità was unquestionable. The use of
an octagonal plan for memorial churches has been sanctified
throughout the Renaissance, and the use of *pietra* *serena*
borders and brick panels both recalled the stylistic traditions of Brunelleschi and implied Roman monumentality for
a building which celebrated the military power of the
Tuscan State.[55] Since visibility either in a city or

across a landscape was a primary requirement for memorial
churches, the raised dome was a simple device which satisfied this condition.

Vasari's involvement in the early stages of the
Capella dei Principi is mentioned in his Autobiography
(VII, 712). Prior to publishing the second edition of
the Lives, Vasari designed a third burial chapel for the
Medici which was to be similar to Michelangelo's New
Sacristy in style. The dynastic function of the building
was not ignored, for Vasari had dispatched one of his
assistants to make a measured drawing of the tomb of
Theodoric in Ravenna.[56] In contrast to the other San
Lorenzo sacristies, however, Vasari's interior was meant
to be decorated with colored marbles and mosaics, perhaps
in emulation of other Ravennate monuments. Throughout
his description of the project Vasari was concerned with
metaphors of power, for the new mausoleum was meant to
be magnificentissimo and veramente reale. Though Vasari's
own design has been lost, the influence of Vasari's lattice
coffering in Pistoia can be seen in a later drawing by
Bernardo Buontalenti (UA 2498) for the same project (Fig.
30).

Vasari's Temple of Victory at Foiano della Chiana
(Fig. 31) is less conservative in design than it would
appear at first glance. Built to celebrate the victory
in 1553 of Gian Giacopo de' Medici over the Sienese forces

of Piero Strozzi, it recalls other memorial churches like
S. Giovanni in Oleo (Rome) and the tempietto at Isola
Bisentina in both form and function.[57] Vasari, however,
was not content merely to replicate Roman models. The
exterior of the Temple of Victory is a variation on the
architectural themes used in Pistoia.[58] Both the brick
panels framed by pietra serena and the triglyph capitals,
and the same cornice was employed at both churches. In
Pistoia, Vasari was not able to successfully combine a
pilastered drum with a ribbed dome, for by duplicating
the pilasters on either side of the base angles he could
not continue the visual thrust of the ribs to the octagonal
base of the cupola. At Foiano, the solution of canting
the corners provides a more direct relationship between
the elements of the exterior and establishes a visual relationship between load and support, a solution totally
impossible in Pistoia. The freestanding temple àt Foiano
crystallized the image of a memorial church for the Medici
in Tuscany; other projects like the church at Colle Val
d'Elsa and later drawings for the Capella dei Principi
also reflect the spirit of Vasari's design.[59]

The political imagery of the dome is more subtle in
Pistoia. The fact that its completion was commissioned by
Cosimo I explains why the drum was raised by eight braccia:
the additional grandeur gained by this decision was fitting
acknowledgement of the cupola's ducal patronage. This was

certainly congenial to Vasari's political and aesthetic
sensibilities, and its obvious source is Brunelleschi's
Cupola in Florence. Brunelleschi's dome provided a powerful and easily identifiable image to painters who had to
depict the city of Florence in symbolic form, as in
Botticelli's Mystical Crucifiction where Renaissance
Florence is portrayed as the New Jerusalem.[60] Several
times in his career, Vasari, too, had been called upon
to produce painted images of Brunelleschi's cupola, and
the great majority of these were painted inside the
Palazzo Vecchio around 1560-1565, thus roughly contemporaneous with the commission in Pistoia.[61] Following traditional practice, each major monument in these views is
exaggerated according to its social and political importance in 16th Century Florence, and among these the
Duomo is always pre-eminent.[62] Although the various viewpoints give the appearance of an exact location in the
hills surrounding Florence, they were always outside the
city walls and fictive in the sense that they were unnatur-
ally high.

Pictorial devices such as these were the primary
means with which Vasari designed the cupola in Pistoia.
Having no pre-determined viewpoint within the city, the
cupola is barely visible from nearby streets and totally
hidden from the Cathedral square.[63] In fact, it was best
seen from viewpoints similar to those used by contemporary

vedutisti or modern aerial photographers (Figs. 1, 2). The
only land-based viewpoint of any consequence was along the
old road from Prato and Florence. In this sense the church
was never meant to be seen as an isolated element in the
fabric of the city. Its height was the result of a conscious attempt to recreate the elements of the Florentine
skyline--Dome, Baptistry, and Campanile--to be seen in contrast to the surrounding landscape and the family towers
within the city. To Vasari's mind the association of
Florence and Pistoia would have been entirely natural.
Pistoia had been under Florentine domination since 1294,
and in the Lives, Vasari singled out the Madonna dell'
Umilità as the most notable modern building in a city
otherwise undistinguished for its architecture.[64]

Vasari consciously chose an appropriate architectural
metaphor for Cosimo's political regime. The cupola of
Florence Cathedral was the most visible architectural monument in that city, and Vasari's long description of its
construction indicates its importance in terms of both
civic pride and art history. In his paintings Vasari
raised the cupola to the level of an artistic concetto:
it was the personification, so to speak, of the domain
of the Duke of Tuscany. In the portrait of Allesandro de'
Medici (1534), the first Duke of Tuscany, Vasari shows the
ruler clad in Maximillian armor staring into the distance
at his city of Florence which is represented, first and

foremost, by the cupola (Fig. 32). Vasari's decorations inside the Palazzo Vecchio repeat this theme on a grander scale where the ruler's territory was now equated with the most prominent monuments and the entire city. The view of Florence as a symbolic representation of the domain of the Duke was even used in an _impresa_ of Cosimo I.[65] The decision to impose the Florentine skyline on one of Tuscany's most prominent cities was not merely Vasari's preference for local forms; it celebrated the political domination which Florence exercised over the entire Tuscan State.

II

THE BADIA IN AREZZO

Giorgio Aretin e quel frate priore (Don Vicenzo
Borghini) sono uno sebben paion due . . .
Benvenuto Cellini[1]

In the second half of the 16th Century church design
was renewed through the vigorous patronage of the religious
orders. Almost every major architect received the opportunity to design a monastic church--Palladio's San Giorgio
in Venice (1566), Vignola's Gesu in Rome (1568), and
Tibaldi's San Fedele in Milan (1569) date from this period.
In general, their broad, vaulted, naves were suitable for
preaching and areas for each aspect of religious services
were separated in their plans with clarity and distinction.[2]
These churches were rarely embellished with frescoes or
sculpture, and their decoration consisted only of architectural membering. The result was the creation of a new
church type where the ecclesiastical space was purged of
elements like rood screens which blocked the visual importance of the main altar, the spiritual center of the
new buildings.[3]

The church of Sante Flora e Lucilla in Arezzo--
usually called the Badia--stands in sharp contrast if not

direct opposition to the other structures (Figs. 33-35).
While recent scholarship has improved our knowledge of
other 16th Century churches, few writers have discussed
this remarkable structure.[4] The renovation and enlargement
of the aisleless, 13th Century Badia was begun in 1565 from
plans provided by Giorgio Vasari and Don Vicenzo Borghini,
but its execution was slow and prolonged due to a continual
lack of funds. The nave was partially completed in 1587,
and in the next century the church still lacked one of its
domes and a facade.[5] The Badia, in fact, never received
a proper facade, and there is no evidence that Vasari ever
planned one. Yet a simple coat of stucco sufficed on the
exterior for many years, and in 1914 it was removed to re-
veal the facade of the original structure.

If the exterior of the Badia is uneventful, its interior (Figs. 36, 37) is a cacophony of vaulted shapes.
The most significant aspect of its nave--the persistent
alteration of dome and barrel vault along the main axis
of the church--is the result of a syncopated plan (Figs.
38-39) made by overlapping two nine-square, Greek cross
spatial units. This solution creates two crossings and
two transepts, and the main altar is located at the juncture of the second transept with the rectangular choir.[6]
In the vaulted intermediary bays, the sides of the nave
are defined by huge Serliana motifs which conceal three-
bay chapels. Each chapel is almost an independent

structure in its own right, with an oval dome and barrel
vaults (Fig. 40) in imitation of the architectural system
of the main part of the church. In theory, the creation
of separate spaces for each religious function accords
with the architectural principles of churches like the
Gesu or San Fedele, but in practice the Badia fails to
conform to contemporary church design. Although the side
altars are distinct in plan and three dimensions, they
are on the same level as the nave. Unlike the other
churches, this would encourage a mingling of laity and
clergy. Moreover, the conception of the nave as a
rhythmic series of spatial units gives more importance
to the spectator's space than to the sanctuary, thus com-
promising any axial drive towards the main altar.

The syncopated spatial sequence of the Badia immediately underscores its roots in Venetian architectural
design, most notably in churches like San Salvatore (Figs.
41-42).[7] To be sure, the architectural features of the
Badia show Venetian inspiration, but they are also less
strict in their application. Venetian designers controlled
the quality of light in their interiors by combining numerous windows with the color and shape of architectural
membering which, like Venetian painting, would give a
decidedly warm and atmospheric character to the space.
The Badia, in contrast, fails to admit light in any way.
This may not be the fault of the designers--numerous

thermal windows were provided for in the design, but several of them were walled up in either execution or restoration. This is particularly important for the South side of the church, for the main body of the structure fails to rise high enough above the level of the adjacent cloister to admit illumination (Fig. 43). Thus lacking the plentiful direct and reflected illumination of the Venetian churches, a neutral light characteristic of the paintings of Vasari's generation pervades the nave of the Badia.[8]

‸ ‿ The design of the Badia cannot be fully explained solely by Cingecento liturgical practice or stylistic analysis. On all counts, the church is stylistically more conservative than its contemporaries--its plan clearly reflects the influence of older Venetian prototypes. Moreover, the solution for the Badia should be seen as a reflection of Vasari's knowledge of architectural history and the needs of the Cassinese Congregation of the Benedictine order to which the Badia belonged. Vasari certainly recognized that patronage was an important factor in religious architecture, and he even praised Michelangelo's response to the requirements of the Carthusian order in the design of Santa Maria degli Angeli in Rome (VII, 261). In fact, Vasari was forced to take these factors into account while preparing his design since his collaborator, Don Vicenzo Borghini, was a member of the Cassinese Congregation. Yet the combination of history and patronage did not constrain

Vasari's imagination; they actively assisted in the creation of an impressive church which was monumental in conception. These qualities appealed to a 19th Century critic like Jacob Burckhardt, who called it Vasari's best work in building besides the Uffizi, a church which was "gracious and original, but profane."[9]

Although the nominal client was the abbot of SS. Flora e Lucilla, the Cassinese Congregation of the Benedictine order to which the Badia belonged, was the patron in a larger sense. The construction of the Badia was a direct reflection of the renewal of monastic life in the 15th and 16th Centuries within the framework of the Cassinese Congregation. The order was organized in 1404 by Lodovico Barbo, who gave up his literary pursuits for religious life as the youthful abbot of the monastery of Santa Giustina in Padua.[10] Although Barbo was devoted to the rebirth of monastic discipline, his patrician contacts were necessary to the spread of the Cassinese beyond their base at Santa Giustina. Their interests were greatly furthered by Eugene IV (1431-1447) who issued over sixty bulls in their favor.[11] In the most general terms, the reform initiated by Barbo was a reinstitution of monastic rule, and the means of accomplishing this was a greater degree of asceticism with intensely active religious scholarship. The order became highly pietistic--each monk had a cell to himself to attend to prayer in the form of a "devotio moderna," an elaboration of the theological mysticism of the Middle Ages.[12] The popularity

of the reforms begun by Barbo is easily measured by the

number of monasteries which joined the Congregation. By

1474, the year of the Badia's incorporation into the order,

thirty-three monastic communities had already been granted

membership, including the influential San Paolo fuori le

mure in Rome.[13] Their most important acquisition, however,

was the ancient abbey at Montecassino in 1504 when Julius

II added it to the Congregatio S. Iustinae, thereby changing

its name to the present form.

A sense of the order's identity was enforced by the

capitoli generali, the annual conventions where all major

issues affecting the monasteries were discussed, and this

included matters relating to building and construction.[14]

Although each monastery was equally important in terms of

its jurisdictional rights, its independence was subordinate

to the body of the congregation as a whole for the achieve-

ment of its religious goals. The election of its officers

mirrored the organization of the Venetian Republic, thus

acutely embarrassing the Serenissima by the existence of

a religious order in Padua modelled on its own oligarchy.[15]

By the 16th Century, the Cassinese were centralized, pop-

ular, and powerful, and their Venetian origins gave them

a sense of unity associated with the mother house, Santa

Giustina in Padua.

The Cassinese were blessed with material goods.

Barbo actively recruited patricians for his order, and this assured financial solvency with money from the Congregation itself. Moreover, Santa Giustina and other monasteries in the order kept their possessions throughout the 16th Century while other orders tended to lose them.[16] Their wealth can be indicated by the fact that they acted as a filter for Papal funds against the Turks in preparation for the Battle of Lepanto.[17] Most of its holdings were in agricultural land, and this was particularly true in Tuscany where its property was extensive, though modest in comparison to properties owned by monasteries in the Veneto.[18] In the case of the Badia, their own wealth was transferred into building, since Vasari's reconstruction of the Badia was financed by money from the sale of grain and by income from the monastery's own flour mill.[19]

The centralized organization of the Cassinese was reflected in their policy towards new construction. In 1440 the Capitolo Generale declared that no new construction could be undertaken without the approval of a majority of deputies of the order, and in 1520 it stated the form, material, and altar location for the new church of Santa Giustina, then under construction.[20] The general policy was more clearly stated in 1490 that modelli had to be sub- for all new buildings erected by the monasteries in the congregation. The modelli--probably meaning plans and not wooden models, which would be difficult to transport--would

then be submitted for judgement by the president and visitors of the congregation as well as two other prelates from
the order.[21] Although the policy of design review by the
congregation would appear to be a powerful stimulus towards
architectural conformity, such actions were the exception
rather than the rule in the capitoli which have been published. In general, they were likely rubber-stamp approvals
of whatever the local abbot wished to do. The great majority of notices deal with the administrative aspects of the
monastery and give no prescription whatsoever for the shape
or form of the church. Moreover, the possibility for diversity in plan and style was increased gy the Cassinese preference for local lay architects since they lacked clerical
architects like the Jesuit Giovanni Tristano who acted as
either architect or consultant for numerous buildings in
his order.[22] While the case for a Cassinese style or
Cassinese church plan is less strong than one for the
Jesuits, both orders shared a sense of communal purpose
and artistic identity even if the mode was not shared by
all churches in the order.[23]

The regimen of the Cassinese and their renewal of
monastic life must have appealed to Cosimo I. His interest
in theology was apparently limited--Cosimo had never heard
of the major reformers. Most matters of religious reform
were an extension of his political activity.[24] Cosimo had
sent several emissaries to the Council of Trent, but his

interest in reform was aroused only when the debates touched
matters close to his own heart, such as the issue of contributions to his Cavalieri di Santo Stefano for the protection of the Italian coast from attacks by infidels.[25] Although Cosimo used the Council for purposes of politics and
diplomacy, he was generally in accord with its religious
decrees. Of particular importance was the Twenty-third
session of the Council which sanctioned the re-institution
of discipline in monastic life. Cosimo had already dealt
with this issue in Tuscany. In 1545, he began his reform-
atio monasteriorum, an intervention into religious matters
which attempted to make monastic rules compatible with
princely powers.[26] However, Cosimo's reforms were more
concerned with religious administration than with church
building, and very often it became bogged down with comparatively minor issues such as safeguarding feminine
honour in the convents. Yet his hopes were still high.
Writing on this matter in 1558, Cosimo said "Evisto che
l'onore di Dio si era maltrato . . . volusto cercar i
deliquinti."[27]

Thus, the commission for the Badia evolved from a
set of historical circumstances somewhat different than
other churches of the 1560's. That Barbo had begun his
monastic revolution a full century before the Jesuits, for
example, meant that Cassinese would appear to be conservative and old-fashioned by comparison. It also meant that

Vasari and other architects who designed churches for the
Cassinese would have to deal with a client who had already
built or re-modelled a number of distinctive churches, and
the order's conservative patronage often tolerated churches
based on older models. In Tuscany, the administration reform of the orders preceded in time and importance the
architectural reform of their churches, and this leant
itself more easily to the renovation of extant structures
like Santa Maria Novella (1565-72) and Santa Croce (1566-
84) than to new construction. In this context, the Badia
was the first Tuscan renovation which involved the construction of an essentially new building. In form the spatial
complexity of the Badia contrasts with the solemnity of
the Florentine examples, thus giving an indication of the
architectural variety which the reforms permitted.

A review of churches built by the Cassinese will show
both the tradition and diversity in plan types used by the
Congregation. The earliest new construction initiated by
the Cassinese was built in the Veneto and Emilia Romagna
during the last quarter of the 15th Century. It is also in
this phase when anything approaching a common plan type
existed for their churches. All of the earliest constructions (San Pietro, Modena, 1476-1506; San Giovanni
Evangelista, Parma, 1489-1540; Praglia, 1490-; Santo Sisto
Piacenza, 1494-   )[28] employ a five-aisled plan with a tri-
lobed presbytery. The outer aisles contain side altars,

and in the case of Praglia, the same chapels are cellular
units separate from each other. In general, their choirs
were located in front of the high altar, and in the 16th
Century they were re-located behind the high altar. But
it is precisely at this point where all similarity ends.
Almost every church used a different structural system--
barrel vault (Santo Sisto), cross vaults (San Giovanni
Evangelista) or flat ceiling (Praglia)--and consequently
the spatial effect of each building is different. Moreover, the five-aisle plan with trilobe presbytery was certainly not unique to the Cassinese--it was a common plan
found throughout Northern Italy during this period.

The most original of the Cassinese churches built at
the end of the 15th Century bears a closer resemblance to
Vasari's Badia. Biagio Rosetti's design for the church of
San Benedetto in Ferrara (Figs. 44, 45) has been characterized as a remarkable blend of Venetian and Tuscan elements,[29]
and its use of alternating barrel vaults and domes in the
nave achieves the syncopated effect which Vasari adopted
more than a half century later in Arezzo. Yet is is funda-
mentally different in conception, lacking the double transepts found in the Badia. It is also doubtful if Vasari
was familiar with any of the buildings designed by Rosetti,
an architect completely overlooked in the Lives.

In the literature on Vasari's architecture, the Badia
is usually compared to Santa Giustina in Padua,[30] the

headquarters for the Cassinese and the "mater et caput" of
the order. Although this view has been restated repeat-
edly,[31] the similarities between the two churches are more
superficial than they are substantive (Figs. 46, 47). The
comparison can be visually seductive--an observer standing
in the nave near the main crossing will see an alternation
of barrel vaults and domes not like unlike the Badia. In
plan, however, the differences are apparent. Santa Giustina
is, in effect, similar to the churches built by the Cassinese
in the Fifteenth Century, but with a far more elaborate
chancel. In contrast to the Badia, the nave of Santa
Giustina is a simple series of shallow domes on pedentives
separated by broad arches. Vasari could have known the
church only in plan since the nave was not vaulted until
the end of the Sixteenth Century.[32]

The priorities which the Cassinese recognized in
their buildings were, in origin, more practical and utilitarian than dogmatic and religious. Churches were built
anew only when the previous structures were inadequate in
size, and in the cases of San Benedetto al Po and Montecassino, they were willing to adapt and renovate an already
extant architectural fabric.[33] Furthermore, church construction was of secondary importance to them. The depopu-
lation of the monasteries prior to Barbo's reforms resulted
in the serious dilapidation of most monastic buildings, and
the later growth of the order taxed the capacity of the

existing structures. In this respect it is important to notice that the construction of housing for the monks preceded the construction of the churches in many Cassinese monasteries, most notably in Arezzo, San Benedetto al Po, Santa Giustina, and San Giorgio Maggiore.[34] In fact, it was the monastery and not the church which was more important to the Cassinese in spiritual terms.[35] Their efforts were devoted to internal reforms within the church and not preaching to the public. This, too, stands in sharp contrast to other orders which were devoted to the reform of society through preaching. In Jesuit churches, for example, the pulpit is given a prominent location on the side of the nave; permanent pulpits are not found in Cassinese churches.

The real priories affected the design of the East end of their churches. The Cassinese saw a direct connection between music and monastic prayer, and even Barbo himself was convinced by the pastoral efficacy of a liturgy celebrated with dignity and enriched with music.[36] The way for musical reform was paved in the Quattrocento when polyphonic music was introduced into monasteries where the Gregorian chant was commonly employed, and the adoption of the new musical form was by no means immediate or consistent.[37] While the contribution of the Cassinese to the History of Music has not been well studied in light of its importance for the order, a number of compositions, often used for

Holy Saturday processions, were written by members of the
order.[38] Furthermore, other scholars have recognized the
significance of the Cassinese in moving the position of
the choir from a position in front of the altar to one
behind it,[39] and the Cassinese interest in music assisted
this change.

The old choir location was ill-suited for the performance of choral music, since the waves which carry
sound were diffused into the nave without being reflected,
concentrated, and given direction by adjacent surfaces,
and this would have resulted in a distinctly muddled sound.
This is comparable to the effect of a band-shell in a park;
if the shell did not exist, then the music would be barely
audible.

Admittedly, these observations are not confirmed by
the statements of the Cassinese or their architects. Yet
Renaissance designers were aware that a proper acoustical
setting was a primary factor in church planning. When Fra
Francesco Giorgi recommended in 1535 that the choir of San
Francesco della Vigna in Venice should be vaulted, he certainly must have been aware of the beneficial effect it
would have on the performance of religious music.[40] Although vaulted choirs had been built earlier--most notably
by Bramante in Santa Maria del Popolo in Rome,--their
acoustic properties would accent the intelligibility which
the Council of Trent demanded in music.[41] Even the

Cassinese suffered from acoustical defects in the design
of their churches. At Santa Giustina, the audibility of
the choir was compromised by excessive reverberation, and,
according to Scamozzi, openings were made in the domes of
the transept and the choir to remedy this situation.[42]

The Cassinese's lively interest in music often lead
to the adoption of elaborate chancels in their churches.
While this was true for the larger (and richer) monasteries
in the Veneto, Vasari's barrel-vaulted, rectangular solution was modest by comparison. At both Santa Giustina and
San Giorgio Maggiore in Venice, choirs are given separate,
vaulted spaces behind the main altar, and passageways connect them to the residential quarters of the monastery.
The Badia's choir lacks any real separation from the main
body of the church as found in the other examples, since
it is connected to the monastery only through the transept.
While this solution was probably dictated by the Badia's
existing structures and its constrained, urban site, the
choir's design resembles more closely Tuscan Quattrocento
models like the Badia in Fiesole or Francesco di Giorgio's
Santa Maria del Calcinaio in Cortona than any solutions
used in other Cassinese churches.

If the Cassinese's contribution to the Badia was the
patronage of a conservative, regimented, Venetian religious
order which tolerated regional diversity in its buildings,
then how did Vasai derive the plan of his church in Arezzo?

Although the syncopated plan used in the Badia is
commonly associated with Venice and the Veneto, it is by
no means confined to that region. Among Renaissance
theorists, Francesco di Giorgio deserves particular mention since he was the first architect to illustrate it in
an architectural treatise. Francesco's illustration in
his Tratatto is not explicitly mentioned in the text (Fig.
48); it is only grouped together with various forms of
columnar temples (prostilos, antiprostilos, peripteros),[43]
and no domes are indicated in its plan. It would be difficult to build a circular dome over the rectangular bays
shown in the plan, but only minor modifications would be
necessary to make this possible. Yet it is easy to see
how Francesco's sketch could have excited the imagination
of other architects. His plan is highly suitable for a
16th Century church, for the main axis emphasizes the
high altar and adequate space is provided for the semi-
circular side chapels. In the Lives, Vasari described
Francesco's architectural projects at length to the ex-
clusion of his projects in painting and sculpture (III,
69-79), and in an earlier project, Vasari had borrowed
architectural motifs from Francesco.[44] In fact, Vasari's
likely consultation of the Quattrocento treatise is not
surprising since he called Cosimo I's copy of it "one of
his most valued books."[45]

The syncopated plan was brought to Rome by Fra

Giocondo in his design for St. Peter's (Fig. 49), and consequently it could light the imagination of architects who
had never seen a Venetian church.[46] In reality, Giocondo
proposed two almost distinct structures, a longitudinal
plan church at the center of the project surrounded by a
choir and chapels which are physically and spatially separate from the nave. Like St. Mark's in Venice, Fra
Giocondo conceived of the nave as a series of domed units
separated by broach arches. This is what obviously in-
terested Vasari--it suggests the alternation of dome and
vault which was used in Arezzo. The other elements of the
plan were not relevant to the commission for the Badia and
were eliminated.[47] The availability of this scheme to
Vasari is unquestionable, since he acquired a drawing for
his Libro dei disegni.[48] Vasari, however, deviated from
his model in two important respects. The first change was
important, since the use of square bays in the nave suggests the continuing influence of Quattrocento models like
Brunelleschi. The second modification was less important;
Fra Giocondo's cross-shaped piers were changed to a more
complex T shape to accommodate the different scales of
vaulting in the nave and side aisles.

The architects and painters who were involved in the
long history of St. Peter's often borrowed freely from Fra
Giocondo's scheme, and its influence extended even into
Vasari's native Tuscany.[49] Around 1533-34 Baldassare

Peruzzi prepared a number of schemes to renovate San
Domenico in Siena, a large monastic church whose interior
had been destroyed by fire. In his first scheme (Fig. 50),
Peruzzi employed a series of saucer domes on barrel vaults
which, in turn, are supported by gigantic, hollow piers.[50]
At first glance, the plan might be seen as a variation on
Alberti's San Andrea in Mantua, but that is not the case.
In Fra Giocondo's scheme, the piers and vaulting of the
nave piers would have probably been built with arches
connecting the vertical supports (like St. Mark's),
Peruzzi's solution was much bolder, avoiding all arcuated
forms below the vaulted ceiling. With its chapes as open
cellular spaces defined by pier and lintel construction,
the clustered piers in San Domenico would have been read
as free-standing sculptural elements supporting prominent
architraves. Unlike its antecedent, Peruzzi's ecclesiastical space would have been more open and flowing, punctu-
ated by the piers supporting the vaulting. While its lack
of massive, space-defining walls was thoroughly un-Roman
in character, its openness would have created some remarkable visual effects. The trabeated construction would
have promoted a conflict of axes by allowing diagonal
glances into the chapels and implying free movement within
the open space of the nave. Although the spectator might
have been somewhat bewildered by the multiple views which
the design offered, in compensation he would have been

offered a scenographic religious space not at all unlike
Peruzzi's stage set designs.[51]

Vasari's design for the Badia in Arezzo shares many
of these qualities. In general, the nave of the Badia em-
ploys the same contrast between axial direction and lateral
views (Fig. 36). Vasari's design is also more confusing.
Peruzzi obviously thought how the lateral views would be
seen by the observer; a small perspective sketch in the
corner of UA 338 attempts to standardize the design for
every possible view. Vasari, on the other hand, seems to
have designed the nave by considering each of its elements
separately. Surfaces are unrelated to their neighbors;
the screen-like Serliana in the nave, the wall architecture
of the arched lateral chapels, and the arch and entablature
connecting them are not consciously bound together by design. Despite the Venetian origin of its plan, Vasari's
design is still Florentine in the sense that it gives primary importance to an architectural system composed of
planes and not walls or individual spatial units. The
Serliana and its flanking piers were meant to be seen
frontally, and there is no change in the size or scale
of structural elements when they are used in the smaller
side transepts. The indecisive character of the interior
is heightened by the choice of bays equal in size for both
domed and vaulted spaces in the nave. While Vasari never
mentioned the schemes for San Domenico in the Lives, his

knowledge of Perazzi's drawings can be taken for granted,
since they contain anticipations of the plan of the Badia
and the tabernacle altars which Vasari used in Santa Croce
and Santa Maria Novella.[52]

Turning to the Badia's details, we can see other
sources of inspiration. Renaissance architects rarely used
the Serliana as a monumental motif; it was generally presented as the central element in a complex rhythmical
system (a Serlian palace facade) or as a small, isolated
element in a larger composition (the window in Raphael's
Fire in the Borgo). Its use in ecclesiastical architecture
was even more rare, but Vasari had two important precedents
to follow. First, Peruzzi had employed the Serliana in
another of his projects for San Domenico (Fig. 51). Likewise, Giulio Romano's renovation to the monastic church at
San Benedetto al Po, begun in 1539, also used the Serliana
as a screen-like element on the side walls of the nave
(Fig. 52). Vasari's turn to Giulio is not surprising in
light of the similar nature of both commissions, and there
were good reasons for Vasari to associate the Serliana with
his client's order. San Benedetto al Po was, after Santa
Giustina, the largest Cassinese monastery in North Italy,
and both Vasari and Borghini had visited it on separate
occasions in the 1540's (V, 549, 552). Its renovation must
have impressed the numerous abbots who had visited it for
the capitoli generali which were almost always held there.

Vasari was certainly impressed by it when he revisited San Benedetto in 1566 in the company of the abbots of Perugia and Arezzo, for a letter to Borghini calls attention to the great pleasure which he received in being there.[53]

Vasari repeated the San Benedetto Serliana without observing Giulio's archeologically derived detail. The architrave profile which Vasari used in the Badia is characteristic of his architectural style, for it is related to the architrave which he used on the ground floor of the Uffizi riverfront loggia (Figs. 53, 54). Yet Vasari was not licentious in his application of the classical orders, for he employed them according to accepted norms. The measurements given in the stonecutter's contract conform to the traditional 1:7 proportion between column diameter and height for the Tuscan order,[54] and the general design of the base column and architrave corresponds to Serlio's illustration of that order in his Fourth Book (Fig. 55), first published in 1537.[55] The only departure is minor but sophisticated: the frieze is eliminated and the architrave is sharply beveled to create a strong shadow line.[56]

The use of the Serliana was also a concession to contemporary taste.[57] In 1560 Ammannati had criticized the correctness of Vasari's design for the facade of the Uffizi (Fig. 56), and, in his words, the solution was meant to show "più ragione d'architettura."[58] His criticism included the inclusion of a Serliana on the ground floor to replace

Vasari's flat entablature. Though Ammannati was equally
free in his use of the orders, the association of the
Serliana with correctness must have been fixed in Vasari's
mind--it reappeared as the dominant motif of the Uffizi
loggia as well as in the Badia. Although Vasari followed
the criticism more in spirit than in rule, choosing the
Serliana had the double advantage of pleasing his clients
and his critics.

The Badia's lack of direct progeny is due to several
factors. First and foremost, Vasari never claimed it in
his autobiography in the 1568 edition of the Lives, and
consequently only members of the Florentine architectural
community would have been aware of his authorship of the
Badia.[59] This was certainly not an oversight on his part;
he had good reason not to mention it at all. At the time
of the writing of the second edition, only the crossing
and part of the choir had been built. The Libro della
Fabrica also indicates a slowdown in construction, and it
probably seemed doubtful if the church would ever be completed. This left room for possible changes in the design,
and Vasari realized that a half-finished project would be
more detrimental to his reputation than one which was never
begun. Moreover, Borghini's collaboration meant that he
never could claim it as totally his own design. Also, it
would have been doubly embarrassing for the propagator of
Tuscan supremacy in disegno to claim authorship of a church

with Venetian overtones even if the direct source lay elsewhere. Vasari had seen Palladio's design for San Giorgio
Maggiore, and he was surely aware of contemporary church
design in both Rome and Milan. In comparison to these examples, the Badia would have been judged old-fashioned in
style and not up to date in terms of contemporary religious
practice.

Despite these difficulties, echoes of Vasari's design
for the Badia are to be found in several places. The clear-
est case of influence is demonstrated by Ammannati's preliminary plan for a large church (Fig. 57) which was included in his La città ideale.[60] Unlike its monastic
counterpart in Arezzo, Ammannati uses the syncopated plan
only for the nave while the sanctuary is designed as a
large, centrally planned structure resembling Bramante's
scheme for St. Peter's. It was designed as an ideal structure in every sense--particularly lacking limitations of
size and economy--and for this reason it is much more elaborate with its use of a five-aisled plan containing free-
standing columns framing the vista towards the sanctuary.
Ammannati rejected Vasari's employment of the Serliana as
a screen-like element in the nave and relegates it to a
subordinate role as a chapel facade in the side transepts,
using the same element which he had used in his criticism
of Vasari's design for the Uffizi. Although it shares the
same plan as the Badia, its alternating rhythm in the nave

bays and development of the pier chapels is more in harmony
with the open spaces planned by Peruzzi for San Domenico in
Siena. With the exception of San Biagio in Fabriano,[61] the
syncopated plan was no longer a source of inspiration for
Italian architects.[62]

In choosing a syncopated plan for the Badia, Vasari
consciously revived the spatial structure of the Oriental
crossdomed church.[63] Stylistically, Vasari had both the
correct model (the Fra Giocondo plan) and its architectural
filiations as aids in accomplishing this. Yet it remains
to be seen why Vasari resorted to a model which recalls the
Byzantine tradition of Venice rather than the forms of
Ancient Rome or Renaissance Florence. Vasari was shrewd
enough to realize that Byzantine Architecture did exist--
he called it the "maniera greca"--but he was both incorrect
and inconsistent in his reactions towards it in the Lives.
In the 1550 edition he never mentioned the subject at all,
but the 1568 edition contained numerous references to the
subject, all part of a more complete, systematic, and fair
approach to the evaluation of medieval architecture. Vasari
reacted with distaste to several monuments in Ravenna. The
palace of Theodoric is chastised for being rich and grand
instead of good (meaning classical) architecture, and structures such as the Mausoleum of Galla Placida, San Vitale,
and San Apollinare in Classe were grand and magnificent but
designed in a clumsy kind of architecture (I, 233-234). Yet

Vasari reserved warm praise for both San Marco in Venice and Santi Apostoli in Florence, seeing both as buildings which were imbued with grace and proportion (I, 235). By comparison, his laudatory statements for the painting in the "maniera greca" were very few. To even the most famous painters the "maniera greca" was always a handicap: the mosaics in the Florentine Baptistry were "designed in the Greek style, but were very beautiful nonetheless" (Vasari-Barocchi, I, ii, 30), and Cimabue's famous Rucellai Madonna was a facile combination of the Greek and Modern styles (I, 254). In any case, the "goffa maniera greca" was certainly not on the same aesthetic plane as the "buona maniera greca antica" (Vasari-Barocchi, II, i, 36). In other words, the architecture of the "maniera greca" was considerably more detached from the critical abuse which had been heaped upon its painting.[64]

In equating San Marco in Venice with Santi Apostoli in Florence, Vasari failed to distinguish between examples of Romanesque and Byzantine Architecture. That the two different styles were comparable to him should not be surprising; it must be remembered that Vasari equated Cimabue ("maniera greca") with Arnolfo di Cambio.[65] This is of the greatest importance for understanding the significance of the Badia. Among the churches which Vasari called "maniera greca" are the seven Badie created in Tuscany at the end of the 9th Century by Count Ugo of Brandenburg, and the first

Badia of Arezzo was one of them.[66] This statement was merely
bad history and not a bad aesthetic judgement. It must be
stressed that all of these churches are Romanesque, a sty-
istic category which did not exist in Vasari's time. Furthermore, he had almost no visual evidence to support his claim
for the style of the churches, since only one of the seven
was still standing in original form during Vasari's
lifetime.[67]

The dilemma which Vasari faced was more philosophical
than architectural. The issue at hand was historical con-
formity--how was he going to renovate a church which he
associated with the "maniera greca"? Vasari had already
faced a similar dilemma when he had to design a Gothic frame
for a drawing by Cimabue,[68] but the commission for a real
building meant that an anachronistic style would be inappropriate. The solution could only be to build in a modern-
ized version of the original style. Certainly the Veneto-
Byzantine affinities of the Fra Giocondo plan would have
been apparent to him, and the must have been its most at-
tractive aspect. Its alternation of domes and barrel vaults
were surely reminiscent of San Marco, and the relatively
large amount of surface area in that type of church meant
that Vasari could employ the most recent and up-to-date
architectural motifs. In this sense Vasari was able to
satisfy the dual requirements of historical conformità and
invenzione. Truly, the plan for the Badia was just as

stylistically correct as the Gothic frame for the Cimabue
drawing. In this way, Vasari's own historical judgement
prevented him from designing a building which was more
Roman or Florentine; he simply had to design a building
which would accord with his own conception of the Badia's
history.

Finally, who was responsible for the design of the
Badia?

Vasari's collaborator on the Badia, Don Vicenzo
Borghini, was perhaps the most influential "artistic consultant" of his generation.[69] Among his achievements were
the iconographic program for the frescoes in the Palazzo
Vecchio, the programs for the _feste_ for the wedding of
Prince Francesco de' Medici to Anne of Austria,[70] and preparation for the funerals of Michelangelo and Cosimo I.
Born into a well-to-do Florentine family, Borghini took
the Cassinese habit at the Florentine Badia, where he
studied Latin and Greek. In 1537-1538 he made his first
trips to Siena and Arezzo, and two years later, he travelled
to Cassinese monasteries throughout the South of Italy.
In 1541, he was ordained and assigned to the Badia in
Arezzo (where he probably met Vasari for the first time),
and in the following year he participated in the _Capitolo
generale_ of the Cassinese Congregation held at San Benedetto
al Po. In 1544 he visited Venice to study Greek manuscripts,
and upon his return to Tuscany he was re-assigned to the

Forentine Badia.

Borghini had an inexhaustable knowledge of humanistic studies which he combined with a keen appreciation for the visual arts. His influence on the artistic programs with which he was connnected has never been questioned, but only relatively recently it has been asserted that Borghini might have prepared drawings for execution, thus providing other artists with the initial inspiration for their creations. The Taccuino in the Biblioteca Nazionale Centrale, Florence, containing sketches for the wedding of Prince Francesco has been interpreted as a series of idea sketches which were given to or copied by the artists who were to execute them and not as a record of decorations already built.[71] In addition, a drawing for the renovation of the courtyard in the Palazzo Vecchio also has been attributed to Borghini.[72] In general, Borghini's drawing style is less sure than Vasari. The heads and figures of his bodies are disconnected and made of amorphous shapes. Borghini also shows a tendency to overindulge in broad areas of ink wash while Vasari uses this technique only sparingly. Moreover, Vasari's architectural forms are drawn with an economy of means while Borghini's are heavy and clumsy in character.

Borghini's intervention in the Badia can be confirmed by both documents and correspondence, and it is even possible that, as an important member of the Cassinese, he obtained the commission for Vasari. Borghini's contributions

date from the first stages of the project when he was mentioned as a collaborator in the preparation of the "modello."
His responsibilities included tasks usually performed by
architects, among them problems resulting from liberties
taken by stonecutters (18 November 1566).[73] At all times,
Borghini must have been aware of the progress (or lack of
it) on the Badia.

With this information at hand, it is tantalizing to
attribute a large share of the responsibility of the design
to Borghini. This temptation should be avoided, not only
for the lack of further documentation on the Badia but also
for Borghini's sketchy and incomplete opinions on architecture. It is known that Vasari and Borghini criticized
each other's work, exchanged drawings, and even offered
each other corrections.[74] Yet Borghini must have desired
a direct relationship between liturgical necessity and
architectural form. He was aware that a clear view to the
altar was contrary to existing conditions in many churches,[75]
and he implies a preference for the longitudinal plan when
he refers to the Florentine Baptistry as being inappropriate to the Catholic service.[76] His critical reaction to
the Florentine churches was never very clear--San Miniato
was "noble and grand and not of bad architecture for those
times" (12th Century), while Santo Spirito was merely "magnificent and beautiful" in form.[77] In his fanciful reconstruction of the Baptistry (Fig. 58) as a Temple of Mars

he echoed Albertian theory by saying that columns up against a wall have no reason for their existence. His fictive reconstruction is archeological in its dryness than correct in its form, and none of its details are applicable to the Badia.

Certainly, Borghini's role in the design of the Badia was more than that of an enlightened friend with whom Vasari discussed his own architectural practice. As a priest and member of the Cassinese Congregation, Borghini was aware of the Venetian origins of his own order, and this must have suggested the appropriateness of a Venetian plan type for the church in Arezzo. As a historian and a philologist, Borghini must have been aware of the history of the Badia in Arezzo, thus raising the question of the appropriate form for a church which had been identified with the "maniera greca." As a designer, however, Borghini's contribution was probably minimal since his experience in this area was limited to temporary structures or large scale decorative programs. All other evidence, both documentary and stylistic, indicates that Vasari retained control of the architectural aspects of the commission.

In conclusion, both participants contributed within their own spheres of knowledge and activity. Like Vasari's other collaborative efforts with Borghini, an intellectual conceit was expressed in an artistic language which was derived from the past. Though Vasari's design can be explained

by the factors which affected the commission, his solution
celebrates the usage of an older architectural type without
starting any new tradition. Had the care which went into
the Badia's design and execution equalled the attention
paid to the philosophical aspects of its planning, the final
verdict might have been more favorable.

III

THE CORRIDOIO

Above (the Ponte Vecchio), the Gallery of the Grand
Duke crosses the river. It was built to connect the
two great palaces by a secret passage, and it takes
its jealous course among the streets and houses with
true despotism; going where it wishes, and spurning
every obstacle away, which goes before it.
                        Charles Dickens, Pictures from Italy[1]

Everywhere in Europe, as soon as the state was established it disciplined the towns with instinctive
relentlessness, whether or not it used violence. .
. . Take Florence for an example. . . . From the
Pitti Palace, a gallery, a secret passage in fact,
allowed the prince to cross the river and reach the
Uffizi. This elegant gallery, still in existence
today on the Ponte Vecchio, was the thread from
which the spider at the extremity of his web super-
vised the town. . . .
        Fernand Braudel, Capitalism and Material Life,
                                        1400-1800[2]

Anyone who has ever read Charles Dickens' description

of the Corridoio in Florence will attest to the evocative

powers of secret passageways connecting distant rooms and

buildings. While secret corridors have captivated the imag-

ination of writers and readers alike, descriptions of them

have colored our perception of this forgotten element of

urban architecture with so much Romanticism that we can

only think they existed to serve the purposes of marital

infidelity and political intrigue exclusively. Recent

interpretations are no less free of this point of view.

Twentieth Century critics like Braudel have emphasized the Corridoio's authoritarian implications,[3] forcing us to believe that every private passageway was built by a wicked ruler to escape riots and protests against his repressive political regime. Surely, each generation of historians has exaggerated evidence to suit its own point of view, but it is equally certain that we have forgotten the numerous significant examples of this building type which flourished during the Renaissance.

The Corridoio is perhaps the best known example of a private system of urban circulation built in the Renaissance.[4] Designed and constructed in 1565 by Giorgio Vasari to connect the Palazzo Vecchio with the Pitti Palace, the Corridoio is a connection of several distinct and different structures, each with a different form relative to its location in the city. While access to the Corridoio was restricted to the Medicean court and its retainers, it was never a secret passageway. To be sure, privacy was specified in construction contracts,[5] but the passageway was conspicuously visible to anyone who passed it. Paradoxically, the Corridoio did not significantly alter the environment surrounding it, and it is likely that most 16th Century Florentines would agree with such a judgement. To appreciate why this is true, we have to understand the Corridoio's form and the circumstances which lead to its construction.

The Corridoio (Fig. 60) begins with an unobstrusive
doorway in the Camera Verde of the Palazzo Vecchio. After
crossing the Via della Ninna, it continues along the second
floor of the Uffizi, passing the galleries which once contained both the Medicean art collection and workshops for
artists.[6] At the Southern end of the Uffizi's Western arm,
a barrel-vaulted stair descends to the piàno nobile of a
medieval house. Crossing the Lugarno degli Archibusieri
on another arch (Fig. 61), it continues along the river
towards the Ponte Vecchio (Fig. 62) as an exposed structure
supported by a series of vaults on piers (Figs. 63, 64).
Fording the Arno by passing over the shops on the Eastern
side of the famous bridge (Fig. 65), the Corridoio man-
euvers around the tower of the Manelli family on beccatelli
(stone brackets) (Fig. 66). Crossing the Via dei Bardi
on a third arch (Fig. 67), it follows the course of an old
alleyway until it passes the church of S. Felicita (Fig.
68), crossing over its steps and creating its present
loggia-like facade. Continuing further along the cloister
of S. Felicita, it finally terminates adjacent to the
grotto facade which Vasari had designed several years
earlier.[7] The Corridoio travels almost a half mile, but
it is visible to the observer only along the Arno and on
the Ponte Vecchio; its integration with the facade of S.
Felicita makes it almost unnoticeable.

Although the purpose of the Corridoio was to connect
the seat of Medicean power (the Palazzo Vecchio) with the
residence of Duke Cosimo I (the Pitti Palace), it performed
several other useful tasks as well. It certainly made the
administration of the state easier since it was passed
through the Uffizi, and it assured the continuity of government in the face of natural disasters like the flood
which destroyed the Ponte S. Trinita in 1557. Moreover,
Cosimo had always sought international recognition for his
young state, and it finally arrived in 1565 when he pro-
cured a royal bride for his son, Prince Francesco de'
Medici. His marriage on 18 December 1565 to Giovanna of
Austria, daughter of Emperor Maximillian II, occasioned
some of the most lavish affairs ever created in the service of international diplomacy,[8] and its numerous foun-
tains, street decoration, and theatrical events were designed to impress the "Signori alemanni."[9] The total cost
for the events was over 50,000 scudi[10]--almost five times
the cost of the Corridoio itself![11] A contemporary description of the wedding clearly states that the Corridoio
was built for these events,[12] and Vasari repeats this in
his Autobiography.[13] Accordingly, the Corridoio would
have connected the place where the most prestigious foreign
visitors were housed (Pitti Palace) with the focal center
for the celebration (Palazzo Vecchio).

This explanation is only partly true. The Corridoio was not built solely for the wedding festivities. There were too few events in either the Palazzo Vecchio or the Pitti Palace to merit the construction of such an urban extravagance.[14] Furthermore, the completion of the connection between the distant buildings did not assure free and easy passage between them. The upper floor of the Uffizi was not begun until 1574, and until that date access to the corridor could only be gained by a makeshift connection across the roof of the church S. Pier Scheraggio (Fig. 69) which was located in the first bay of the Uffizi.[15] When seen in the context of the wedding, the purpose of the Corridoio must have been more symbolic than utilitarian. Braudel correctly asserts that it was a symbol of ducal power, but the Corridoio was more likely to impress Cosimo's guests than his subjects. The ancient connection between the place where one ruled and where one resided never died; it existed unbroken throughout the Middle Ages and the Early Renaissance, and the Corridoio was one of the last examples of this building type to be erected.

The privacy which Cosimo had desired by erecting the Corridoio was a privilege of rulers since the Golden Age of Greece. Cosimo's passageway was sanctified by ancient precedent, but like its equivalents in Gothic novels, they were often the result of literary license without the benefit of architectural imagination. A passage in Virgil's

Aeneid has been cited as the means of inspiration for the
Corridoio.[16] In Book II, Aeneas' narration of the sack

of Troy, we are told that

> There was a secret access to the palace gained
> through a concealed entrance, a doorway never
> noticed by passers-by, which communicated be-
> tween the mansions of King Priam's family. In
> the days of our empire poor Andromache would
> often walk this way, unattended, to Hector's
> people, when she took little Astyanax to see
> her grandfather.
>
> (Lumen erat caecque fores et pervius usus
> tectorum inter se Priam, postesque relicti a
> tergo, infelix qua se, dum regna mangebant,
> saepius Andromache ferre incomitata solbat ad
> soceros, et avo puerum Astyanaca trahebat.[17]

What is enchanting about Virgil's description is the con-

nection betwen two palaces for familial reasons (Cosimo

resided in the Pitti while the newlyweds lived in the

Palazzo Vecchio); what is disappointing is the failure to

specify its length and architectural form. In all, it

offers scarcely any help in reconstructing the appearance

of the link. Without any other information, we can only

conclude that it was little more than a hidden doorway

(caecae fores).

  Other ancient passageways show a typological similar-

ity to the Corridoio in both form and function, and they

are all described in Suetonius' Lives of the Caesars. Nero's

first house, the Domus Transitoria (or literally, the House

of the Passage) connected the Imperial Residence on the

Palatine with the Gardens of Maecenas on the Esquiline, but

it was burned in the Great Fire shortly after its completion.[18] Almost immediately, it was rebuilt as the Domus
Aurea. The descriptions of the later palace are precise
enough to identify its component parts; we know that it
had a vestibule "large enough to contain a statue of the
Emporor 120 feet high, and it was so extensive that it
had a triple colonnade a mile long (tanta laxitas, ut
porticus triplices miliarias haberet)."[19] Presumably,
the last feature of the Palace connected the extremities
of the complex on the Palatine and the Esquiline. If
both Neronian structures are taken together, they suggest
an ancient prototype for the Corridoio: an arcaded, three
story facade connecting two residences, one a seat of power
and the other a place of enjoyment.

While these models suggested a definite form for
ancient passageways, they were still elements of single
buildings which did not extend beyond the palace complex.
However, another ancient passageway connected distant
elements in the city. While describing Caligula's divine
ability to discourse with the Gods, Suetonius remarked
that "he was even invited to live with the Gods, (and) he
built a bridge over the Temple of the Deified Augustus,
and thus joined the Palace to the Capitol (et in contubern-
ium altro inviatus super templum Divi Augusti ponte trans-
misso Palatium Capitoliumque coniunxit.)"[20] With this
act, the private passageway became an urban architectural

element related to the administration of the affairs of state. If Cosimo and Vasari did consider these passages while designing the Corridoio, we can be certain that they disregarded Suietonius' characterization of their patrons Neither Caligula's bridge nor Nero's villa were presented in the most favorable light. The former was one of his acts which earned the title "monster,"[21] while the latter was "damniosor" than his palaces![22]

Finally, Roman Florence once accommodated a struc-ture, which, like the Corridoio, was composed of a series of high arches which marched over and across the fabric of the city. The structure was the aqueduct which brought water from Monte Morello, and its terminus was located near the present-day Palazzo della Parte Guelfa (Fig. 70).[23] Vasari surely associated the Corridoio with ancient aque-ducts which were built with rectangular sections for carry-ing water. This was not accidental, for every few years aqueducts did carry people--to clean out the deposits of salt and other mineral substances conveyed by the water. Furthermore, its remains could still be seen during the Cinquecento.[24]

Like the examples of ancient passageways, the Floren-tine aqueduct was one of a number of related structures which Cosimo and Vasari knew through literary sources. It would be fruitless to argue whether they consulted any specific ancient model in the design of the Corridoio.

With the exception of the Florentine aqueduct, none of these
examples can be accurately reconstructed. Likewise, the
correspondence between Cosimo and Vasari is never explicit
as to why such a seemingly fanciful project was begun in
the first place.

The key to understanding the Corridoio lies in the
political principles of Cosimo I. While Cosimo would have
been morally outraged by the excesses of the Emperors, he
certainly stood in awe and admiration of the power which
they wielded in the administration of the Empire. As
Cochrane has warned, the term absolutism must be used with
considerable care whenever evaluating Cosimo's deeds.[25]
Unlike traditional rulers such as Cesare Borgia and
Sigismondo Malatesta, Cosimo never considered himself
superior to statutory law. The concept of building a new
Palatine must have been morally inimicable as well as impractical to him, particularly since he followed the path
of least resistance in laying out the Corridoio. The project involved scarcely any demolition, and Cosimo paid for
whatever structures he destroyed.[26] For these reasons it
is more likely that Cosimo would have adopted a single,
useful element from the complex of Palatine structures and
not the whole ensemble. In this light, Caligula's solution
could be considered appealing indeed. As such, antiquity
could only be used as an additional justification for the
Corridoio, something which, as we shall see, was almost

commonplace in Italian ducal cities during the 16th Century.

While ancient authors confirmed the existence of private passageways, Quattrocento architectural theorists convinced Renaissance patrons that a secret means of circulation was a necessary element of a princely palace. The most complete commentary on this subject is found in Alberti's De re aedificatoria. It is no small wonder that Alberti's ideas were still current at this late date; Cosimo Bartoli, who later became the Medicean agent in Venice, published the first Italian translation of the Quattrocento treatise in 1550 as a "pendant" to the first edition of Vasari's Lives.[27] To Alberti's mind, two kinds of secret doorways or passageways were necessary. The first was merely a convenience so that the prince could receive messages and advice without the interruptions of friends and family.[28] The second kind, however, was more vital to princely power.[29] Alberti indicated that the prince needs a place of refuge which could offer escape in difficult moments. Of these, the Corridoio falls into both categories, offering Cosimo both efficiency and escape.

Filarete, on the other hand, relied on images to convey his ideas about passage design (Fig. 71). In the chapter on bridges, he told his patron in detail how to span a river of 200 braccia.[30] While he failed to mention passageways in the text, his illustrations evoked the kind of structure which was desired by Alberti and achieved by

Vasari. In this case, Filarete shows a bridge which connects two palaces located on opposite sides of a river.
Lacking all decoration, its plain style is not unlike the
utilitarian architecture of the Roman Empire. It offers a
striking resemblance to both Roman aqueducts and Nero's
porticus triplices, but now offering open circulation below
for the general public and reserving its upper level for
princely personages. This construction should be considered
as an urban building type--it is hard to imagine it isolated
in the countryside as Filarete illustrated it.

Filarete's project is considerably different from
Alberti's proposal. To accomplish his goal, Alberti would
only have to rearrange a small number of residential spaces
while Filarete would have to rebuild an entire city.
Alberti's passageway could be built in a private palazzo;
Filarete's extravagant bridge could be executed only under
the patronage of a powerful ruler. Alberti's construction
could be easily hidden within the fabric of a single building; Filarete's solution is a visible symbol of the power
of his patron.

Filarete's design can be contrasted to the numerous
Medieval corridors which existed throughout Europe. In
general, they were neither urban nor always related to the
affairs of state. The private passage which joined the
ruler's residence to the Palatine Chapel was a characteristic feature of Medieval palace design. In Constantinople,

a private passage connected the Chalke gate with the South

Gallery in S. Sophia, and numerous references to it in

Byzantine literature assured its survival in Medieval

architecture.[31] It reappeared in several Russian churches,[32]

but the most famous example was the open, wooden "porticus"

which connected the Regia and the Palatine Chapel in

Aachen.[33] It seems to have been a necessary feature for

an Emperor's palace; as late as 1550 a private passageway

was built connecting the Hofburg in Vienna with the

Augustinierkirche (Fig. 72).[34] In general, the combination

of palace and church occurred mainly in the North; Southern

examples are either lost or totally obscured by later con-

struction.[35]

Italian princes rarely adopted the passageway as a

link between the palace and church since they were not in-

vested with both spiritual and temporal power of a Pope

or a Byzantine Emperor. Whenever the passageway was adopted,

its purpose was always secular and usually built for reasons

of defense or convenience. The most famous example was

the corridor which connects the Vatican with the Castel

San Angelo (Fig. 74). Built into the walls of Leo IV

(847-855), the "passetto" (as it is known today) has no

certain date of construction although the name of Alexander

VI (1492-1502) is generally connected with it due to his

numerous restaurations.[36] His work continued well into

the Cinquecento. Antonio da Sangallo[37] executed repairs

for Julius II while Paul IV (1555-1559) reenforced the entire structure with new arches in its walls. Although the passageway is famed for its aid in the escape of Clement VII during the Sack of Rome, its purpose was to facilitate the movement of military troops which were stationed in the Castel. This was certainly its function during Vasari's time, for the renovations made to the "passetto" by Paul IV were preceded by the repairs made in the 1540's to the walls surrounding Vatican.[38] It proved to be a convenient model for other courts. An overhead passage five bays in length still connects the Castello with the Este residence in Ferarra (Fig. 76),[39] and an even more extensive system of circulation existed in Sabbioneta.[40] A similar structure in Turin also used the city walls as a base for a passageway connecting the Castello and the Palazzo Reale.[41]

The corridor of convenience was equally common. In Urbino, a secret gallery across the giardino segreto (Fig. 75) connected the separate suites of the Duke and the Duchess.[42] It was only a method of communication, but it was still considered unique enough in the Cinquecento to deserve mention in Vasari's Lives (VI, 320).

The most influential corridor of this kind was Bramante's Belvedere. Garden and theater, museum and villa, it was the most convincing testament to Julius II's avowed goal of reinstating the political and artistic primacy of Rome. While the Belvedere is usually analyzed as a "cortile," Vasari emphasized its function connecting the Vatican Palace with the Villa of Innocent VIII (IV, 158). In his biography of Bramante, Vasari continually called the Bevedere a "corridore." With this in mind, Frommel has suggested that the original plans included only a single raised corridor crossing the valley between the palace and the villa. The evidence supporting this point of view is convincing; early documents refer to it as a via and not a villa.[43]

One of the distinguishing characteristics of the Corridoio is that it connects an urban palace (Palazzo Vecchio) with a garden (the Boboli) across a river. The most ambitious project of this sort was never built-- Michelangelo's suggestion to connect the Palazzo Farnese in Rome with the gardens adjacent to the Villa Farnesina across the Tiber.[44] Although this project is more in the realm of garden design than urban architecture, it might have been at the back of the client's and designer's minds at the moment of conception for the Corridoio, particularly since Vasari is our only source on this subject (VII, 224).

The private passageway became a typical expression of papal power. In the 1530's, Paul III (1534-1549) Michelangelo's patron for the Palazzo Farnese, began the construction of a corridor connecting the Palazzo Venezia to his Summer retreat in the villa adjacent to S. Maria

in Aracoeli.[45] Its design (Figs. 77, 78) continues the
tradition of the raised passageway as an undecorated,
utilitarian structure, and over time it became invisible
as adjacent buildings obscured its view. Less than ten
years after the death of Paul III, Paul IV contemplated
the construction of an elaborate set of three stairways--
the first and last covered--which would extend from San
Silvestro al Quirinale to San Marco.[46] Thus what once had
been a personal caprice had become a papal compulsion. In
the course of a half century, three popes had planned or
built private passageways, and several others sponsored
repairs on the existing passage to the Castel San Angelo.
Cosimo and Vasari certainly knew these examples in Rome
and other cities, and it is not improbable that they knew
of similar passageways in Vienna and Paris.[47] By contrast,
Florence must have appeared woefully inadequate, lacking
a private system of urban circulation which other cities
enjoyed. With the construction of the Corridoio, Cosimo
brought Florence a step closer to becoming an up-to-date,
16th Century capital city.

Both tradition and the nature of the commission
limited the expressive possibilities at Vasari's disposal
when he designed the Corridoio. According to the models
which were available to the designer, a private urban
passageway was a utilitarian building lacking architectural
detail. Like modern railroads, it sought the easiest and

most level connection between two points. A church could
contain a monumental interior space or a palace could present an imposing facade for its urban setting, but the
Corridoio only had to provide an extended, enclosed space
of no great architectural distinction. This does not
belittle Vasari's accomplishment in designing the Corridoio;
but it indicates the limited means which he had at his
disposal.

The North Arm of the Corridoio along the Arno is
both the most imposing and the most visible section of the
structure. It has always been impressive. An earlier
generation admired it for its rugged simplicity in contrast
to the Uffizi;[48] a modern critic might admire the Corridoio
for its ability to coalesce with the fabric of the city
of Florence. Yet not all of its design determinants were
visual. Francesco di Giorgio had already suggested that
a city divided by a river ought to build piazze and continuous porticoes on either bank,[49] but the Corridoio's
connection to the Quattrocento theorist is perhaps more
accidental than deliberate. In 1558 Cosimo built the
Loggia di Pesce at the Northern end of the Ponte Vecchio,
but in 1565 it was pulled down for the construction of
the Corridoio.[50] Since Cosimo had demolished one of the
most important commercial structures in the city, the
merchants had to find another location in Florence. In
compensation for this act of deliberate destruction,

another Loggia for the fish market was built in 1568 by
Vasari[51] on a site in the center of town. To wait three
years for new space was too long for most merchants, and
it is very likely that some might have never left while
others moved into the area to take advantage of the favorable location. Like any market loggia, the arcades of the
Corridoio were a natural means for protecting trade from
inclement weather. The commercial value of the spaces
under the Corridoio became so great that in 1570 they
were walled up to contain permanent locations for botteghe.[52]
The shops under the North Arm existed until their removal
at the end of the 19th Century.[53]

The design of the space within the passageway was
not problematical. Size posed no great difficulty. With
the exception of the Ponte Vecchio arm, Vasari maintained
a constant width of about 3.30 m. along the entire distance.
This assured convenient and easy access throughout the entire structure, but privacy and visual monotony had to be
reckoned with. Vasari had planned to use arched windows
on the river side of the North Arm, but shortly after construction began, he changed his mind and used square windows instead.[54] The reason was probably aesthetic and not
financial. It contrasted the different architectural functions of the two sides of the corridor: the city side with
small bull's eye windows affording privacy from observers
in adjacent palaces[55] while the river side had large,

square windows permitting the occupants of the Corridoio
to enjoy the view. The only place where this system was
broken was at the center of the Ponte Vecchio where an
arrangement of rectangular windows focused down river at
the Ponte S. Trinita.[56]

The Roman-like character of the North Arm was rendered necessary by the extreme height of the Corridoio.
The floor level was determined by the height of the shops
on the Ponte Vecchio; from that point the land slopes down
to a lower elevation near the Uffizi, creating an actual
need for the base on which the composition sits. The real
problem was to design a structure which could withstand the
forces of the winds along the unprotected riverbank, and
in this case simple columnar supports probably would not
have sufficed. The aqueduct-like design was the perfect
solution, answering all structural difficulties by the use
of mass. Lessmann has asserted that the continuous alternation of barrel vaults and piers pierced by transverse
vaults recalls utilitarian Roman architecture like the base
of the Temple of Jupiter Anxus at Terracina,[57] but it is
more likely that the actual sources for Vasari's treatment
of the North Arm can be found in the other passageways
which he saw in Rome. In fact, the Corridoio repeats the
arched forms of the Castel San Angelo and San Marco corridors. Like the Corridoio, both are merely enclosed passageways on vaulted substructures, and the only difference is

that the Castel San Angelo corridor is solid on one side
since it was a part of the defensive walls of Rome.   In
this case, then, the closest Ancient prototype would be
the Aurelian walls of Rome which employed a similar structural configuration.[58]   Yet the ultimate effect of the
Corridoio is not Roman.   The large surfaces of plaster
(hiding the rubble construction), the strapwork around
the arches and piers, and the bull's eye windows lend
an air of papery insubstantiality to the entire structure.
What Vasari has created is a marriage of the scale and
forms of the Roman Cinquecento with the simplicity and
delicacy of the Florentine Quattrocento.

Other features are derived from Florentine Medieval
architecture.   The stone brackets used by Vasari to support
the Corridoio when it passes the tower of the Manelli are
primary examples of this.   Derived from sporti, the above-
ground projections into the public space of streets, the
brackets are given Renaissance respectability by treating
their horizontal cross-beams as architraves and adorning
the intersection to the diagonal strut with some of
Vasari's favorite and over-worked guttae.   Beginning in
1295, projections like this were outlawed in some of
Florence's public thoroughfares (Via Maggio, Piazza del
Duomo),[59] but they were employed throughout the Renaissance
as well.   Vasari himself already had used similar brackets
on his porch attached to the Palazzo del Parte Guelfa,[60]

but he was not exceptional in this respect. Projecting
brackets are found on several Florentine palaces, most
notably on the Palazzo Cocchi-Serristori and the Palazzo
dell' Antella, both the Piazza Santa Croce.[61]

Similarly, the Corridoio gave Vasari the opportunity
to design his only completed church facade. Before the
construction of the Corridoio, the facade of S. Felicita,
like so many other Florentine churches, was a plain, unadorned wall.[62] Vasari only allowed the Corridoio to pass
across the front of the church, for it is highly unlikely
that he could have built an entirely new facade to dis-
guise the passageway without radically changing the architectural vocabulary which he used on the North Arm. Despite the double limitation of time and technique, Vasari
still made an effort to make the Corridoio less obtrusive
to its neighbors and more integral with the church. This
was achieved by the manipulation of floor levels. Vasari
certainly wanted to give to the arches in his facade a
"classical" proportion which was neither too squat nor too
elongated, and for this reason the floor level of the
Corridoio rises considerably between the Ponte Vecchio and
the church. In addition, the use of a different cornice
and the introduction of a colossal pier at the North end
of the loggia distinguish the facade of the church from
the passageway. Yet the effort does not seem totally convincing. In a forward-looking decade which produced the

facades for the Gesu in Rome and S. Francesco della Vigna
in Venice, Vasari's solution by comparison shows more af-
finity with Medieval Florentine churches like S. Jacopo
than its own contemporaries.[63]

The significance of the Corridoio in the social and
political history of Florence is notable for the lack of
objections to its construction. That it was a curiosity
cannot be denied; a 17th Century guide to Florence emphasized its regal magnificence and gave the Corridoio
a description equal in length to the Uffizi.[64] Furthermore, an official biographer stressed Cosimo's fairness
during its construction by passing around the outside of
the Manelli family tower, thus not destroying their an-
cestral family residence.[65] Yet admiration was not uni-
versal, since the Corridoio's construction necessitated
the destruction of the botteghe of many artisans and the
removal of some beautiful houses which dated from the
Trecento.[66] Despite any censorship which might have been
imposed in the Cinquecento, it is unlikely that the last
opinion is exceptional. One explanation for the surprising
lack of criticism has already been discussed: since the
construction of the Corridoio necessitated little demolition, there was scarcely any reason to begrudge its
existence.

Any conflict with the fabric of the city was prevented by following the established route of communication

between the Palazzo Vecchio and the Pitti. The pattern
of circulation between these two points would have been
almost the same even if Cosimo I had not built the linkage between the two palaces. In modern terms, this would
be seen as a stroke of genius, for the construction of the
Corridoio involved no change to the environment surrounding it. For a building of such size and length, the
Corridoio had little if any effect on the urban evolution
of Florence.

Despite its Roman ancestry, the Corridoio continued
Florentine urban traditions. Florence was, and still is,
to a large degree, a veritable matrix of overhead passageways. The clustering of buildings belonging to a single
family was a characteristic feature of Medieval domestic
architecture in Florence,[67] and overhead construction,
either as passageways or habitable space, was their means
of cohesion. Such volte abound throughout the city, and
the most visible examples belonged to the Peruzzi near
Piazza Santa Croce and the Girolami directly opposite the
Corridoio's North Arm.[68] Yet no significant passageway
of this kind was built after the 16th Century. With the
concentration of power in individual rulers, the different
functions of ruling and residing were accommodated in
larger residences like Versailles, and structures like the
Corridoio were made obsolete by the straight streets of
Baroque cities and the growing use of covered carriages.
By the 17th Century, it had become a relic of an earlier age.

IV

THE LOGGIA IN AREZZO

In August, 1570, Giorgio Vasari toured the Grand
Duchy of Tuscany with Prince Francesco de' Medici.[1] When
they visited Arezzo, they must have been struck by its
ruinous condition. Only a month earlier the Cancellaria
of Arezzo expressed the desire to construct a building
to beautify the city.[2] The most logical site for it
was on the North side of the Piazza Grande where many
buildings had been damaged or destroyed by the reconstruction of the fortress located just to the North-East of
the Piazza.[3] They must have realized that Arezzo had
built no new public buildings since the Fourteenth Century,
and that its most recent churches--late Quattrocento designs like Santissima Annunziata and Santa Maria delle
Grazie--were located at the periphery of the city or just
outside its walls. While there is no evidence that Vasari
made any suggestions about the Loggia which he ultimately
would design, it is very likely that he would have been
consulted for advice on the largest building to be built
in Arezzo, the city of his birth. Francesco, on the other
hand, must have maintained a guarded interest in the project,
and two years later he gave it his definite approval.[4]

The Loggia was meant to be an imposing building (Figs. 79, 80). More than a hundred meters long, its twenty bays extend from the Corso Italia on the Northwest to the Southeast corner of the Piazza Grande, and to the North is a modern park adjacent to the old fortress. Immediately to the South were the two major religious and fraternal institutions in Arezzo, the church of the Pieve and the Misericondia (Figs. 81, 82). The Loggia's patron was the confraternity of the Misericordia and its economic purpose was to provide income for their works of mercy.[5] Its twenty bays contain botteghe on the piazza level, while the upper floors of the Western half contained offices for the Monte di Pietà of Arezzo, the Dogana, and the Cancelleria. Five rental houses were built on a repetitive plan in the Eastern half (Fig. 84). An ingenious use of the sharply sloping site permits access to both shops and houses at street level from opposite sides of the building (Fig. 83) and these two areas are connected by a stair in the eleventh bay which possibly was once the location of a street. Other functions were accommodated over time, namely a theater and the official printings offices for the city, which were added in the 18th Century.[6] Since all of these functions were directly concerned with the administration of the city, the Loggia became in effect a second communal palace for Arezzo.

1. The Political Background

The Loggia's sober facade hides a history of political
turmoil. Vasari's Loggia was one of his few buildings un-
encumbered by previous construction, and this opportunity
was the result of systematic destruction carried out under
the orders of Cosimo I. The fortress begun in 1502 by
Giuliano da Sangallo was totally rebuilt from 1539 on,
and much of the reconstruction (Fig. 79) involved demolition of the area just to the Northeast of the Piazza
Grande.[7] This project forged an important link in the
chain of fortifications in Southern Tuscany, and at the
same time, removed an important symbol of independence
from the Aretines. Arezzo had been under Florentine
domination since 1384, but its history indicates a continuous series of reactions to foreign subjugation.[8]
The medieval Palazzo del Commune, located just to the
North of the site of the Loggia, already had been demolished in 1533 (I, 273). Other buildings of civic importance did not escape the needs of the State. The
destruction of the 11th Century Duomo Vecchio on the opposite end of the city raised the anger of the Aretines
who pleaded for its preservation, but Cosimo remained
steadfast.[9] It had to go, and it, too, was destroyed
in 1561. The motivation for these acts was primarily
political. The Palazzo del Popolo was probably the most

important symbol of Aretine freedom, and in 1554, Piero
Strozzi, commander of the Sienese army, occupied the Duomo
Vecchio while at war with Florence.[10] Although there are
no views which show the result of this massive destruction
before the construction of the Loggia, the irregular cornice
lines and facades behind San Rocco in Bartolomeo della
Gatta's altarpiece (Arezzo: Pinacoteca, 1479) accurately
show the character of the Piazza Grande as it existed at
the end of the Quattrocento (Fig. 85).[11]

The history of the Loggia's site indicates that political aspirations and public architecture were inseparable
in Medicean Tuscany. Already in the 14th Century, Florence
controlled a territorial state which included both Pisa and
Arezzo.[12] Almost two centuries later, Cosimo I enlarged
this area through the conquest of Siena in 1555-1559. The
scope and authority of the new regional state considerably
exceeded that of its predecessor, and to administer his
domain, Cosimo replaced self-government with a class of
bureaucratic functionaries who ruled in his name.[13] The
state was subdivided into a series of regional units, and
among the largest was Arezzo, with over 70 towns and vil-
lages under its control.[14] But Cosimo's yoke was not ab-
solute. Within this larger framework, the local nobility
retained a major role in the governmental process. Arezzo
avoided complete Florentine domination in the Quattrocento,
and in the Cinquecento the General Council continued to

function with over 30 members drawn from the local aristocracy.[15] As in other Tuscan cities, the closed hereditary
ruling class excluded other citizens from participation in
this political body. The councils provided one means of
aristocratic control; the others are memberships in the
various fraternities and the Monte di Pietà.

The members of this administrative class needed both
office space and housing, and the architectural program of
the Loggia was meant to supply this. The earliest documents indicate that the Loggia was conceived to include
housing, office space for the Monte di Pietà, and rentable
botteghe, and it was not until construction was well under
way that the Dogana and the Cancelleria became tenants.[16]
The accommodation of several distinct functions became an
important feature of the Loggia--in the upper level the
offices and houses are clearly differentiated in plan and
are separate from each other.

The Loggia's patrons and occupants played complementary
roles within the political context of Arezzo. The nominal
patron was a private institution, the Confraternity of the
Misericordia, which provided for the social welfare of the
city.[17] Similar functions were carried out by the agencies
which occupied the Loggia's office space, and the most important one was the Monte di Pietà. In general, monti were
created in the 15th Century as a reaction to the exorbitant
rates charged by Jewish moneylenders. They offered loans

to both cities and individuals, but their funds were generally employed in the interests of the community as a whole.
They were usually forbidden to add income from their interest
charges to their capital, and their profits were generally
distributed in the form of public works or dowries. In general, they made small loans and often stored valuables.
While the charitable activity of monti was controlled by
their charters, the Florentine monte (and probably Arezzo,
too) engaged in commercial speculation to aid the growth
of the Tuscan State.[18] In nuce, monti were municipal loan
banks which became the major financial agents in their
communities.

The Dogana and the Cancelleria, the other tenants, collected customs and taxes and provided notorial services
which linked Florence with Arezzo. While most of these
positions were filled by Aretines, their actions now represented not the power of the individual families but the
larger goals of the Tuscan State. Taken together, the
Misericordia and the Monte were key elements in achieving
one of Cosimo's major goals--economic stability. Moreover,
the connection between these institutions was physical as
well as symbolic, for Vasari's design included an overhead
bridge which connects the Misericordia's palace with the
Monte's offices in the Loggia.[19]

The developing institutions of the Tuscan State needed
an appropriate set of forms and symbols, and Vasari found

his solution in a selective combination of elements from
Ancient and Cinquecento architecture. While he never
claimed to have revived the forms of antiquity in his
buildings, Vasari was certainly conversant with Vitruvius
and classical architectural grammar. He must have known
that the loggia and the unified arcade were features of
ancient fora as described by Vitruvius and Alberti, and he
was definitely aware of examples like Vigevano and the
Piazzo San Marco in Venice which are derivative of this
tradition.[20] Vasari, however, modified these considera-
tions to suit his own purposes. With its government functions and location on the principal piazza of a city, the
Loggia was the Cinquecento equivalent of a Roman basilica.
While Roman examples never had an enclosed upper story
in their facades, Cesare Cesariano reconstructed the
Vitruvian Basilica at Fano (Fig. 86) in this manner.[21]
Vitruvius also said that the stalls of money changers
were located under the porticoes of basilicae surrounding
ancient fora.[22] This was an apt analogy for the Loggia
in Arezzo, since the Monte di Pietà was the major tenant,
so to speak, in the new structure.

Despite these similarities, the sources for the Loggia's
design can be found in Renaissance models. To Vasari's
mind, the most important determinant for the Loggia must
have been the presence of the Monte di Pietà. The utilitarian requirements for monti were minimal--a few rooms for

offices and sometimes a chapel--and consequently this did
not justify a separate architectural tradition. Monti were
usually given space in existing structure, and only in the
largest cities did they ever achieve the size and wealth
to merit their own buildings. Vasari, however, could easily
claim expertise in this field since he had already converted some rooms in the Palazzo del Parte Guelfa into
offices for the Florentine monte.[23]

Certain features reappear in the buildings which housed
monti, and the most common elements are the siting on a
major square, and the inclusion of a ground floor portico
or shops. While the Arezzo monte was the only one in
Tuscany which necessitated new construction, buildings for
this institutional client abount in Northern Italy. In
Brescia, the Palazzo del Monte di Pieta was built in 1484
using an open ground floor on the Piazza della Loggia, a
scheme which is directly related to North Italian communal
palaces (Fig. 87).[24] The monte in Vicenza took a slightly
different   form--a closed block with the ground floor
devoted to shops--but with an equally important site on
the Piazza della Signoria opposite the Basilica (Fig. 88).[25]
But the monte most similar to Arezzo was designed by
Falconetto for Padova in 1530 (Fig. 89).[26] Nine bays long
and two stories high, the Paduan example anticipated the
Loggia facade not only in its general character and bay
proportions but in some details as well--the tabernacle

windows on socles are readily apparent. The stylistic
similarities between Vasari and Falconetto are perhaps
accidental, but the choice of the loggia form in Padova
seems to be a deliberate act to reinforce the importance
of the Monte di Pietà as a public institution and as a
public building equal in importance to the Palazzo Communale. The architects of buildings for monti found the
loggia form to be a convenient model for their own build-
ings--it signifies its public importance as a communal
institution in the same way Roman models implied Imperial
wealth and strength for banks built in the Beaux Arts
style. Perhaps with similar thoughts in mind, Alberto
Alberti was sent to Arezzo to copy Vasari's Loggia as a
model for his design of the Palazzo dei Laudi in
Sansepolcro, a building which also happened to contain
the offices for the monte of that city (Fig. 90).[27]

The Loggia is indebted to Ancient Architecture in a
more fundamental way. Almost all Italian piazze lie on
flat ground or on the top of a hill; the Piazza Grande in
Arezzo and the Campo in Siena are the only major spaces
built on hillside sites. Renaissance architects rarely
had to design urban buildings on sharply sloping sites
such as the Loggia has. A drawing from the Peruzzi circle
is particularly important for the Loggia (Fig. 91). Reconstructing one of the hemicycles adjacent to the Forum
of Trajan, the drawing shows a building in the upper left

corner which is comparable to the Arezzo Loggia in both
the anonymous character of its facade and its three story,
three part section. Vasari certainly would have admired
how the Roman architect placed his building on the sloping
site, and the square mezzanine windows over the shop entries
in the Loggia as executed recall similar features in the
ancient model. It is probable that Vasari knew of the
Peruzzi drawing (or even the original if it is a copy),
since in the Lives Vasari indicated familiarity with
Peruzzi's architecture in general and with his studies of
ancient architecture in particular (IV, 604). By choosing
to study Trajan's Markets where the complex problems of
urban planning were similar to projects like the Uffizi,
Vasari captured the pragmatic spirit of ancient design instead of the details of classical buildings.

2. Architecture and Political Administration

The primary functions of the Loggia--administrative
headquarters for the Monte di Pietà and rental space--were
the co-determinants of its architectural form. In his
letters Vasari recognized this distinction, for they are
normally addressed to the building committee for the Monte.
More important, however, is the observation made by an
Aretine just before the completion of the Loggia that it
was very similar to the Uffizi in Florence, thus implying

not only a formal connection because of their extraordinary length but also a similarity in their use as government office buildings.[28] Despite its sophisticated observations, this comment should not be taken to construct a fixed, immutable typology for administrative structures. While political bodies and charitable organizations constructed buildings which were used for the discharge of their functions, the rich and varied solutions to this problem reflect the different requirements of site, function and iconography as presented by the client. It is important to note that additional functions often were accommodated in 16th Century office structures, botteghe and rental housing being the most common subsidiary requirements. In both form and use the administrative structures with which Vasari was acquainted were hybrid structures often with overlapping functional requirements. This was directly reflected in the kinds of uses which were accommodated in the Arezzo Loggia.

Porticoed structures including administrative offices had been common in Italy throughout the Middle Ages, and they existed wherever a representative form of government permitted the delegation of political power. In Medieval Italy, the characteristic form of expression for civic administration was the communal palace. While all palazzi communale are not alike, the Loggia and several of its Medieval predecessors share common features: they are

located on the main squares of their respective cities,
and their ground floors are given over to commercial while
the upper floors were reserved for administrative space
and living quarters. Numerous examples of this building
type are found throughout Northern Italy--Cremona and
Piacenza to name two examples--and in form they descend
from Carolingian and Ottonian court architecture.[29] Of
the buildings in this tradition the 13th Century Broletto
in Milan (Fig. 92) is most comparable to the Loggia. Its
most important features can be appreciated only in three
dimensions. Sitting in the middle of a market square,
the Broletto is only two bays deep in its plan. In contrast to the communal palaces which had loggie grafted on
to palace plans, the Broletto's shallow depth permitted
only office and warehouse space on the upper floor. Unlike the communal palaces, its size and location made it
unsuitable as a residence for a political leader. This
tradition did not die at the end of the Middle Ages; it
continued well into the Cinquecento. Cesariano's reconstruction of the Basilica at Fano was, in reality, a North
Italian communal palace decorated with the language of
Antiquity.[30] Similarly, Michelangelo's renovation of the
Palazzo dei Conservatori on the Campidoglio recognized the
problem of historical continuity by using a portico on its
facade, a feature found in numerous town halls built in
the Papal States during the Quattrocento.[31]

Any major change in the form of a structure used to
house administrative offices had to await a change in the
administration of the State itself. The communal palace
was an appropriate solution for housing the simple governmental functions of a Medieval town. While it could
contain the administrative structure for a single city
in the 15th Century, it provided neither the space nor
the flexibility needed for housing the numerous offices
of trade and government which were characteristic of
larger 16th Century regional states. Its closed form
presented two drawbacks to the development of an administrative architecture. First, the generous size of rooms
and internal courtyards in the earlier structures created
a large amount of wasted space which was more suited to
ceremony than efficient administration. Second, it was
difficult to rationally accommodate diverse uses like
housing or shops which would produce rental income for
the building's owners. To efficiently administer a regional state, on the other hand, it was necessary to
bring together into a single structure the numerous
agencies which were scattered throughout the city. Efficiency of administration was one of the characteristic
features of the Tuscan State under Cosimo I,[32] certainly
the most notable office structure in 16th Century Italy.
Yet Tuscany was not unique in resolving the conflicting
demands of administration and income, for comparable

projects could be found wherever a highly developed system of administration existed.

The Venetian Republic was the first state in Italy where a complex administrative system brought about the creation of unique office buildings. The division of administrative offices exactly mirrored the division of the State. The office of Procurator of St. Mark's was only second in importance to the Doge, and by the 16th Century, its vast wealth forced the division of the office into three parts, two of which were concerned with the administration of private estates, while the third was responsible for all of the holdings in the area of the Piazzo San Marco.[33] Consequently, the goals and purposes of the Procuratie were not altogether different from the Misericordia in Arezzo. Prior to the construction of the Library and Sansovino's proposed renewal of the entire square, the most notable architectural accomplishment of the Procurators was the Procuratie Vecchie (Figs. 93, 94) on the North side of the Piazza, built by Bartolomeo Buon after a fire in 1512 had destroyed an earlier building on the same site.[34] Two stories high and 50 bays long, the building was not an administrative structure in the strictest sense. It contained shops on the ground floor and rental apartments on the upper floor, while the Procurators lived in the small houses on the other side of the Piazza.[35] It is not certain whether the Procurators used their own

houses or the new apartments for the discharge of their
official functions, and they did not acquire their own
offices on the upper floor of the Library until the end
of the 16th Century.[36] Although the Procuratie Vecchie's
construction on the site of an existing building precluded
the possibility of a clearly repetitive plan for the entire structure, the layout of the building still included
one housing unit every four bays with a light well in its
center. A similar plan was followed for the Procuratie
Nuove. In reality, then, the Procuratie Vecchie was a
series of linked palaces, and for this reason it has been
characterized as a true forerunner of the Uffizi.[37]

The Rialto, on the other hand, had always been the
center of trade and administration in Venice. Its eminence
in the city was assured by the fact that it was the earliest
settlement in the city, and its position on the grand canal
made it easy to move goods in and out of the market by
water. As early as 1305 the city had exercised the right
of eminent domain for the construction of new buildings and
the enlargement of the market square.[38] These measures
were not merely utilitarian, for the city wished to give
greater dignity and propiety to the area.[39] Yet the demands of trade kept the area in flux. New construction in
the 15th Century included further enlargement of the piazza,
the construction of a new loggia, and a landing area for
zentilhuomini.[40] These buildings also contained the

administrative and jurisdictional offices for fiscal and tax matters. Jacopo de' Barbari recorded their form in his map of Venice (Fig. 95). Shallow structures only a few bays deep surround the campo, their porticoed shops surmounted by two floors for offices and storage.

The history of the Rialto in the 16th Century is well known. After a fire destroyed the entire area in January, 1514, a special committee of seven nobles solicited designs from several architects for the reconstruction of the district, and among them were Fra Giocondo and Antonio Scarpagnino. The former's design is known to us through a passage written by Vasari, who apparently had seen the drawings for the scheme (V, 269-272). His model included a church dedicated to Saint Matthew in the center of a symmetrical, foursided square surrounded by a street of commercial shops for the silk and wool trades. The shops on the square were to contain bankers and jewelers, and the food markets were confined to the waterfront canals on all four sides of the project. The upper floor would have contained offices and warehouses. The grandiosity of the project was its downfall, for the State could not afford it due to expenses incurred in the War of the League of Cambrai. Instead, Scarpagninio's plan was chosen because it involved neither the acquisition of new property nor the construction of costly foundations. Curiously, aspects of the executed scheme were not substantially

different from Fra Giocondo's proposal, since the campo is
defined by a series of arcuated, slab-like buildings which
focus upon the church of San Giacomo di Rialto (Fig. 96).
Like the Procuratie Vecchie, the financial purpose of the
complex was to build rental space for the gain of the State.
Construction on the Rialto never really halted in the
Cinquecento. The Dogana was built in the 1530's,[41] and
more space for storage and shops was gained in Sansovino's
Fabbriche Nuove di Rialto, begun in 1554.[42]

Sixteenth Century architects had buildings like this in
mind whenever they had to design large commercial structures
which included office space. The shallow loggia was a
rational response to the problem of making a building with
limited vertical growth and unlimited horizontal expansion
along a street or a square. Its repetitive facade could
be expanded or contracted according to the limits of the
site, and its varying depth meant that only a minimal amount
of land had to be acquired for its construction. The inclusion of botteghe on the ground floor meant additional
income for its owners, and it had the added advantage of
making an easy graft onto the fabric of existing palace-
like structures, as in the case of Palazzo dei Conservatori
in Rome. Yet, as we have seen in the Rialto, this kind of
juncture rarely occurred whenever rental space was a primary determinant in the architectural program of a project
which also included office space. Even in cities like

Florence or Venice, the shortage of space and the cost of
land meant that such buildings, like the modern skyscraper,
could only rise vertically once the horizontal dimension
had been set. The result was the creation of a slab-like
commercial structure whose upper floors could be used for
numerous functions--housing, administration, storage, etc.
This also would have been the appearance of the Loggia had
it been built on a flat site. In contrast, buildings
which housed government functions exclusively tended to
stay in the tradition of the communal palace--the Palazzo
dei Conservatori on the Campidogio in Rome and the monti in
Padua and Borgo San Sepolcro are examples of this. Given
the nature of Vasari's task in Arezzo to incorporate offices,
residential, and commercial space into a single structure,
his problem could be characterized combining residential
aspects of the Procuratie Vecchie with a building whose site
and economy dictated building section not unlike those used
at the Rialto.

Vasari and the architects of other multi-use buildings
faced similar design determinants. Two other projects--
the Osteria (Fig. 97) designed by Antonio da Sangallo for
Castro (1537)[43] and the Palazzo dei Giurconsulti in Milan
(Fig. 98) designed by Vicenzo Seregni[44]--recognized the
adaptability of the shallow Loggia form. While neither
project can be considered a direct prototype for the Loggia
in Arezzo, the histories of both commissions further clarify

the problems of design and patronage which Vasari faced.
In form, both structures are akin to the Loggia since
they are extended porticoes which sit alongside a public
piazza. This already had the theoretical blessing of
Alberti who emphasized the features of the loggia as a
convenient shelter from the elements and as a place for
the transaction of business.[45] Like the Arezzo and Rialto
projects, their patronage assured a distinctly political
character to their function and meaning--Papal in Castro,
civic in Venice, and fraternal in Milan. With the exception of the Palazzo dei Giureconsulti, financial motives
were present in every case. Documents for both the Rialto
project and the Arezzo Loggia clearly state the shops or
houses would produce necessary income for its owners,[46]
and a plan drawn by Antonio da Sangallo the Younger for
Castro indicates the division of ownership of the shops
between the "Osteria" and the "Capitano." These structures
were generally built on sites which were either virgin
(Castro) or destroyed by disaster (Venice, Arezzo). Hygiene
and cleanliness proved to be another common goal, for the
removal of unkept meat markets in Venice and Arezzo provided
at least temporary insurance against disease.[47] After these
goals had been achieved, it was simple to collect all of the
public offices into a single location. This was the motivation of Cosimo I for the construction of the Uffizi, and
it was apparently shared by Don Ferrante Gonzaga and Pius IV

for the construction of the Giureconsulti.[48] The inspiration for centralizing administrative offices in a single
building comes from modern Rome. According to Vasari,
Julius II wished to bring together in Bramante's design
for the Palazzo dei Tribunali in Rome all of the Papacy's
curial offices which previously had been scattered throughout the Vatican.[49] This, too, was also a primary motivation for the construction of the Uffizi.

Another element common to these structures--the loggia
facade--was borrowed by Sangallo for the "Osteria" at
Castro which served not only as a hospice for visitors to
the Farnese court but also as a residence and office for
the "Capitano" as indicated on its plan. The "Osteria"
contains another feature found in Arezzo--an overhead
bridge used as a private system of urban circulation connecting the "Capitano" with the Palazzo del Podesta.

The Rialto buildings are closer to the Loggia in both
form and concept. Both schemes tend to avoid closely
architectural ornament, and both were designed mainly as
utilitarian buildings, responding more to the necessities
of inexpensive buildings than to the needs of architectural
symbolism or political dogma.[50] In conclusion, Vasari's
administrative structures in Tuscany provide an interesting
parallel to their forerunners in Venice. The Uffizi, like
the public buildings on the Piazza San Marco, was obviously
meant to be a conscious display of the power

of the State, while the Loggia in Arezzo, like the Rialto
buildings, was reserved for the mundane functions of public
administration.

3. Vasari's Architectural Practice and the Execution of the Loggia

The history of the Loggia offers unique insight into
Vasari's professional relationship with his clients.
Throughout the design of the structure, both the patron
and the architect lacked any clear knowledge of all of the
functions and the extent of the new buildings and throughout the documents they refer to as the Fabrica. This was
not without effect on the wooden model which Vasari sent
in 1572 (Fig. 99). It only shows two bays of the building, and it gives no clear indication of the spaces behind
it, thus showing that Vasari's concerns were limited to
the general effect of the building on the sloping site.
Nonetheless, it hints at the sequence of the construction
of the Loggia, which was built bay by bay from the Western
end of the site near the Misericordia towards the East.
With his financial acumen, Vasari foresaw that construction could have been held up or even stopped. Other loggie
begun in the Cinquecento were still unfinished,[51] and there
was no guarantee that the fate of the Loggia would be any
different.

Vasari's participation in the design of the Loggia

was limited to the features shown in the wooden model. In
paintings and large scale decorations, Vasari delegated
the responsibility for actually designing his pictorial
projects to members of his workshop, and in the case of
the renovations of Santa Croce, the altar tabernacles were
designed by Francesco da Sangallo.[52] The concept of a
workshop, however, cannot be applied to the execution of
the Loggia. Too much was left to be designed, and this
required the services of an architect rather than a builder
or capo maestro. Vasari recognized this in a passage at
the end of Alberti's biography in the Lives:

> Since architects cannot always be at the site, it
> is of the utmost advantage to have a faithful and
> friendly assistant, and if no other knew this, I
> know this well, and by long experience. (II, 546)

This responsibility fell on Alfonso Parigi the Elder,
Florentine architect and father of an architectural dynasty
which lasted until the end of the next century.[53] Parigi
had already worked for Vasari on the construction of the
Loggia linking both arms of the Uffizi in Florence, and
the difficulty in building it was probably the reason why
Baldinucci characterized him as an architect well grounded
in technical matters.[54] In the Loggia, however, he was
forced to exercise his skills in architectural design.
Parigi was involved in the construction of the Loggia from
its inception, and after Vasari's death in 1574 he planned
all of the spaces behind the facade.[55] The facade was
built mainly according to Vasari's design, but there were

some minor changes probably introduced by Parigi which
accentuated the severity of a building already largely
without architectural detail. For instance, the dimensions of the piers were reduced in construction (2 m. in
scale compared to 1.74 m. as built). This decision altered the more squat proportions of the model and made
an already tall building seem excessively vertical. Other
changes included the substitution of square windows for
round ones in the attics of the botteghe, (creating an
effect almost exactly like the doors to the tabernae in
Trajan's Markets) and a preference for windows more square
in proportion in the attic of the facade. The most notable
change was a re-working of the zone just above the arches
to include a keystone. All of Parigi's changes involved
the substitution or elimination of simple features in an
already simple facade, and they all point to the desire
to construct an inexpensive and economical building. In
fact, Parigi repeated several of the Loggia's motifs in
his best known design, a monastic cloister at Santo Spirito
(Fig. 100).

Vasari's correspondence on the construction of the
Loggia gives an indication of his ability to organize and
carry out large artistic projects. Vasari directed the
preliminary planning and design of the Logga from Florence;
he stopped only once in Arezzo during this period, on a
trip to Rome.[56] In no case did Vasari ever allude to the

existence of presentation drawings or construction sketches;
he probably assumed that details would be worked out by the
capo maestro. The delegation of artistic responsibility
also required administrative ability, and this is where
most of Vasari's energies went. His clients were quick to
make use of his connections to the court in Florence. At
the initiation of the project Vasari was explicitly asked
to seek princely approval of a financial contribution to
the project, and he was later asked to seek permission to
re-use material from the old fortress.[57] Yet Vasari's
time was not always devoted to the Loggia. After the project had been approved in 1572, the patrons lacked a
wooden model, and in reply Vasari promised to send both
the model and a capo maestro only after apologizing for
his absence from Florence due to a trip for the inspection
of fortifications with Cosimo I.[58] Within two months the
model had been made and delivered to Arezzo, but Vasari
was consulted again when the authorities in Arezzo noticed
a defect in the design where the building would tend to
slide down the hill into the Piazza Grande.[59] Apparently,
this matter did not bother Vasari. In his reply he con-
fidently asserted that several bays and shops would be
vaulted within the year, and that the project would be a
benefit for a poor and destroyed city like Arezzo.[60] But
Vasari's bright predictions were not universally accepted,
and soon ill-feeling developed between all parties. In

response to a simple demand for a list of expenditures
made on the project, Vasari expressed both confusion and
distaste for a project which is overseen by two different
administrative bodies.[61]

In his letters Vasari indicated no real grasp of the
technical problems involved in the execution of his design.
Similar problems were routine for other 16th Century architects, but Vasari's conception of architectural practice
did not require any participation outside the realm of design and administration. In general, Vasari's practice
resembled those of other architects in the lack of detailed
drawings and in the liberal aid from assistants who would
not meddle in design.[62] There are fundamental differences
as well. Unlike his contemporaries, Vasari was never ap-
prenticed to another architect, stonecutter, or engineer,
nor is there any evidence that he studied ancient architecture with the conviction of a Sangallo or a Palladio.
Most of his design skill in architecture seems to have been
intuitive and self taught, and the lack of any direct training in architecture perhaps explains Vasari's dependence on
executants for his buildings.

The concentration of political and temporal power exemplified by Cosimo I monopolized almost all major artistic
commissions in the hands of the State, and almost all of
Vasari's architectural work was directly or indirectly in the

service of Tuscany. His position demanded utmost facility and flexibility due to the wide range of designs which he was required to produce. Moreover, his position as court architect brought him in contact with almost all major building projects in Tuscany. To execute them, Vasari had to combine the skills of a Quattrocento courtier-architect with the administrative ability and technical knowledge of a 16th Century professional like Sangallo the Younger. To a large degree, this became a problem of time, and thus Vasari's participation in any project had to be limited to the most essential aspects of design and execution. This is borne out by the absence of architectural drawings in Vasari's hand for his buildings, and it can be accounted for in two ways. First, Vasari's presentation to the client always included a wooden model, and the preparatory drawings necessary for it were probably summary in form and were destroyed by the modelmaker. Second, Vasari's major commissions (other than the Uffizi) were located in cities other than Florence, and it is likely that the plans and other drawings were lost or destroyed by Vasari's executants. Although it is not certain if Vasari maintained a permanent office as such, he could clearly notice talent in others, and he could draw on their time and technical skills which he lacked. While the artistic breadth of his work anticipates a Bernini or a Le Brun, Vasari's volume of work and limited

involvement with the design process points to the modern
architect-businessman, resembling McKim more than
Michelangelo.

4. Style and Sources

The problems which Vasari faced in designing the Loggia
were not suited to the inventive spatial composition and
planning found in other buildings from the last half of
the 16th Century. He merely had to design a single facade
to unify two separate buildings which would be different
in plan and function. In addition, the Loggia had to harmonize with the Misericordia's own palace opposte the
Loggia (Fig. 81). To build a columnar facade would have
been inappropriate, since it would have distracted interest
from the Pieve and the Misericordia's own palace, the most
important religious and fraternal structures in the city.
Instead, Vasari chose to harmonize the new building with
the structure owned by his patrons. To achieve this,
Vasari transferred the ABA compositional of the older building to the ground floor elevation of the Loggia's arcades,
altering it only to accept the dimensions of the botteghe
behind the facade. There are obvious differences between
the facades--particularly in Vasari's use of closed elements
where his model exhibits windows or niches--yet their common denominator is a uniform sense of scale obtained by the
reputation of a basic unit of approximately the same height

and width as its model along the entire face of the square.
Yet his re-interpretation of the older facade scheme indicates a sensitivity to both neighboring buildings and to
architecture of an earlier time, a surprising fact for an
architect who is generally considered to have been unsym-
pathetic to gothic design.

While Renaissance architects rarely adapted the facades
of their buildings to accommodate neighboring structures,
Vasari was unusual but not unique in this respect. The
Portico dei Banchi in Bologna (begun 1561) designed by
Vignola had to unify with a single facade several buildings
which were built in the previous century (Fig. 101).[63]
Some of its utilitarian and urban aspects are strikingly
similar to the Loggia. Its upper floors, too, were apparently used for apartments, and the ground floor contain
two story botteghe. Furthermore, the term banchi refers
to the fact that the shops once contained offices for
numerous moneychangers, thus making the basilica-like
structure the financial center for Bologna. Yet its most
important resemblance to the Tuscan structure is in its
urban siting. Since both buildings are located on the
main squares of their respective cities, they had to relate in design and scale to other institutional structures
which were immediately adjacent to their sites. In the
case of the Portico dei Banchi, the height and scale of
the adjacent Palazzo del Podesta was repeated by Vignola

in the lower floor of the newer structure (Fig. 101), thus
assuring visual continuity between two buildings which
were different in date of construction and architectural
style.[64] This is precisely the same device which Vasari
used ten years later in Arezzo. It is even possible that
the Portico dei Banchi provoked the construction of the
Loggia. In comparison to the modernization of the main
piazza of the second city in the Papal States, the main
square of Tuscan cities must have looked woefully old-
fashioned.

Vasari relied on other Cinquecento buildings for the
details of the facade. Baldassare Peruzzi was one of
Vasari's most consistent sources of inspiration, and he
already had adapted elements from the Palazzo Massimi for
the facade of the Uffizi. In the case of the Loggia, the
inspiration for the socle-window surmounted by a smaller
opening for the attic level comes from the same palace
(Fig. 102). Vasari's use of carved motifs is much more
dry and abstract than his model, particularly in the attic
zone where the removal of a secondary frame around the
window indicates Vasari's desire to use only the most
simple architectural details.

The design of the lower level of the facade has a more
unlikely source--Girolomo Genga, the early 16th Century
architect and painter from Urbino. It is very likely that
the sunken courts designed by Genga for the Villa Imperiale

in Pesaro provided the inspiration for the Villa Giulia,
a project with which Vasari was associated during its
initial stages.[65] Vasari certainly must have been familiar with the architecture of the Villa Imperiale. In
his life of Genga, Vasari gives a concise description of
Genga's addition to the 15th Century villa (VI, 318). Almost every detail in the lower level of the Loggia facade
can be traced to Genga's exterior facade of the sunken
courts (Fig. 103)--the panelling on the piers, the continuous string course of stone on the level of the spring
points of the arches, even the continuous band of socles
on which the windows are placed. These similarities seem
to be more intentional than accidental. Genga's son
Bartolomeo had studied in Florence and was on amicable
terms with Vasari.[66] Moreover, two of his students,
Baldassare Lancia and Giovanbattista San Marino, had been
called to Florence to work on fortification design for the
Tuscan state, thus giving Vasari ample opportunity to study
Genga's work through drawings.[67] In Genga, Vasari must have
seen an architect whose career anticipated his own. Both
practiced architecture, painting, and theatrical design
concurrently, and Genga's work for Francesco Maria della
Rovere must have required the same multiplicity of skills
which Vasari used in the service of Cosimo I. Their common preference for flattened forms without architectural
membering was conditioned in part by the element of dryness

in their painting styles, and these simple forms had the
added advantage for a court architect that they could be
erected with almost no supervision, thus leaving time free
for other courtly activities.

What differentiates Vasari's approach from Genga and
Peruzzi is the greater degree of severity in the design
of the facade. The Loggia is the most abstract of Vasari's
buildings in its avoidance of the orders, relying instead
on planner surfaces for its effect. Vasari was certainly
aware of the powerful visual effect of the unending repeti-
tion of the shops underneath the portico of the Loggia,
for their original design appears in painted form as the
background in his painting of the Forge of Vulcan (Florence:
Uffizi, ca. 1570. Fig. 104). Despite the fact that a
three dimensional model of the Loggia had been built,
Vasari's design is essentially two dimensional in character,
avoiding niches and other references to antiquity which were
used by Genga. In one sense, Vasari's facade is a giant
painting where all elements--large and small, receding and
protruding, horizontal and vertical--are resolved into a
neutral composition. With its sources in the work of two
architects eminent in the first decades of the Cinquecento,
the Loggia shows a tendency toward regularity and order-
liness commonly found in many buildings dating from the
middle of the 16th Century.[68]

5. The Loggia and Row Housing

The Loggia is a valuable contribution to the understanding of Cinquecento residential architecture. From
its inception the Loggia was meant to contain a number of
rental houses whose income would benefit the works of the
Misericordia. Rental housing was well known throughout
the Middle Ages and the Renaissance, and the Misericordia
was one of the largest landlords in Arezzo with over
seventy houses in its ownership.[69] They were mainly the
result of legacies and bequests to the Misericordia, and
their scattered locations throughout the city precluded
the possibility of any large scale urban design. In fact,
this was the case with most housing built in Italy during
the Renaissance. Fifteenth and 16th Century row houses
were built in small, separate groups of only a few houses;
larger projects are more scarce.[70]

When Alfonso Parigi the Elder provided the modello
for the rowhouses in the Loggia, he designed a housing unit
for which there were several comparable projects in Italy,
but none of these were copied exactly in the design of
the Loggia. Florentine houses tended to be tall and vertical ever since the Middle Ages, and this was mainly due to
the relatively narrow width of the building lots in comparison to their unusual depth. Numerous examples like
this must have existed throughout the entire city, but one
Quattrocento house bought by the Gianfigliazzi family was

recorded in an 18th Century plan.[71] Its facade faced the
Arno, and all of its spaces on the ground floor were connected by a corridor parallel to one of the party walls
of the house (Fig. 105). This plan type was often employed when large sites were subdivided for the construction of repetitive housing. From the developer's point of
view, this was a logical strategy whereby he could build
the maximum number of houses on any given site.

One of the earliest large scale subdivisions (Fig.
106) was begun by the Arte della Lana and the Arte dei
Mercanti on the via dei Servi on the site of a tiratoi,
a long, narrow building used for the carding of wool.[72]
Their plans (Fig. 107) resemble earlier and smaller
houses where a light-well courtyard separates two zones
of the building each two rooms deep. In scale and character these structures were more like row palaces than
row houses, for their height is approximately twice that
of the Loggia's houses and other contemporary examples.
The palazzo analogy also holds true to a larger extent,
since they were planned as smaller versions of signorial
residences. Their street facades are comparable to larger
contemporary buildings like the Palazzo Guadagni, and in
plan they tend to regularize the features of a palazzina:
androne, eccentric courtyard, and servants quarters at the
rear. The planning of the row palaces made it imperative
to provide at a smaller scale the same features found in

a larger residence, and such conveniences were probably in
the mind of a nobleman like Sansinetto de Bardi who purchased two of these houses in 1521.[73] The significance of
the houses on the via dei Servi is that they formed the
spine of a newly developing residential neighborhood whose
focus was the Church of the Santissima Annunziata, and
this expansion towards the North created another incentive
for the construction of the Servite Loggia designed by
Antonia da Sangallo the Elder in 1516.[74]

The Servite Loggia is the building in Tuscany most
comparable to the residential portion of the Loggia in
Arezzo (Fig. 108). In form, it emulates (but does not copy)
Brunelleschi's facade of the Ospedale degli Innocenti across
the square, and in function each of its three bays contains
two row houses between party walls. A plan in the Uffizi
very similar to the executed project shows the houses' internal layout (Fig. 109).[75] After entering the main door,
the entry hall leads the visitor to a small courtyard with
an open loggia on one side. The main flight of stairs
opens from the courtyard and leads to the main salone overlooking the Piazza; a secondary stair leads to a separate
suite of rooms which were probably reserved for servants or
rented out to other tenants.

The distribution of spaces combines features from both
traditional housing and the Quattrocento Florentine palace.
Lacking knowledge of antique housing of this size and scale,

Early Renaissance theorists failed to make any contribution
to our knowledge about row housing, and consequently no
really new features are found in their plans. Elements
like the androne, courtyard, and grand stair were all
present in Quattrocento palaces, and Sangallo's achievement
was to adapt palace features to a more economical plan for
a smaller house. A three part plan was a standard solution
for the design of small urban housing in the 16th Century.
The central courtyard would provide light and air to both
zones of habitable rooms, and the location of the stairs
between these zones provided a clear means of circulation
throughout all parts of the house. These features, too,
are generic and are not the invention of Antonio the Elder.
Although their parent-age belongs to anonymous buildings
like the Gianfigliazzi house, Giuliano da Sangallo used
the three part plan in an undeveloped form to denote repetitive housing in his plan for a Medici palace on the via
Laura (UA 287).[76] A modified version of the Servite plan
appears on a sketch attributed to his nephew Antonio da
Sangallo the Younger for a row palace in Rome (Fig. 110).[77]
Moveover, palatial features at a domestic scale appear
in a Roman palazzina like Palazzo Ferrari or sketches by
Baldassare Peruzzi (UA 489r, UA 496) where a symmetrical
facade with a central entry is married to the three part
scheme of an Italian house. Although Parigi's plans for
the Loggia houses employ more or less the same features as

his predecessors, it certainly lacks their clarity and
livability.

The row houses in Arezzo must be seen in contrast to
these models (Figs. 83, 111). A hallway leads from the
rear (or uphill) side of the Loggia to the main salone
overlooking the Piazza Grande. Unlike the other examples
where room sizes are differentiated according to their importance and use, the spaces in the Arezzo residences are
cellular units of roughly the same size. Only the hall
and main saloni were vaulted; the other rooms have simple
wooden floors and ceilings. The most curious feature of
the houses is their relationship to their exteriors. Since
they were forced to conform to a pair of unrelated facades,
the Loggia's fron and rear windows sit at different
heights relative to each other and to the Piazza, and
the result was a split level section where a uniform floor
height could not be obtained. Although Parigi's solution
contains more or less the same features as its predecessors,
the excess amount of space devoted to circulation and the
rigid adherence to evenly spaced structural bays created
a series of cellular, almost equally sized rooms which
compromised the flexibility and livability of the earlier
examples. However, this is less the fault of the designer
than an indication of the variety of house plans found in
Cinquecento Italy. The same plan types can be found in
other Italian projects, for the differentiated layout of

the Servite houses reappears in smaller palaces designed
by Antonio da Sangallo the Younger while the units in
Arezzo reflect a cellular plan common to smaller houses.[78]

Finally, the row houses in the Loggia were designed
for a specific type of occupant--the governmental administrator or professional whose status required dignified
housing but whose financial means excluded the possibility
of a private palazzo. The small number of houses in a
building as large as the Loggia hints at their exclusive
character, and their yearly rent was generally five times
that of other houses owned by the Misericordia.

The occupants of the houses were on a different plane
socially as well as physically. The "Bargello" or jailer
of the city, Nicolo Stacesiori rented (at a reduced rate!)
one of the houses which was only a few steps from his
offices in the Palazzo del Podesta.[79] Other tenants included members of the Aretine nobility and officers of the
Misericordia. It seems likely that the other tenants belonged to the same class of civil administrators, and at
the end of the 16th Century a law was passed protecting
the interests of the inhabitants of the Loggia. The
Council of Arezzo forbade "plebs" to pass under the Loggia,
in essence reserving it for the same class of people who
lived and worked in it.[80] Montaigne later noticed that it
was common for the Florentine nobility to meet at mid-day
under the loggia of the Mercato Vecchio, and something

similar must have been normal practice in Arezzo, as the law suggests.[81] With a larger view to its civic environment, the Loggia became both the social and administrative center for the city. Like the via Giulia in Rome and the Strada Nuova in Genova, the Loggia was an attempt to create an aristocratic district in the center of Arezzo.

Writing at the end of the 14th Century, Matteo Villani said that loggie signify tyranny and not a free people.[82] Although he was comparing the public aspects of the Loggia on the Piazza della Signoria to private family loggie, his words are still important for a fuller understanding of the structure in Arezzo. The legislation regarding the Loggia attests to its aristocratic and isolated position in 16th Century Arezzo. Like the Early Renaissance family Loggia, the Late Renaissance "public" Loggia once again became the realm of the aristocracy and those who worked for it. It is not without some irony that Federico Barocci painted the Aretine Loggia in the forms of the Ducal Palace of Urbino in the Madonna del Popolo, commissioned by the Misericordia of Arezzo and once having hung in its chapel in the Pieve (Figs. 112, 113).[83] With its paradoxical combination of an innovative building type with its restricted housing and use, the Loggia in Arezzo represented the best and worst aspects of the Medicean state.

V

VASARI'S THEORY, CRITICISM AND
ARCHITECTURAL STYLE

The three most important factors in the formulation
of Vasari's architectural style were his career as a
painter, his sophisticated criticism in the Lives, and
finally, the location of his practice in Tuscany. Vasari's
training as a painter assured the creation of an essentially planar architecture which accords with his style in
painting. Collecting information for the Lives, on
the other hand, introduced Vasari to the entire range of
artistic accomplishment in the Renaissance. Vasari seems
to have acquainted with almost every major artistic figure
of the Mid-16th Century, and whenever he travelled the
Italian peninsula, he was a welcome guest of his colleagues.
The importance of this is twofold. First, it permitted
Vasari to see a number of projects and drawings not accessible to other artists. Second, and perhaps most important,
is that his own collection of drawings, the Libro de'
disegni, became another possible source of design ideas.[1]
Vasari's bias towards Tuscany and disegno meant that these
ideas could be cast into the more conservative architectural
styles of 16th Century Florence. The result was the

creation of a surface style in architecture which was
equally indebted to the Quattrocento and Cinquecento alike.

In contrast to the planar architecture of the Quattrocento, the architects of the Roman High Renaissance
emphasized the continuity and plasticity of the wall as a
major expressive element in their designs. This was due
in large part to Bramante, who, in the words of Serlio,
revived the principles of good architecture which had
been buried since Antiquity.[2] In his designs for Saint
Peter's, the function of the wall was space moulding and
not just space defining. The relationship of this conception to the classical orders is clearly shown in the
Upper Court of the Belvedere where the physical depth of
the wall is defined by the successive superimposition of
several layers of architectural elements--Corinthian piers,
the plane of the wall behind them, and the inner layers of
both the rectangular niche and the panel above it. In the
Tempietto at San Pietro in Montorio, Bramante also consciously used a strapwork system on the exterior of the
drum of the dome. Taken together, these innovations suggested to later architects a wealth of possibilities for
wall articulation and composition.

The significance of Bramante's innovations for Vasari's
buildings can be clarified by comparison with two important
contemporary architects--Palladio and Vignola. Unlike
Palladio's Basilica in Vicenza, for example, Vasari's facades

(the Loggia and the Uffizi in particular (Figs. 114-115)
use architectural elements as decorative accents to a
neutral background. The only classical members in Vasari's
facades--i.e., Tuscan columns--are never integrated into a
larger composition of load and support which would give
the rich texture of light and shade found on the facade of
the Basilica. Vasari's surface style, however, would not
have been inimical to Palladio, who was elected a member
of the Florentine Accademia del disegno in 1566.[3] Palladio
certainly would have been attracted to the repetitive regularity of the Uffizi and its use of a window type (aedicule
with balcony) which he had employed on several palace facades. Other common approaches shared by both architects
are indicated by the facade of the Loggia. The unadorned
surface of the Aretine structure is similar in kind to
many of Palladio's villa facades where expensive temple
fronts are replaced by arcaded porticoes and aedicule
windows (Villa Godi, Lonedo, ca. 1540; Villa Caldogno, ca.
1560; Villa Saraceno, Finale, ca. 1560). Any direct stylistic connection between the two architects is, however,
accidental. While Palladio's abandonment of classical
orders in facade design reflects the teachings of Alvise
Cornaro,[4] Vasari's disavowal of traditional architectural
ornament reflects the simplicity and frugality of Quattrocento architecture in his native Tuscany.

Vignola's Portico dei Banchi (Fig. 116) provides
another important contrast to Vasari's buildings. Throughout its entire length Vignola emphasized the multiple
layers of its architectural membering. Its surface is a
particularly dense lamination of architectural motifs--
pilasters and entablature on the first plane, two layers
of strapwork moulding on the second. In both cases the
exterior surface of the facade is established by the continuity of trabeated elements, and within this frame, so
to speak, all areas have been subdivided by windows or
relief panels. Its design emphasizes the depth of the
wall surface and in principle it accords well with the
spirit of Bramante's innovations.

Vasari's surface style was directly opposed to the
principles of Roman High Renaissance architecture. One of
the characteristic effects of Vasari's facades is a sense
of sharp relief. While Vignola attempted to contain the
wall surface within the trabeated frames, Vasari always
emphasized its continuity as a neutral background for the
addition of windows, balconies, consoles, and other elements.[5] The difference in their approaches can be seen in
how they handled a single element like strapwork moulding.
In Vignola's design it is one of the primary elements of
the facade; in the Uffizi it is co-planar with adjacent
wall surfaces, creating continuity rather than division.
Grappling with the problem of articulating a long facade

of repetitive elements, Vasari broke the surface only between each three-bay magistracy office, but the visual importance of this small cesura is less than that of the
elements placed on the surfaces surrounding it. The same
effects are even more apparent in the facade of the Loggia
which, confronts the viewer with the basic surfaces of the
Uffizi facade but without its decorative additions. Like
the Uffizi, the Loggia's facade is generated outward from
the plane of the building towards the exterior. Both
facades are hard, brittle, and decorative; nowhere is there
any indication of mass and depth.

Vasari's approach to facade design is essentially
pictorial. In method it is similar to the addition of
paint on a canvas, since each element was composed to achieve an effect somewhere between classical balance and
Michelangelesque tension. Central Italian Painting of
the same period shows the same characteristics of style:
ornamental forms which exhibit a jeweller's sense of precision are composed on a planar surface, always building
outward and giving a sense of reference to the entire composition.[6] Neither Vasari nor his contemporaries were
consistent in the way they depicted fictive architectural
backgrounds,[7] but in Vasari's later work painted architecture often corresponded to structures which were actually
built. The importance of Vasari's paintings for the genesis
of the dome of the Madonna dell' Umiltà in Pistoia has

already been discussed. Other examples include the altarpiece Saint Benedict and the Angels (Perugia; San Benedetto,
1566, Fig. 117) which has the same spatial sequence as the
Badia in Arezzo.[8] Similarly, a huge Serliana motif is found
in the middle ground of The Incredulity of Saint Thomas
(Florence: Santa Croce, 1569, Fig. 118). The Forge of
Vulcan (Florence: Uffizi, 1570) reproduces the underside
of the Loggia in Arezzo. For these reasons, Vasari's
architectural style demands a painterly analysis.

The similarities between Vasari's paintings and
buildings are important for a fuller understanding of his
surface style in architecture. First, the human figures
are always placed in front of the architecture and effectively not in it. The painted constructions are in reality
a foil for the figural compositions in the same way that
the surface of the facades becomes a reference plane for
the elements which project from it. In Vasari's paintings
and buildings there is a tendency for forms to adhere to
well-defined planes and surfaces. The figures in The Forge
of Vulcan exist in their own space independent of the architectural background (Fig. 104), and they could have been
changed or removed without significantly altering the character of the composition. The same principle applies to
the facade of the Uffizi where details like the tall window
frames are the most important elements of the facade; any
variation would not create something different in kind, but

the design would be merely less elegant and sophisticated.
Similarly, details are also brittle, and the wall structures to which they are attached show scarcely any gravity
or weight. The Uffizi facade is visually effective in
light or shadow; like Vasari's paintings, it does not de-
pend greatly on light for its effect.

In contrast to Vignola and Palladio, Vasari's approach to architectural design was conditioned by contemporary developments in painting. In paintings, where he
was free from the restrictions of budget and use, Vasari
created architectural compositions which were considerably
different in style from those which he constructed. In
The Incredulity of St. Thomas, he employed a correctly
formed Doric order; while in his executed projects he always used the Tuscan. The Saint Benedict and The Forge of
Vulcan are more plastic in their conception of the wall,
using the breaking of entablatures and the manipulation of
vaulting to create an architectural construction more com-
pelling than the painting itself. Though the dates of the
pictures generally accord with the construction of their
corresponding architectural projects, there is no pattern
to the order of their creation: the Saint Benedict was
painted well after the construction of the Badia while The
Forge of Vulcan possibly preceded the design of the Loggia.[9]
This gives a key insight on an important aspect of Vasari's
art theory: in both design and execution Vasari's practice
indicates that the arts were interchangeable while in theory

he supported the ancient primacy of architecture over painting and sculpture.[10]

The relationship of painting and sculpture to Vasari's
architecture is invariably linked to the nature of his
artistic dependence on Michelangelo. While Vasari certainly
appreciated the significance of Michelangelo's architecture,
he also expressed caution on imitating the Master, noting
that his boldness had caused other architects to make im-
itations which bordered on fantasy rather than reason or
rule (VII, 193). Vasari's own designs followed this warning, for his indebtedness is generally limited to details
and never to entire structures. Of the four projects under
discussion in this study, only the dome of the Madonna
dell' Umilità is directly linked to Michelangelesque prototypes, and this is prominent only in the design of the
lantern and the articulation of the drum. In fact, only
Vasari's earliest architectural designs attempt direct emulation of Michelangelo. The organ loft which Vasari designed for the Duomo in Arezzo (Fig. 119) is certainly
unthinkable without the precedent of Michelangelo's tomb
for Julius II.[11] Its size is overwhelming; Vasari's criticism of Michelangelo's followers would certainly be applicable to this work. Likewise, Vasari's early designs for
the Del Monte Chapel in San Pietro in Montorio drew on the
New Sacristy at San Lorenzo for inspiration, but this solution was criticized by Michelangelo and consequently the

design was changed.[12] Unfortunately, there is no documentation on Michelangelo's intervention in the design of the
Villa Giulia on which both Vasari and Ammannati participated.[13]

Michelangelo's criticism must have been more effective
than Vasari indicated (VI, 201-202). Taken together with
the criticism of Michelangelo's followers, first published
in the 1568 edition of the Lives (VII, 193), both events
provided a strong impetus to move away from a Michelangelesque mode of architectural design. This is precisely what
happened in Vasari's later projects where his ascetic surface style become the primary mode of architectural expression. Accordingly, Vasari's sources for his architectural
designs go beyond the limited number of projects which
Michelangelo planned or executed in Florence.

The greatest extent of Michelangelo's influence on
Vasari after 1550 is shown in the Uffizi, and it is largely
confined to this project. Recent criticism has shied away
from the conception of the Uffizi as a transposition of
the Laurentian Library reading room to the out-of-doors,
and instead it has been analyzed as a street of repetitive
houses.[14] Some elements of Vasari's architectural grammar
are obviously derived from Michelangelo.[15] The windows
and the doorways under the portico are free essays on the
windows of the reading room of the library, and the raised
panel on the window entablature derives from the same
source, too. Vasari's preference for sharply-defined entablatures also can be linked to Michelangelo's designs.

For example, the Tuscan order was employed on the ground floor of the Uffizi, but its entablature is closer to Ionic models, and the effect of the projection of this composite design was utilized by Michelangelo, too, on the Lantern of the New Sacristy at San Lorenzo. Nor did Vasari limit himself to Michelangelo's Florentine structures,[16] for the entablature which circumscribes the interior of the Badia is similar in form and effect to the massive architectural framework supporting the Ignudi on the Sistine Ceiling.

If much of Vasari's architectural vocabulary is Michelangelesque, his sentence structure was composed of elements commonly found in Roman designs.[17] The trabeated ground floor elevation of the Uffizi openly recalls the courtyard of Peruzzi's Palazzo Massimi, and the general composition for the facade is anticipated in one of Peruzzi's sketches (Fig. 120) for the facade of the same structure.[18] Similar features (most notably the articulation of the piers flanking the Serliana) can be found also in Alessi's facade for S. Maria del Popolo in Perugia (Fig. 121).[19] At the same time, other features of the Uffizi facade (ground floor portico, enclosed second floor, open roof loggia) were suggested by Sangallo's revised design of the Lower Court of the Belvedere (Fig. 122). Other elements of romanità are absorbed in Vasari's designs. The Uffizi's full length balcony windows were employed on

Bramante's Palazzo Caprini while the Loggia's socle windows
can be found on numerous Roman palaces from the Quattrocento and Cinquecento. The chromatic effect of its composition, however, is particularly Florentine in its abun-
dant use of pietra serena for the exterior facade, a fact
which Vasari proudly noted (I, 126). In short, Vasari's
complex web of stylistic sources covered the world of the
Italian Renaissance. While the facade of the Uffizi reflected Roman and Florentine models, the cupola in Pistoia
and the Badia in Arezzo respectively borrowed from Medieval structures and recent buildings in the Veneto. In fact,
the origins of Vasari's buildings are so widely scattered
that it appears he wished to repeat the achievements of
Raphael, who, in Vasari's words, formed a distinctly personal style out of numerous sources (IV, 11).

The sources of Vasari's architectural motifs do not
necessarily explain the acceptance of a surface style in
his buildings. Actually, this mode of expression which
was born in Quattrocento Florence, never died. Tuscany
had never fully appreciated the principles of Roman High
Renaissance Architecture. The patronage of Julius II had
drawn numerous Tuscan artists to Rome, and the political
instability of Florence during the first decades of the
16th Century produced few significant architectural commissions, Michelangelo's work in San Lorenzo excepted.
What is more significant is that Florentines continued to

build in a mode similar to Brunelleschi throughout the 16th

Century. In fact, both Quattrocento and Cinquecento styles

existed side by side in 16th Century Florence. For example,

the construction of the central bays of the Servite Loggia

was roughly contemporaneous to the construction of the

Uffizi.[20]

The taste of Quattrocento forms and motifs even af-

fected innovative architects like Ammannati. These char-

acteristics are most striking in the palaces and cloisters

attibuted to him. For example, the Palazzo Giungi on the

Via degli Alfani incorporates into its main entry a rusti-

cated archway found on several earlier palaces.[21] In

another case, the flat forms of a late Cinquecento monastic

courtyard built for the Camaldolesi at Santa Maria degi

Angeli is scarcely different from cloisters executed in

the Quattrocento.[22] The reasons for this probably reflect

the conservative taste of the local patrons, for Vasari

informed us that Baccio d'Agnolo Palazzo Bartolini was

ridiculed by Florentine wits for its Roman architectural

vocabulary (V, 321).

While this episode identifies a Florentine reaction

to an imported style, the survival of older forms during

the age of Cosimo I became a glorification of the Tuscan

State. Cosimo saw himself comparable to the Pope, the

Holy Roman Emporer, and the Kings of France and Spain,

and thus he had to establish Tuscany's political and

artistic identity within the theater of European politics.[23]
With this task at hand, the use of Roman architectural forms
in Cinquecento Florence became even less likely. One of
the primary motivations for writing the Lives was the glorification of Tuscany and its artists, and Vasari proudly
boasted this in a letter which was appended to the first
edition of the Lives (I, 1). The sense of an identifiable
Tuscan style was not confined to the arts, either, since
the Accademia della Crusca established the Tuscan dialect
as the standard for the Italian language.[24] By designing
in a historicizing style, Florentine architects could ap-
pease patrons and critics alike--the regional forms would
heighten the artistic and political identity of the Ducal
regime while satisfying its critics by evoking memories
of Republican Florence.

Vasari was not immune to using Quattrocento forms.
The Loggia del Pesce (1568), originally built in the Mercato
Vecchio and now standing along the via Pietrapiana (Fig.
123), was inspired by the chaste forms of Brunelleschi's
Foundling Hospital.[25] Similarly, Vasari's completion of
the pilgrimage church Santa Maria Nuova (1553, Figs. 124,
125) in Cortona[26] repeats many features from Francesco di
Giorgio's Santa Maria del Calcinaio (Figs. 124, 125) in
the same town. The interiors of both churches utilize
a grey on white color scheme, and they employ similar details for their entablatures at the crossing of the

churches.[27] This was not accidental, since Vasari bestowed considerable praise on Francesco in the _Lives_. The biography (III, 69-75) is riddled with erroneous attributions--among them the design of both Pienza and the Ducal Palace in Urbino--but this does not diminish the importance of Vasari's critical commentary. Vasari's opinions on Quattro-cento architecture were generally limited to the orders and their application--that the best architects had rediscovered the proportions of Ancient architecture and were able to distinguish the various orders and the differences between them (II, 104). According to these principles, only two men were cited for recognition in these matters--Filippo Brunelleschi and Francesco di Giorgio! Curiously enough, this commentary was included in the 1550 edition, while Francesco's biography (in the same edition) fails to mention his architectural achievements at all. The pattern of influence exercised by Francesco was more important than the borrowing of a few motifs by one architect from another, for it clearly shows the influence of Vasari's _Lives_ on his own buildings.

By recalling the Quattrocento forms of Francesco di Giorgio, Vasari followed his own criticism which he had already written in the 1550 edition of the _Lives_. Both structures are similar in their religious function (pil-grimage churches) and both act as visual pendants located on opposite sides of the same hill which is crowned by the

town of Cortona. The religious and historical parallels
were certainly apparent to Vasari; all he had to do was
to make them visually similar in style. In addition, the
renewal of Vasari's interest in Francesco brought about
by the commission in Cortona accounts for a greatly expanded and revised biography of Francesco in the second
edition.

The Lives also contain Vasari's theoretical statements on architecture. They are generally confined to the
Introduction and his theory is neither systematic nor
original.[28] This was not the result of any flaw in his
intellect, for his statements on architectural theory were
written for the 1550 edition, well before Vasari could
claim any competence as a practicing architect. Only
slight changes were made for the 1568 edition, and hence
Vasari's architectural theory is less sophisticated than
any of his executed buildings.

The Introduction is divided into three sections, Dell'
architettura, Della scultura, and Della pittura. In each
chapter, theory and practice are roughly equivalent in importance, for their subjects are almost equally divided
between the two concerns. The titles and organization of
the Introduction recall Alberti, whose De re aedificatoria
was published in Italian translation at the same time as
the first edition of the Lives. For this reason, Vasari
could not make his theoretical section look too similar to

Alberti, and any direct connections to the Quattrocento theorist had to be obscured. Consequently, the chapters of Vasari's section on architecture were modelled on Vitruvius in their subject matter, but their sources or equivalents are more diverse. The composition of Vasari's "treatise" is best expressed in chart form:

Vasari Chapter	Subject Matter	Equivalent or Source
I	On the Different Kinds of Stones Used by Architects	Vitruvius, II Alberti, II, ix
II	Description of Ashlar Work	- - - - - - - -
III	The Five Orders of Architecture	Vitruvius, IV Serlio, Libro Terzo
IV	Vaults and Centerings	Vitruvius, VII
V	Rustic Fountains	- - - - - - -
VI	On Pavements	Vitruvius, VII Alberti, III, xvi
VII	Principles of Architectural Judgement	Vitruvius, III

While Vasari acknowledged his debts to Vitruvius and Alberti (I, 107), he did not necessarily repeat the information contained in their writings. To a large degree, this was due to the different purpose of Vasari's "treatise," since he wished to describe the techniques and methods of his own time, not those of Antiquity. For this reason, he listed the stones available in 16th Century Italy, not in the Rome of Virtruvius. When discussing vaulting technique, he points out the use of Roman construction methods in the re-construction of St. Peter's. It must be added that Vasari never discussed any of these subjects in depth; he was satisfied to identify a few techniques which were applicable to both ancient and modern design. In no way did he clearly describe how to construct a building or its parts, for in the Introduction Vasari evaluated methods of construction in the same way in which he judged artists in their biographies.

Vasari's section on the "Principles of Architectural Judgement" is more complex in its structure and in its ideas (I, 145-148). Like Alberti, Vasari attempted to formulate a number of criteria for recognizing a good building. Vasari's standards were more practical than ideal, for the building had to serve its patron and accommodate its site. The site held particular significance for Vasari, since a building could not be too large for its location. Recalling Alberti's dictum that nothing could be added or subtracted from a perfect building, Vasari also noted that every detail must be suitable to its own place.

Vasari's verbal description of a palace served as his paradigm of good design. In it, he echoed Vitruvius when he said that "the building, like human bodies, has to be arranged and distributed according to the kind and variety of the structures themselves" (I, 146). The courtyard

of the palace, like the trunk of the human body, was to be
at the center of the building and square or 2:3 in proportion.   Otherwise, Vasari is unclear about the effect of
the human body on his palace.   Unlike Vitruvius, no further
system of proportions was given which would clearly relate
all parts to the whole.   It was to be anthropomorphic in
the sense that the locations of its major features were to
reflect the face of a man.   Like the mouth, the door was
to be low and in the middle of the facade, while the windows,
like the eyes, were to be equally disposed about the central
vertical axis of the facade.

Michelangelo, on the other hand, used the same metaphor in a letter of unknown destination and date.[29]   To
him, the "nose which at the center of the face has no com-
mitment to one or another eye, but one hand is obliged to
be like the other and one eye is obliged to be like the
other in relation to the sides of the body."   Unquestion-
ably Vasari was aware of Michelangelo's ideas, Vasari himself states that Michelangelo had suggested the study of
architecture to him (VII, 672), and ideas similar to this
must have been discussed during Vasari's numerous visits
to the aging masters in Rome.

Yet the descriptions used by both architects under-
score different points of view.   Using the nose as a reference Michelangelo located all features radially from this
point.   No fixed set of relationships was established since

the distances are relative to the other members of the
body, thus establishing a dynamic relationship between the
component parts of the architectural composition. In contrast, Vasari's facade is static and immobile, every element
is clearly related to a fixed central axis. Unfortunately,
Vasari's metaphor was unworkable in terms of architectural
design, because the requirement for an even number of
windows relative to the central axis of the facade would
place a solid wall over a void opening. In the end,
Vasari's paradigm is really a paradox, since he brought
to facade design what Michelangelo meant to apply to a
building's plan.

Vasari was somewhat more successful in dealing with
the orders, but this was due to the source for his descriptions, most of which were derived from Sebastiano
Serlio's Fourth Book. Serlio was perfect for Vasari's
needs: A concise description of the origin of each order
is followed by designs which show their application in
various situations. Vasari's borrowings were always
limited to Serlio's first paragraph on each order. Throughout the discussion Vasari invoked Vitruvius, but Serlio
in particular provided Vasari with the bulk of ideas.
For example, Vasari adopted the idea of association of
the orders with the personal characteristics of the gods.
Both Serlio and Vasari cite the Doric order as proper for
Jupiter, Mars, and Hercules, while they concur that the

Ionic was more appropriate for Diana, Bacchus, and Apollo.
In fact, Serlio seems to have dictated the examples which
Vasari chose, for both use the Theater of Marcellus in
discussing the superimposition of the Ionic over the Doric
orders. The similarity is even more apparent in their discussion of the Corinthian:

Vasari: Il lavoro corinto piacque universalmente molto
           ai Romani . . . ma molto piu bello e il
           Panteon, detto la Ritonda di Roma, il quale
           è il più ricco e l'più ornato di tutti gli
           Ordini detto di sopra. (I, 134-135)

Serlio: Ma gli antichi Romani dilletandosi molto di
           questo specie Corinthia . . . ne scielerò
           una nel più bello edificio di Roma, che è
           il Pantheon, detto la Ritonda, ponendo in
           Regola tutte le sue misure.[30]

Though these similarities are not plagiarism in the strictest sense, they clearly indicate that Vasari consulted
Serlio's Fourth Book while preparing the first edition of
the Lives. Since Vasari's professional experience in
architecture was limited at the time when this section was
written, it is understandable that Vasari would go to the
most recent text book to cover a field which he had never
adequately studied.

The importance of Serlio's publications for Vasari
goes beyond the classical orders. Serlio's eclecticism
has been likened to Vasari's theory of copies in art;[31]
both architects certainly felt free to draw on the architectural resources of Italy or France to create a single
style from numerous sources. Serlio's illustrations even

served as inspirations for some of Vasari's designs. This
can be seen in the civic decorations designed in 1565 by
Vasari and Borghini for Prince Francesco de' Medici's
wedding. The decorations had to be designed and completed
over a short period of time, and one of the easiest solutions was to consult Serlio's pattern book for appropriate designs. Though the decorations have long since
perished, their essential features have been preserved in
a sketchbook which is now in the Biblioteca Nazionale,
Florence.[32] Ornaments for the facade of the Palazzo
Ricasoli are similar to a fireplace from the Fourth Books
(Figs. 128, 129) and an archway at the Canto dei Carneschi
is derived from a combination of the arch at Benevento
from the Third Book with a doorway from the Libro
Strordinario (Figs. 130, 132). The list of comparisons
could go on, but it is important to remember that Vasari
never adopted Serlio's architectural style in toto. Avoiding the heavily rusticated frames illustrated in his model,
Vasari's forms are always more flat and delicate, always
avoiding whatever was plastic and robust in Serlio. Their
common stylistic language also produced similar results.
In the Seventh Book, certainly unknown in Italy before its
German publication in 1575,[33] Serlio illustrated a design
for a villa portico which corresponds almost exactly with
the ground floor elevation of riverfront Loggia of the
Uffizi (Fig. 132). Admittedly, Vasari's skimpy and unfair

treatment of Serlio in the Lives is unpardonable, but
Vasari's bad opinion of his source was tempered in the
later edition. In 1556, he claimed that the Fourth Book
was almost totally written by Peruzzi (Vasari-Ricci, III,
172). in the 1568 edition, he states only that Peruzzi's
drawings of antiquity were useful to Serlio (IV, 607).

Vasari's architectural criticism and practice were
mutually interdependent. Almost all of Vasari's architectural activity falls between the publication of the
two editions of the Lives, and his greater sophistication
in dealing with architecture in the second edition should
be attributed to the emergence of his own architectural
career. Vasari devoted more text to architectural subjects
in the second edition, and nowhere is this more apparent
than the Proemio to Part I where he discusses Medieval
Architecture (Vasari-Barocchi, II, i, 22-27). At first
Vasari had dismissed all Medieval architecture as having
lost the "modo buono" of Antiquity, but later he altered
his position, proposing that the decline was less rapid
and was caused by the departure of the Emperors from Rome.
Vasari was perceptive enough to note the Medieval foundations of Florentine Renaissance architecture when he
praised Santi Apostoli in Florence, noting that it had
served as the model for both San Lorenzo and Santo Spirito.
Likewise, Vasari became more appreciative of the personalities who created Medieval buildings. In the second

edition Vasari gives an entire chapter to Arnolfo di Cambio, the "architetto fiorentino" who previously had been slighted as a "tedesco architettore" (Vasari-Barocchi, II, i, 27). While Vasari's sympathy to Medieval architecture may be lukewarm at best, it is also manifest in his design for the Loggia facade where he clearly attempts to relate his structure in form and scale to its Late Medieval-Early Renaissance neighbor.

Vasari also became more adept at describing buildings in the later edition. In the earlier edition, he avoided this task, and his description of the "ideal palace" in the Introduction clearly was the work of a rank beginner. Generally, Vasari's method of revising his text was to append new paragraphs to the earlier edition, but in some instances he completely rewrote entire chapters. Michelozzo is a case in point where the minimal biography of the first edition has given way a full study which includes a sophisticated description of the Medici Palace in terms of the location of the household functions. Filarete's architectural career is totally new to the second edition. In both cases, Vasari mentioned in the first edition that both had practiced architecture, but in the second he gives an extended account of their careers.

To a large degree, Vasari's criticism is anti-theoretical and delights in professional and technical aspects of architectural practice. At one point, Vasari

clearly says that theory, when separated from practice,
amounts to very little (Vasari-Barocchi, III, i, 283).
These factors colored the expanded biography of Leone
Battista Alberti (Vasari-Barocchi, III, i, 283-290).[34]
While Vasari admired his theoretical writings, he clearly
deplored the lack of technical knowledge in projects which
he attributed to Alberti. In the case of Rucellai Loggia,
the difficulty was caused by the architect's inability to
turn an interior corner with the vaulting, thus creating
different profiles for the interior vaults (Vasari-Barocchi,
III, i, 287). To Vasari, this lacked sound judgement in
architectural design, a quality which was the result of
practice added to general knowledge. Alberti was also
chastised for the design of the choir of the Santissima
Annunziata, where, in Vasari's terms, the arches appeared
to fall backwards. This, too, was a faulty design judgement; Vasari implies that the arches were too high for the
width of the space.

Not surprisingly, Vasari identified himself with professional architects like Antonio da Sangallo the Younger.
Vasari did not share Michelangelo's venomous dislike for
the Sangallo clique, or at least he did not show it in
print.[35] Actually, Vasari's admiration for Sangallo grew
in the second edition, for he adds unequivocally that
Sangallo was worthy of praise as an "eccellentissimo architettore" (V, 472). In both editions Vasari told the story

how Sangallo built the foundations for San Giovanni dei
Fiorentini on the banks of the Tiber. In the second edition
he added that it was stupid to spend all that money to get
only an additional 20 braccia in length by building in
such a rapid river (V, 455). Vasari at least had knowledge
in this field, for the Uffizi was one of the most difficult
and dangerous projects which he faced since the foundations
had to be laid partially in the Arno (VII, 703). Fast work
was another positive attribute. Compare the following excerpts from the Lives on Sangallo's fortress in Ascoli
Piceno and Vasari's construction of the Corridoio in
Florence:

Sangallo: Fece ancora la fortezza in Ascoli, et quella
              in poichi giorni condussi a termini, che elle
              si poteva guardare. Il che gli Ascolani et
              gli altri non pensavano gia mai che si potesse
              fare in motli anni. (V, 477)

Vasari: Il quale corridore fi condotto in cinque mesi
              con mio ordine e disegno, ancorchè sia opera
              da pensare che non potesse condursi in meno
              di cinque anni. (VII, 704)

Vasari also borrowed from Sangallo's technical proficiency
when he shored up the underside of the chapel arches in the
Madonna dell' Umilità just as Antonio had done to the crossing of the church in Loreto. The reason was obvious--Vasari
said that Antonio's buildings never show a crack (V, 459-
460)! Criticism, however, is a double edged sword. Though
Vasari excised from the second edition a derogatory passage
about Antonio's private life (Vasari-Ricci, IV, 318-319), in

1568 he was also more critical of Antonio's design for
Saint Peter's (V, 467).

If Vasari's criticism is anti-theoretical, his architecture is equally anti-Humanist in its explicit avoidance
of Classical Antiquity. Though Vasari claimed to have made
over 300 drawings from ancient architecture and sculpture
on a single trip to Rome (VII, 663), the fruits of these
studies rarely appeared in his own buildings. Vasari's
avoidance of the orders is due to the fact that his own
contemporaries became a substitute for Antiquity which he
could excavate for design inspiration. This, too, is a
result of the influence of Michelangelo, who also borrowed
from Antiquity only whatever he needed.[36] If Michelangelo
had already surpassed Antiquity (IV, 13), what was the
reason to return to Ancient sources? This, too, corresponds with the practice in painting of Vasari's generation
where direct quotations tend to come from the supreme
authorities of the 16th Century,[37] but there is a fundamental difference between the two arts. In painting, this
created a style which was more uniform in its general characteristics (the Maniera), but in Vasari's architecture
the same principles of stylistic selection result in buildings which vary in style from Quattrocento revival (Loggia
del Pesce) through the inventive classicism of Peruzzi
(the Loggia) to buildings which are unique in their own
right (the Uffizi). In contrast to Palladio and Vignola,

this was certainly the outcome of a painter's approach to architecture. Ironically, it is important to note that Vasari, to whom we are eternally indebted for our knowledge of Italian art, rejected the artistic consequences of the revival of Antiquity, one of the most important principles on which the Renaissance was largely founded.

Vasari's most important contributions to architecture were the ability to provide specific solutions to the unique building needs of the Tuscan State and the facility to take on large scale projects which would be responsive to their environment. In the Lives, Vasari seems to be slightly self-satisfied with this achievement; but history prevented him from influencing subsequent generations of significant designers. Perhaps the most important factor in this respect was that Vasari's preference for specifically Florentine solutions did not accord with the developing pattern of patronage in Italy. His surface style was certainly antithetical to the Roman preference for a massive and malleable wall architecture derived from Antiquity. Since Vasari's choice of forms was essentially personal in nature and political in their service to the Tuscan State, his solutions lacked any larger meaning outside their regional context. Nor was he helped by the fact that some of his most interesting designs were built in inaccessible provincial centers like Arezzo and Pistoia. Had Vasari built in Rome, his architectural style might have been altogether different. Had he chosen to publish his own designs in addition to the biographies of artists, his fate would have been less ignominious. Yet these shortcomings are easily forgotten standing in front of the Uffizi, inside the Badia or the Madonna dell' Umilità, or in the piazza at Arezzo. These projects surely indicate that Vasari went a long way towards achieving the perfection which a sense of history demanded of him (IV, 7).

APPENDICES

I

THE CUPOLA OF THE MADONNA DELL' UMILITÀ, PISTOIA

A. THE HISTORY OF THE CHURCH

On 17 June 1490, a group of women were worshipping a frescoed Trecento image of the Madonna and Child, painted by Giovanni di Bartolomeo Cristiana on the wall of the church of S. Maria Forisportae. Shortly thereafter, the image began to give forth beads of sweat which ran from the head of the Virgin to the crown of the infant, and finally to their knees, where it divided into three beads. One of these was still visible at the end of the 19th Century (Beani, 1890, 17). The event was proclaimed a true miracle. The Bishop and the Rectors of the city examined the fresco, and they decreed that it could not have been caused by condensation from within the walls of the church.

To commemorate the apparent miracle, the Council of Pistoia ordered the construction of the Church of Santa Maria dell' Umilità, commonly called the Madonna dell' Umilità. According to Sanpaolesi, a model was presented on 27 October 1492, and Giuliano da Sangallo aided in its preparation (Sanpaolesi, 1939, 254). In 1494, four deputies were elected to oversee the construction of the church (Beani, 1890, 24), and construction was begun in the Spring of the following year. The construction was entrusted to

Ventura Vitoni, a local architect who had already built several structures in that city. He was the sole executor of the project, but both Antonio da Sangallo the Elder and Antonio Pollaiolo were called upon for consultation regarding the project (Sanpaolesi, 1939, 256).

The construction of the new church was subject to frequent interruptions. Between 1496-1497 and 1499-1501 construction was halted due to the bloody family warfare involving the Cancellieri and the Pantiatichi (Fossi, 1973, 85). The atrium of the present church probably lies on the foundations of S. Maria Forisportae (Dami, 1914, 1-40), thus accounting for both its unusual size and its function as a church nave before the consecration of the octagonal tribuna in 1582. It was the first part of the church to be completed; a stone at the South-West corner of the octagon exterior bears the date 1509. Construction was interrupted again in 1522 when the octagon had been built as far as the third level. In 1530, Pistoia lost what few freedoms it enjoyed by its inclusion in the new Medicean state, and thus the project was doomed to oblivion if patronage from Florence was not forthcoming. In 1540 and 1547, the Council again deliberated the completion of the church, but no definitive action was taken (Beani, 1890, 54).

According to tradition, Cosimo I visited Pistoia in 1555, to see the fortifications which were then under construction, and at that time he was impressed by the beauty of the unfinished church (Chiti, 1952, 33). Although there are no documents to corroborate this, the Council of Pistoia

may have resumed discussion of the church as early as 1559.

On 5 December 1561 the Council requested permission to built

the church (Bargiacchi, 1890, 34-39; Doc. 1); it is granted

in March of the following year (ASF, Practica Segreta di

Pistoia, Libro di lettere, 490, 118). There is no mention

of an architect in any document of this period; Vasari must

have received the commission shortly after this date. His

contribution to the Madonna dell' Umilità can be documented

only through his letters and scattered documents, since

the book of payments for the Madonna during Vasari's time

has been lost.

B. VASARI'S CONTRIBUTION

29 November 1561:   Fossi has asserted that Cosimo's decision to complete the cupola dates from this period. In
a letter to Donato Tournabuoni, the Florentine Commissioner
in Pistoia, the Practica Segreta makes an explicit reference
to a project to roof the Madonna (Fossi, 1977, 129-130).

25 April 1562:   In a letter to Vasari, Cosimo mentions
the architect's recent visit to Pistoia to complete the
cupola (Frey, I, 670).

21 July 1562:   A letter from Cosimo to Vasari mentions
he is satisfied with the design and that it should be executed (Frey, I, 683).

19 January 1563:   In a letter to Borghini, Vasari notes
that he just returned from a trip to Pisa, but it is likely
that he passed through Pistoia to make preparations for the
renewal of construction (Frey, I, 693).

20 January 1563:   In a letter to Cosimo I, Vasari re-
ports that his design for construction of the dome pleased
the Practica Segreta, and all of the moneys alloted to it
would be spent. In a rare moment of philosophical

reflection, he says "ora é tempo da murare in cielo col dar del pane ai poveri in terra," an obvious reference to the philanthropic duty which the Opera of the Madonna dell' Umilità exercised in Pistoia (Frey, I, 697).

10 May 1563:   In the Ricordanze, Vasari notes that the construction of the dome began on this day (Ricordanze, Frey, III, 37).

18 April 1564:   There were frequent interruptions to the construction of the cupola. The Monte di Pietà in Pistoia, who had the authority to disburse funds for the completion of the project, were slow in paying for com- pleted construction. In a letter to Cosimo, Vasari noted the adverse effects of the two previous winters on the fabric of the cupola (Frey II, 74). The work was begun again in July, but several other interruptions occurred during the next few years (Fossi, 1977, 133-134).

20 January 1565:   Vasari made another trip to Pistoia to check up on the progress of the Dome. He left on Epiphany (January 6), and when he returned, he reported that the cupola had been built as high as the tambour. In this letter to Cosimo I, Vasari indulges in more than the usual amount of flattery. He notes that the patronage of this project would result in a magnificent work in honour

of God, and that at that moment, there appeared to be no difficulty in achieving it. Reflecting on future glory, he adds that it will be a work of great importance, too (Frey, II, 144).

2 February 1565: The final design for the cupola still had not been settled. Vasari sent a design to Pistoia, and it was subjected to criticism. This design, now lost, proposed a major change in lighting the tribune. The majority of those who viewed the design were not in favor of closing any windows, but they preferred to broaden them to allow more light to make the paintings visible (Frey, II, 149).

Fall 1566: Another trip to Pistoia was possibly made during this period (Frey, II, 270).

25 January 1568: The shells of the cupola were built in record time; the sloppy nature of the internal constructions bears this out. In only three years the dome was raised to a level near the lantern. On this date Vasari signed a contract with several scarpellini for the construction of the lantern which caps the cupola (IV, 167). The correct date is 1568 and not 1567 (Fossi, 1973, 85) since it was written in Florence and dated according to Florentine conventions.

<u>28</u> <u>March</u> <u>1569</u>:   The entire project was nearing completion by this date, when, the Operai and Deputies of the Madonna dell' Umilità sent an envoy to establish how much Vasari was to be paid for his efforts on their behalf (ASP, Fondo Madonna dell' Umilità, 514, 155v). It is likely that all work had not been completed by then, and that the payment might indicate a halt in the work due to the lack of funds (Fossi, 1973, 85-86). There is no evidence to support or refute this assertion.

<u>28</u> <u>June</u> <u>1569</u>:   Cosimo I authorizes a <u>donativo</u> of 100 scudi to Vasari from the authorities in Pistoia (Gaye, III, 276).

<u>27</u> <u>October</u> <u>1572</u>:   In a letter to Vicenzo Borghini, Vasari mentioned that he had been ordered to Pistoia by Cosimo on matters pertaining to the cupola. Though the reason for the trip is not explained, Fossi has speculated that this might have been the first indication of structural problems in the dome's fabric (Fossi, 1977, 136).

C. DOCUMENTS

1. 19 December 1561

Proviso of the Council of Pistoia (ASP, Fondo Archivio
Communale, Libro di riforme e provisioni, 91, 149 verso)

Li stupendi et apparenti miracoli fatti de la Regina del
Cielo P.C. nel nostro venerabile oratorio di Santa Maria
dell' Umilità sono stati potissima causa che è, nostri
padri cominciando, suo honor et gloria, a edificar un
ornatissime et splendissimo tempio nel quale sin a, qui
si è speso a lire a 60,000: né essendosi potuto fornir
per no' maneggiar la città, le sue entrate publiche comé
per il passato, si é recorso a S.E.I. che si degni operar'
che decta fabrica, non vadi male rispetto a li venti et
pioggie et che si degni darli la sua perfettione in qualche
miglior modo che paio espertente. Percio si elleghi deputati
li huomini che debbino haver cura a la perfettione di essa
fabrica in qualche miglior modo che appar per Signori del
Magistro Consiglio et practica segregata di S.E.S. . . .

This is the record of the final deliberation of the Council

on the subject of the Madonna dell' Umilità. It had been

discussed as early as 23 October 1559.

2. 3 June 1575

Proviso of the Council of Pistoia (ASP, Fondo Archivio
Communale, Libro di riforme e provisioni, 91, 241 verso).

L'Operai di Santa Maria del Humilità, et li deputati sopra
la fabrica di detto luogho fano intendere, comé la detta
muraglia ha patito, et patice di continuo, per la pioggia
che la molestano, per il pel' vecchio che giornalamente
si vede crescere, et per altri che di nuovo appariscono
per il danno, che va fece la saletta nella lanterna della
copua (sic) di maniera che alla giornata si puo pensare. . .

This unpublished notice is the earliest record of the prob-

lems which were to plague Vasari's cupola. It is also the

most complete description of the crack which Ammannati was

to repair. The poor quality of the construction is alluded

to by the reference to the effect of the bad weather on the

cupola's fabric.

3. 6 July 1576

Letter from the Deputies of the Madonna dell' Umilità in
Pistoia to Ammannati in Florence (ASP, Registro di lettere,
Fondo Madonna dell' Umilità, 511, 6 verso).

In margin: Al' Amannato per finire la cupola

Per una vostra delli 24 di Maggio prossimo passato, demo
aviso a V.S. Magnifica del stato della fabrica quale pensavamo
li fussi stata consegnata et ne aspettavamo riposta ma per
quanto oggi ritraghiamo dal nostro proveditore. Crediamo
non l'habbia riscevuta onde per questa nostra di nuova.
L'advisiamo comè s'è seguito l'ordine da lei datone, et per
gratia di dio et dell Gloriosa Sua Madre è a buon porto,
cioè finite. Le capelle posti li altari con predelle et
l'ammattonato con i quadroni (è) tutto finito salvo che la
meta di un ottangolo che domanda sera sara finito. Li
denari sono consumati; ora ci resta come sa benissima V.S.
Magnifica a fare le finistre invetriate e l'occhio sopra
l'altare grande che secondo si dicono i frati gesuiti saranno
di spesa 250, o più, a fare di vetro bianco col' adornamento
et di spese. Ancora restare serrare le finestre grande di
sopra et farli li occhi secondo la nostra fece fare. Inoltre
ci resta da rasettare la lanterna et fare le panche intorno
alla chiesa della detta muraglia del coro, con il mettere
La Madonna dove ha da stare che secondo ci disse Maestro
Francseco sara di grande spesa. Inperò desideremo la sua
risposta. Et con questa li bacciamo li mani, che Dio la
guardi.

Di Pistoia il di 6 di Luglio 1576

Di Vostra Signoria Magnifica affezionatissimi

                    Li Deputati sopra la muraglia

This important document was overlooked by Fossi in his

publication of Ammannati's letters regarding his repairs to

Vasari's cupola. It is a veritable "punch list" of most

of the contributions made by Ammannati to the Madonna dell'

Umilità. It confirms Frey's opinion that circular panels

in the fourth level of the octagon were originally windows

which bathed the interior with even more light than there

is today. (Frey, I, 675) Other contributions were of

relatively minor importance. Taken together with the

other documents, this letter indicates that Ammannati's

contribution to the cupola was less extensive than the

"radicale sistemazione" which Fossi attempted to portray.

II

THE BADIA

A. THE HISTORY OF THE CHURCH

The renovation of the Cassinese monastic church of SS. Flora e Lucilla was begun in 1565 from designs furnished by Giorgio Vasari. The original 13th Century church was too small and in need of repair: the earliest contract related to the renovation describes the project as "de volentis restaurare, atque et amplionem et maiorem facere" (See Appendix II: Chronology, 12 February 1565). Several houses were demolished (See Chronology, 24 April 1565) and some foundations were laid before Vasari was paid for a modello in 1565 (See Appendix II, Document 1B). Construction proceeded at a constant rate through 1567, but it slowed down and came to a complete halt by 1570. This was probably due to the lack of cash; the Badia financed the construction from its own income in agricultural investments, not from substantial contributions made by wealthy individuals. At this time, the church was approximately half finished; the bay closest to the entry was completed in 1578 (Viviani-Fiorini, 1941-1942, 81, and Appendix II: Document 3) and the church was roofed in 1580 (Viviani-Fiorini, 1941-42, 80). Yet the church was still incomplete.

A report written for Innocent X noticed that the Badia
lacked a facade and one of its domes (Document 4). The
campanile was built in the same year by Simeone da Lugano
from a plan given to him by the abbot. Its use of panel
decoration and framing strips suggests that it was built
from a Cinquecento design, possibly made by Vasari himself.
Around 1700 the dome closest to the choir was painted with
an illusionistic fresco similar to illustrations in Fra
Andrea Pozzo's Perspective pictorum et architectorum (Rome,
1693) and this is usually attributed to Pozzo himself. In
1944, two sides of the adjacent cloister were destroyed by
bombing, and concussion from the blast destroyed the roof
tiles, causing rain to seep through the vaults and flood
the church. After the War, both roof and vaulting were
repaired (Hartt, 1949, 118-119).

Vasari's enlarged plan necessitated the construction
of an entirely new North aisle added to the fabric of the
medieval church. The modello of 1565 must have been incomplete, for only two years later Borghini wrote the Abbot
warning him that it would be a mistake to allow the
scarpellini to continue from designs which were only preliminary (Viviani-Fiorini, 1941, 79). In any case, the
severe detailing corresponds to Vasari's architectural style
of the 1560's, and the dimensions of the architectural details concords with the stonecutter's contract of 26 April
1565. For example, the length of the architrave is 2.62 m.

according to the contract and 2.49 m. as built; the remaining .13 m. is probably used for bonding with the adjacent pier.

Although Vasari's drawings for the Badia have been lost, a plan of it was drawn by Giorgio Vasari il Giovane (Fig. 59) for inclusion in his La città (UA 4877). Since the plan generally accords with the existing construction, it is tempting to regard this as a statement of Giorgio Vasari's intentions. However, his nephew probably took the liberty of making the plan appear more regular than it is. The deep side chapels could never have been built since any construction would be limited by Giuliano da Maiano's Quattrocento cloister. Giorgio would have certainly been aware of this fact. Other changes include the addition of side doors into the nave and the deletion of doors into the sacristy and cloister.

B. CHRONOLOGY OF THE CONSTRUCTION

12 February 1565:   The monastery makes a contract with
Gianella d'Arezzo to supply sufficient bricks and lime for
the renovation of the church. No mention is made of either
modello or architect, but the nature of the project is expressed as "de volentis restaurare atque et empliorem et
maiorem ecclesiam facere." (ASF, Conventi Soppressi, No. 7,
SS. Flora e Lucilla, filza 6, 191).

31 March 1565:   Vasari makes a trip to Arezzo, most
likely to discuss the new church with his clients, and the
expense for his return in the company of the capo maestro
are paid by the monastery (Appendix II: Document 1A).

24 April 1565:   The monastery pays y 83.13.4 "allevar
il terreno della chiesa et della strada" (ACV, Libro della
Fabrica, filza 58, 14 right). Demolition expenses continue
throughout the following year, and they often include work
on buildings other than the church itself.

26 April 1565:   Contract between the Abbot and the
stonecutters Iacopo di Mariotto (called Bagella) and
Giovanni di Andrea Marzolini. This was to be done according to the modello "data o darsi per lo eccelentissimo
maestro Giorgio Vasari pictore architectore aretino"
(Viviani-Fiorini, 1941, 217).

1 May 1565:   Money is made available to Giovanni
"a far le colone et architravi secondo la scritta di M.
Vicenzo Torri, cioe le collone con sue zoccoli, base, et
capitelli per XXII scudi et mezzo l'una, et i architravi
per scudi 17 et mezzo l'uno." (ACV, Libro della Fabrica,
filza 58, 25 left).

29 June 1565:   Another contract for "tutti i lavori
et pietro concie et collini et architravi." It goes on at
length to renegotiate the terms of payment, and neither
Vasari nor the modello are mentioned. For some reason
Bagella removes himself from the contract and leaves all of
the work to Giovanni (ASF, Conv. Sopp., N° 7, SS. Flora e
Lucilla, filza 6, 221).

29 September 1565:   Vasari is paid for the modello which the
capo maestro, il Maiano, brings from Florence (Appendix II:
Document 1B).

21 November 1565:   The date of the first request to obtain
space from a public right of way for the Badia. This is
the first direct mention of Borghini's official involvement
in the project (Appendix II: Document 2A). Work on foundations begun in March (before the arrival of the modello?)
now totals y 696.8.8 in cost (ACV, Libro della Fabrica,
ilza 58, 19 left and right).

<u>16 January 1566</u>:   The second request for the right of
way is not granted. Again both Vasari and Borghini are
named as those who supplied the <u>modello</u> (Appendix II:
Document B2).

<u>29 January 1566</u>:   The request for the right of way
was important enough to send the cellerario of the monastery
to Florence to oversee matters regarding this subject.   On
this date he is reimbursed for his expenses (ACV, <u>Libro
della Fabrica</u>, filza 58, 29 left).

<u>22 March 1566</u>:   On this date, Vasari writes from
Arezzo to Borghini in Florence that "ne' gli è detto niente
nella mia cosa d' Arezzo" (Gaye, III, 202).

<u>1 April 1566</u>:   In a letter to Borghini in Florence,
Vasari writes that he will meet with the Abbot on the matter of the chiasso (right of way) (Gaye III, 204).

<u>June 1566</u> (?):   Vasari is paid y 13.17.0, probably
for his meeting with the Abbot (Appendix II: Document A4).

<u>2 October 1566</u>:   From Arezzo, Vasari writes to
Borghini that "oggi comincero a fermare i conci con lo
Abbate di Badia, chi resta fin mal sattisfatto" (Gaye, III,
228).

<u>18 December 1566</u>:   Writing from Florence to the Abbot in
Arezzo, Borghini says "Accademi mettervi anchora in

consideratione . . . che quelli primi disegni et schizzi
che si danno, sono solo accennati et non hanno nelle
scornicature et intagli et altre simmetrie quella fine che si
dà poi nel disegno grande et che si fa poi per l'appunto,
bastando solamente accennare in quelli un certo che della
invenzione et della forma; onde se quel nostro scarpellino
non ha avuto questa consideratione, avvertite che e' non
sia preso un granchio" (Viviani-Fiorini, 1941, 79). The
importance of this letter is twofold: it indicates that
some details had not been designed and that the stonecutters
might have taken artistic liberties in their execution. It
also shows that bad feelings might have existed between
client and patron.

27 March 1567:   On this date, when he had to repay y 64
(probably for bad workmanship), Vasari was probably passing
through Arezzo returning home from Rome, where he had given
consultation on the construction of St. Peter's (Appendix
II: Document 1C; also Frey, II, 330).

21 June 1567:   Writing for Pope Pius V, Mons. Sangaletti
tells Vasari in a letter that "Signor Giorgio, io ho hauto
d'Arezzo la pianta della chiesa della abatia, come e stava,
et come e oggi ridotta, et ne ho qualche fede, ma no' mi
bastano. Avisate, si volete, vi mandi la pianta che il faro"
(Frey, II, 340). This was in the context of the planning for

the church at Bosco Reale. Evidently Vasari's design for
the renovation of the Badia was of interest to the Papal
Court. The drawing has not been located.

23 December 1570:   Writing to Vasari in Rome, Borghini
says "delle monache non vi dico altro se non che a me par'
che le cose vadino di male in peggio" (Frey, II, 557).
The subject of this exchange has not been identified. It
probably refers to the Badia (monache or monache neri often
signify the Cassinese in their correspondence), particularly
with the indication of bad feelings on all sides.

14 May 1578:   Numerous payments are made on this
date for work on the nave of the church. At this time the
choir was far advanced in construction, three windows of
earlier church were walled up, and there is mention of work
on numerous pilasters (Appendix II: Document 3A). The
last four columns and architraves were begun or ordered on
this date, but they were not finished and put in place until
before 16 December 1586--the date on which the scarpellino
was paid for his work (Appendix II: Document 3B). Another
notice says that the last columns were put in place during
1587 (Viviani-Fiorini, 1941, 81).

C. DOCUMENTS

1. DOCUMENTS PERTAINING TO GIORGIO VASARI

A. <u>31</u> March <u>1565</u>:

12 left

Et adi detto y 20 et 20 p per andar a Firenze M. Giorgio
et il capo maestro et cavalcatura a nolo, et allogar
la sera alla malsa, a cassa ac 3   y 20.20.0

<u>Libro</u> <u>della</u> <u>Fabrica</u>, ACV, filza 58.

B. <u>29</u> September <u>1565</u>:

20 left

Et adi 29 7bre y 70 (zero) p a mandarsi a M. Giorgio per
il modello a cassa ac 26   y 20.0.0

26 right

Et adi 29 detto y 70 per il modello porto col il Maiano
ind (ebito) a legnami ac 20   y 70.0.0

<u>Libro</u> <u>della</u> <u>Fabrica</u>, ACV, filza 58

C. <u>27</u> March <u>1567</u> and <u>15</u> March <u>1568</u>:

30 left

M. Giorgio pittor d'Arezzo dedar adi 27 di Marzo 1567 y
sessanta quattro (et zero) p quali si sono spese in
sua faccie per mano di Fr. Ansano come appariscie per saldo
fatto di Felice Ottaviani, et Baptista di Salvatore, Maur
(ator) i d'Arezzo, arbitieri di M. Giorgio, et Fr. Ansano,
come appariscie per mano di Ser Pompeio di Ser Camillo
Calderini, et in q(est)o numero non é y 14 quale Ser
Pietrino mele misse a co(n)to delle y 50 che q(uel)li pristai
quando si co(m)p(er)o capacciuolo. Et che i(n) tutto
havebbono a esser y 70, ma d(etti) arbitieri non ce le
hanno fatte buono per non esser i(n) sul libro. Questo
saldo appariscie a lib(r)o d(i) d(etto) M. Giorgio, sotto
scritto di suo mana et nostra ac 34   y 64.0.0.

30 right

M. Giorgio di casa di haver' adi 15 di Marzo 1568 y
sessanta quattro (et) zero p(icco)le a 1 V: P B Giovanni
Baptista: allo stracciafoglio di sudetto p ac in di casa
ac 46   y 64.0.0

46 left

Et adi (15 March 1568) posti per error perch dedar la y
64 in tutto a M. Giorgio in questo ac _____ y. 64.0.0

D.   June 1566 (?):

Et piu y 13 et 17 p tanti spesi di M. Giorgio Vasari per
mano di Fr. Ansano come per la lista di suoi conti appar
(iscie) a casa ac ___32_____ y 13.17.0

N.B.   y = lire

2. DOCUMENTS PERTAINING TO VICENZO BORGHINI

A. <u>21 November 1565</u>:

Supplica made by the Abbot and the monks of the Badia in
Arezzo to the Capitani di Parte in Florence for permission
to build over a public street adjacent to the church. ASF,
<u>Capitani di Parte</u>, filza 718 nero, p. 181.

<u>21 9bre 1565</u>:

Li humili servi di V.F. Abbate e Monaci della Badia di Sta.
Fiora e Lucilla di Arezzo desiderosi di ampliar il cuto div-
ino, a honore di Sua Maesta, et di V.E. et andro della sua
citta, expongo a quella come gia molti anni essendo dietro a
loro Chiesa un' chiasso, chi rispondera nella strada maesta,
fu loro concesso dalli ufficiali delli torre della citta
di Firenze che potessino serrar' detto chiasso con un'
murato quadrato della Chiesa, o poco manco, chome hoggi si
vedi per la insegna della torre. Et perche detta serrata
sino a detta strada maestra rimasse di circa braccia 22 al
canto il loro cimeterio. Et forse perche in quella sboccava,
come anchora hoggi sbocca il chiassuolo, che viene dietro
a 7 o 8 case. Et havendo hoggi detti supplicati dato principio a voler', a honor' di Dio, accresier la loro chiesa,
molto brutta et mal conditionata, secondo un' modello fatto
secondo il disegno del S. Prior' degli Innocenti, et di
Messer Giorgio Vasari Aretino, et havendo gittati fondamenti et alzati mure di X braccia, fa il bisognio per condurre a perfettione detto disegno pigliare detto chisso
circa 7 o 8 barccia. Et non per questo si viene a serrare
che chi volessi passare non ci reste da due braccia e mezzo,
ovvero 3, il restare come prima. Et perche detti vicini
non hanno mai usato detto chiassuolo, ne con bestie, ne
con persone di tanto tempo in questo non vi e, memoria in
contrario, atteso che maggior' commodita li e, lo usar le
loro parte di nanzi che hanno nella strada maestra, come
manifestamente si vede per una portuccia che e intesto di
detto chiasuolo, non solo infino a questi tempi, e stata
serrata et confitta, ma ancho con terra abastionata,
accio non si ussasi, e tutto con volonta di detti vicini.
Come cosa che non sene suono et che gli rende le loro case
piu sicure dalla banda di dietro, et toglie occasione
a chi volessi fare, o gittare, qualche bruttura. Et per
tanto desiderosi detti supplicati di mandar inanzi detto
loro impresa secondo detto modello, ricorono avanti le
piedi di V.Ex. supplicandi humilamente che la si degni
sieno accomodati i dette chiasso di quel tanto che fa di
bisognio a una tanta opera buona et pia, et ancho bella,

della quali tutti cittadini se ne rallerono, accio con
la gratia di Dio, et con la benigna parola di qulle si
possa condure al fine, et a perfetta tanta buona opera,
ricivedo tutto per gratia, con pegior al solito loro il
Signore Dio per la sua conservatione.

at bottom:

A Capitani di Parte chi informino

B. 16 January 1566:

Supplica by the Abbot and Monks of the Badia in Arezzo to
Prince Cosimo de' Medici for permission to build on a public
way. ASF, Capitani di Parte, filza 718 nero, p. 180. The
document is frayed along its right hand edge, and consequently some of it is either illegible or missing.

*

Illustrissimo et Eccellentissimo Signore Principe

L'Abbate et Monaci di Santa Fiora d'Arezzo supplicanti chi-
eggono a I.E.V. che li facci grazia di farli concedere 7 o 8
braccia d'un chiassuolo che non ha riuscita p'essere condurre
a perfectione la nuova fabrica della chiesa secondo il modello et disegno, dato dal spedalingho degli Innocenti et
Messer Giorgio Vasari dove spendiamo buona soma di denari,
dicendo non fare prejudicio.

Supplicano alli mesi passati un' altra volta alla presente
a V.F. et dopo la fatt in (illegible) per Illustrissimo
magistrato. Dicendoli che l'opera sarebbe buno, et bella,
ma che comincini che rinscriverro con le loro case della
banda di dietro non se ne consenteranno a legendo che in
detto chiassuolo (illegible). Rescrisse che non voleve
serrare la strade.

Ricorreno di nuovo chieggendo il medesimo, et dicendo che già
molti anni sono ottenero dalli ufficiali di torre in quel
tempo licentia di possere et sindere detto chiasso per quanto teneve detta chiasso la Chiesa come sine per l'arme della
torri. Et che ne me rimassa circa (vacant) braccia dove
sbocca il detto chiassuolo nel quale uscino 7 o 8 che non se
ne serrano a cosa della una.

Per Possere dare vero raguauglio a V.E.S. habbiamo mandato
tal luogho Messer Baptista Battaghioni, uno di capi maestri,
persona intelligente per vedere tutto con fare (illegible)
ci riferisce detto chiassuolo essere largo dove 5 et dove 6
braccia et che in vicino otto case et non consta che ne
serino a cosa a le (illegible) et servandose supplicati per
condurre a perfettione detta la chiesa che sara molto bella
in resta per ogni modo due braccia et mezzo di spazio a tale
che le (illegible) ma non gia le bastie cariche in possono
passare commodomente, et che senza dubbio detto chiassuolo

si'apriono al pubblico, cioé a questo Magistrato, et che
li particolari non hanno chi fari, et li supplicati non possono condurre alla dubito perfectione il modello fatto da
Messer Giorgio Vasari se non si serrono di una parte di
detto chiassuolo. Il medesimo anchora aferma il Commune
di quel luogho, dicendo che tal cosa non fa prejudicio a
nessuno, ma ornamento al belleza a quella città et accio
che V.E. possi vedere et considerare tutto. Si manca la
pianta et il disegno fatto dal detto capo maestro, et questo
e in questo per informatione. Possiamo dire a V.E. alli
quali ci humilissimi ci raccomando che idio da l'ogni
felicissima. di Firenze 16 Gennaio 1565

at bottom, in another hand:

      non havendo il consenso decomincini
      non accede altro

3. THE COMPLETION OF THE NAVE

<u>14 May</u> 1578:

Various construction notices. ACV, <u>Libro</u> <u>della</u> <u>fabrica</u>, <u>filza</u> 58.

A. page 25 right

Et più d'havere p(er) in conto fatto sera in Celleraio, cosi d'accordo adi 14 di Maggio 1578 con il Ven.P.D.Gio.Bap. Sacietti, priore e D. Sebastiano Celleraio, d'avere y quaranta tre, p 17, sono per braccia nover et 3/1 di pietra lavorata posta in opera su il cantone del Campanile, cioé y 4, p 4 il braccio _____ y 43.17.0

Et più d'havere y ottanta sono per la valuta di tre occhi murati, uno grande posto sopra la finestra del choro prezzo di y 40-42 piccioli, uno posto sopra la capella riscontro al forno, et l'altro nel campanile, per prezzo di y venti l'uno _____ y 80.0.0

Et più d'havere y quaranta sono per la valuta della finestra posta sopra la capella riscontro al forno stimato cosi d'accordo _____ y 40.0.0

Et più d'havere y trenta nove sono per la valuta di tre capitelli per gli architravi uno de quali e in opera nel pilastro sotto l'organo, e gli altri 2, sono in terra in chiesa stimati d'accordo y 13 l'uno _____ y.39.0.0

Et più d'havere y quindi y sono p immo d'havere y trenta sono pe la valuta del primo ordine del basamento di amenda i pilastri chi sostentano l'arco della capella del choro quale per esser cosi imperfetti si sono stimati y 15 l'uno d'accordo _____ y 30.0.0

Et più d'havere y trecento settanta tra sono per la valuta di 4 basamenti per i pilastri, tre di quali sono in opera uno, stimati d'accordo y otto e mezzo il braccia, sono di braccia, 12 l'uno che monterebbano y 10 l'uno, e in tutto y 408, ma app.ce ne e uno cioé quello e dall'organo accato agli scalini o gradini della chiesa, al quale uno poco d'accordo _____ 7 393.0.0

B.   page 64 left

M. Giovanni di Maestro Andrea Mazzolini d'Arezzo scarpellino
d'ebbe dare questo di 14 Marzo 1578 y trecento novanta
quattro p 13 tanto sono per saldo e resto di una sua ragione
come appare in questo _____25_____y 394.13.0

page 25 right

Et più d'havere y trecento novanta quattro p 12 che finite
sono poste dare in questo 64 resto e saldo della confrater-
nita _____y 394.13.0

page 64 right

M. Giovanni per conto d'havere adi 16 di Dicembre 1586
y trecento quattro sono y resto et saldo dello conto fatti
nel prezzo di quattri coloni et quattri architravi con i
suoi capitelli et abbasamenti _____y 394.13.0

page 25 right   _____

                                        y 1028.13.4

N.B.   y = lire

4. THE BADIA IN 1650

La Chiesa e sotto titolo, e invocatione delle sopradette
S.S. Flora e Lucilla, conservandosi in essa i di loro
sacri corpi, sotto l'altare maggiore, e detta ha la sua
sagrestia, reliquario, oratorio, e lavamani: e l'anno 1565
fu dato principio a rinovarla fabricandola nuovo modello,
e adesso compita per di dentro: resta pero da fabricarsi
una cupola sopra il santuario, et un catino nel mezzo il
pavimento, a la facciata et anche da campirsi il campanile
e l'ornemento dell' organo, e d' alcun altari, che sia tutti
sono dieci. . . .

LSP, Status Monasteriorum cassensis, anno 1650 (ms.), 212.

III

THE CORRIDOIO

A. THE HISTORY OF THE BUILDING

The history of the Corridoio is relatively straight-
forward. Its construction was begun in March, 1565, and
it was complete by December of that year. The only exception to this is the connection with the Uffizi (see Text:
Note 13). Vasari's claim that the construction took only
five months probably refers to the superstructure (VII,
703-704); the remaining months were used to finish the
exterior and interior surfaces with plaster and to complete
the roof. It seems to have been in continual use throughout the entire Gran Duchy of Tuscany, but its history after
the 1799 invasion by the French is not clear. It suffered
considerable damage in World War II (Hartt, 1949, 128) when
the angle to the North side of the Ponte Vecchio was severely
damaged, the roof was totally destroyed, and the part between the South end of the Ponte Vecchio and S. Felicita
was completely obliterated. The Corridoio has been recently
restored and the area South of the Ponte Vecchio to S.
Felicta is new. At the moment it is used as a gallery (in
the French sense: see Note 3) for the display of numerous
paintings in the Uffizi collection, mainly artist's self-
portraits and Italian schools of the 17th and 18th Centuries.

After four centuries, its original function now can be appreciated by the public at large.

B. CHRONOLOGY

19 March 1565:

a.

Adi 19 di Marzo in lunedi a ore 18 in circa si comincio a
gettar il primo fondamento del primo pilastro del corridore
e di mano a mano tutti li altri che vanno a trovare il bello
Palazzo de' Pitti, e che attraversa il Ponte Vecchio. Quel
pilastro fu di getto, e ja ja e calcina, e fue quello che è
rimpetto alla volta de' Girolami, lungo Arno. Fu finito
detto corridore di tutto punto, per insino al Palazzo de'
Pitti, per tutto Novembre 1565; e di Gennaio 1570 si comin-
ciorno a fare, sotto detto corridore, le botteghe che vi
sono dirempetto alla casa de' Girolami.

A. Lapini, Diario fiorentino di Agosto Lapini dal 252 al
1590 (ed. G. Carrazini), Florence, 1900, 145.

b.

Addi XIX di Marzo 1564 lunedi
A ore 19 in circa fu cominciato a gettare il primo fondamento del primo pilastro p(er) fare un Corridore che dal
Palazzo de' Pitti andasse a questo di Piazza, che fu già
dell' Antica Signoria di Firenze; qual pilastro fu di getto
ed aja e calcina, e fu quello ch'e dirempetto alla Volta
de' Girolami Lungarno

ASF, Diario di Francesco Settimani, Ms. 128, III, 311v.

20 March 1565:

Addi XX di Marzo 1564 Martedi

Il Duca Cosimo fece rovinare la Loggia del Pesce fatto
pochi mesi avanti sul Ponte Vecchio, dove p(er) in
avverenza de' Capi Maestri rovinavono tre colonne con la
morte di un Muratore e due manuali; sopra detta Loggia
doveva passare il Nuovo Corridore.

ASF, Settimani, Ms. 128, III, 312 r.

27 March 1565:   From Seravezza, Cosimo writes to
Vasari on the subject of the Corridoio. He makes his
wishes clear that he wants it done as soon as possible
and that he wants all areas to be worked on concurrently
to speed construction (Frey, II, 154-155).

28 March 1565:   A court secretary writes from
Seravezza to Vasari in Florence. In it, he informs the
architect that his change of the windows from arched to
square has been approved by the Duke (Frey, III, 100).

1 August 1565:   On this date Vasari writes his
"recordo" for the corridor. Here he uses the phrase about
completing in five months what normally would have taken
five years--this is repeated in his Autobiography in the
Lives (Frey, II, 878). The cost is given as 11,000 scudi.

21 September 1565:   Vasari writes to Borghini that the
Duke is satisfied with the Corridoio (Frey, II, 210).

30 June 1567:   220 scudi are paid to Carlo di
Nicolo Paganelli for his house on the Via de' Bardi which
was demolished for the construction of the Corridoio (del
Badia, 1902, 9).

12 April 1570:   The Corridoio was the cause of romance
in the life of Cosimo I; on this date he married Cammilla
Martelli, the daughter of Domenico di Girolamo Martelli,

the owner of a house contiguous to the passageway (del

Badia, 1902, 11).

Il Granduca si era invaghito della sudetta Cammilla Martelli,
qual er allora di circa 20 anni, essendo nato 1547, ed era
bella della persona, bianca, e bionda, coll' occasione che
fece fare un Corridore dal Palazzo Vecchio a quello de'
Pitti, il qual Corridore passava per le case di alquanti
cittadini, che bisognio per farsi strada, bucare fra le
quale fu di detto Antonio Martelli, la quale era contigua
a detto Corridore sopra l'ufficio del proconsolo.

ASF, Settimani, Ms. 128, IV, 12v.

1 January 1571:   From Rome, Vasari writes to Prince

Francesco, telling him to take care of some repairs on

the Palazzo Vecchio. The cause, apparently, was Cosimo's

wish to spend as little money as possible. This also

applied to the Corridoio, for Vasari said that now the

roof was leaking in many places (Frey, II, 558).

30 December 1575:   50 florins are paid to the Ricci for

their house which was demolished for the Corridoio. Their

residence was in the Torre della Parte Guelfa, on the Via

de'Bardi opposite the Torre dei Manelli (del Badia, 1902,

9).

30 October 1883 to 21 November 1883:   The Communal

Council of Florence proposes and approves the demolition

of the botteghe underneath the vaults of the North Arm of

the Corridoio. A Royal Decree declares the work to be of

public utility, and the work is completed in November, 1885

(del Badia, 1902, 10).

IV

THE LOGGIA

A. HISTORY OF THE BUILDING

The Loggia on the Piazza Grande in Arezzo was conceived and built as a multi-function, rental building containing shops, government offices, and houses. Financed
mainly by the Confraternità di Santa Maria di Misericordia
of Arezzo with contributions from the city and the Ducal
government in Florence, the Loggia owes its existence to
the generosity of Mariotto Cofani, an Aretine businessman
who left a substantial amount of money and property to the
Misericordia in 1564. Although its construction was deliberated as early as 1570, the project was held up for more
than two years due to the lack of approval from Prince
Francesco who, at that time, had assumed many of the functions of Duke Cosimo I. It was finally begun in January,
1573, and its construction lasted well into the 1590's.
Like most buildings of its kind, the Loggia was built bay by
bay, and the Misericordia was buying land for the building
as late as 1596. The Western portion of the building was
begun first, and hence it was completed earlier.

*

<u>1570</u>: The rectors of the Misericordia petition to the

Consiglio Generale of Arezzo to make use of the funds left
to them by Cofani (Appendix IV. Doc. 1). The nature of the
project is described as faciendo novas fabricas in civitate
Aretii pro decore civitatis et comoditate civi ad utilitate
fraternitatis, and the funds were to be used pro fabricis
faciendis et ne plus ultra. The Council accepted the
petition, and it repeated the Misericordia's Vitruvian
description of the project, calling it con utilita di detta
fraternita et anchora ornamento et decoro detta citta. In
addition, they stipulated that four citizens would be
chosen to oversee the project. The site is not mentioned
until October 17 when it is officially designated as such,
and it is mentioned that the design will be made by Vasari
(Appendix IV: Doc. 4). At the same time they write to
Vasari describing the ruinous condition of the site, and
they ask him to intercede on their behalf for a contribution from Cosimo I for the cost of the Monte di Pieta (Frey,
II, 538). In addition, they ask for a small amount of land
for the project.

1572: Vasari directed the preliminary planning and design
for the Loggia from Florence; he stopped in Arezzo only once
during this period, on a trip to Rome. His clients must have
foreseen Francesco's approval of the project. The book of
the Fabbrica was dedicated on July 1, and by November
demolition was well underway (Gaye, III, 342). Yet the

design had not been set. The authorities in Arezzo lacked
a wooden model of the Loggia, and the design was to be
bella, honorata, e gratiosa on its site (Frey, II, 691).
Almost a month later Vasari replies that he had been busy
working on fortification design for Cosimo, but he would
send the model and a capo maestro to Arezzo soon (Appendix
IV: Doc. 5). The deputies were pleased, and they asked him
to intercede on their behalf again, this time for permission to re-use the stones from the recently demolished
fortress in their building (Appendix IV: Doc. 8). In
October the site was surveyed and the model was delivered
(Appendix IV: Doc. 10).

1573: Vasari continued to conduct the affairs of the
Loggia by letter. At the end of the previous year, the
authorities in Arezzo noticed a defect in the design
whereby the building would tend to slide down the site and
fill up the Piazza below it (Frey, II, 735). Apparently,
this did not bother Vasari, who wrote that several of the
bays and the shops would be vaulted within the year. In
Vasari's terms, the Loggia would be a benefit to a "poor
and destroyed city" (Frey, II, 758). On January 27
construction was begun (Viviani-Fiorini,1941-42,115) and
at the same time Alfonso Castelli (Parigi) signed a contract as murator et architect to complete the building
according to the designs of Vasari. Payments were made to

Parigi regularly and consistently for his work on the
Loggia until his death in 1591, but they are recorded
by trade ("muratore") and rarely give any indication of
what was built.

The construction proceeded slowly but consistently.
Vasari's contribution to the project was in the realm of
administration rather than technique or design. Shortly
after the commencement of construction ill-feeling developed between all parties. Within six months Vasari had to
write a letter with glowing terms of praise for Parigi
(Frey, II, 796), answer for defects in the stone used in
wall construction (Frey, II, 810), and was finally agitated
enough to write a letter showing the difficulty in working
for two separate clients--the Misericordia and the Deputies
for the construction of the Loggia. This was possibly
provoked by a letter from the Misericordia demanding
detailed records of expenses and salaries (Appendix IV.
Doc. 11).

1574-1580: Most of these problems must have been due to
Vasari's continual absence from Arezzo--only this can explain the abundance of documentary information on the
Loggia. After Vasari's death in June, 1574 Parigi divided
his time between Florence and Arezzo. This arrangement must
have satisfied both the Misericordia and the Deputies--no
other conflicts arose during the construction of the Loggia.

In 1575 the Misericordia deliberated the location of the
offices of a new tenant--the Dogana of Arezzo--and the
design for the distribution of office space was ordered from
Parigi (Appendix IV. Doc. 12). A year later the Fraternita
appealed again to Florence for permission to use more stone
from the old fortress, and an itemized list of masonry work
indicates that ten piers and their vaults had been completed
by then. In 1579 nine shops under the Loggia were substantially complete (Appendix IV. Doc. 13).

1580 to Completion: The Loggia was almost half complete,
but it also had no other remaining possibilities for governmental tenants. In 1583, Parigi was paid for the design
of the houses above the Loggia which are entered from the
present day Via della Torre Rossa (Appendix IV. Doc. 14).
Work proceeded smoothly but still slowly while awaiting the
purchase of more land, and by 1590 ironworkers were paid
for the catena dell' ultimo pilastro (Appendix IV. Doc. 15).
A year later, the rectors were able to report that almost
everything had been completed (Appendix IV. Doc. 17).

Parigi's contributions to the Loggia ended on April 13,
1591; after that, all payments were made to Sano da
Bastiano Bertacchi who had worked as Parigi's assistant
(Appendix IV. Doc. 18). By 1593 a small amount of roofwork
remained to be completed (Appendix IV. Doc. 19) but payments
for masonry work were made as late as 1596 (Appendix IV.

Doc. 20). Like most other buildings erected as a commercial
investment, the Loggia was prone to renovation and change
in interior organization. Small changes were probably
made from time to time, but the only major restauration
was done in the 18th Century. Although the botteghe on the
Piazza Grande have held their original function, the houses
designed for a single family have become apartments for
three or four. The offices of the Monte di Pietà underwent
a major renovation in the 19th Century when they became
the Corte d'Assize. The facade has been recently restored
by the Soprintendenza degli Monumenti of Arezzo.

B. THE WOODEN MODEL

The wooden model for the facade of the Loggia, now in the Casa Vasari in Arezzo, is the only existing evidence which shows Vasari's preliminary design for any of his buildings. It is built to a recognizable scale (1:40), and it is in good condition. Its side and roof are modern repairs; they are both plywood and may not reflect the original condition of the model. It is built in three pieces--piers, bottega facades and vaulting, upper floors --and the reason for this was probably ease and safety in transportation from Florence to Arezzo. No other pieces have survived which might indicate alternative features interchangeable with the present design.

Vasari's clients did not request a wooden model of the Loggia until July, 1572 (Appendix IV. Doc. 5). Vasari continued to correspond with the authorities in Arezzo throughout this time, and on 13 August 1572 he mentions that a model will be made (Appendix IV. Doc. 7). It was completed and delivered to Arezzo by October 18 of the same year; on this date Lutio Guasparri was paid 70 lire for building it (Appendix IV. Doc. 10). This is the only instance in the entire history of the construction of the Loggia were a wooden model is mentioned. The payment in

1582 to Parigi refers to a <u>modello</u>, not a <u>modello</u> <u>di</u>
<u>legno</u> (IV. Doc. 14). Hence the model in the Casa Vasari
is the 1572 model.

C. DOCUMENTS

1. 23 June 1570

Excerpts from the petition of the Rectors of the Misericordia to the Consiglio Generale of Arezzo to make use of
the funds given to them by Mariotto Cofani. FDL, 1484,
Deliberazioni dal 1564 al 1571, BB 85, fol. 269.

Petitio ad Cons(siglium) Generale pro erogando introitus
hereditatis Mariotti Cofani in frat(ernità).

. . . qui provenient de hereditati Marriotti de Cofanis
expender, et erogare in construendo et faciendo novas
fabricas domos in civitate Aretii pro decore civitatis
et commoditate civi ad utilitate frat(ernitat) is in illis
. . . et debeat fructus hereditatis . . . aliis pecunis
depositis in cassone fraternitatis, servendo faciendis pro
fabricis, et ne ultra.

2. 6 July 1570

Excerpts from the petition presented by the Misericordia to
the Magistro dei Priori for the construction of the Loggia.
ASA, <u>Deliberazioni</u> <u>del</u> <u>Magistro dei</u> <u>Priori</u> e <u>del</u> <u>Consiglio</u>
<u>Generale</u>, 1385-1863, no. 26, 1567-1571, fol. 272 verso.

*

La fraternita per molti anni con li fructi di essa fraternita
fabricasse sui case et edifici li qiali (illegible) di una,
dua, o più ragionevole prezzi, et havendo poi anchore fra
di loro stessi consider(atione) questo fatto, et parendosi
che il mandato ad esecutione fosse senza danno anche con
utilità di detta fraternita et anchora ornamento et decoro
della città li quali per li nuovi edifici si abellisce et
comodo grande ai cittadini chi hanno di bisognio di pigliar
casa . . .

in margin: petitio fraternitatis super fabrica nove per
            facienda.

3. 21 July 1570

Letter from Prince Francesco de' Medici in Florence to
Mario Tolosano, Cancelliere of Arezzo, ABC, Manoscritti
della Fraternità dei Laici, Ms. 85: Jacopo Buriali,
Memorie storiche aretine dal 1502 al 1600, fol. 60.

Don Francesco De Medici
Principe di Toscana

Magnifico nostro Carissimo

Ci pare Molto Buono Pensamento Quello de Rettori di
Fraternita di volere co(n) li Ava(n)zi della Heredità di
Mariotto Cofani ornare quella città, di qualch(e) fabrica,
et Poich(e) Voi co(n) la Vostra di x ci scrivete essese
di co(n)se(n)so di tutto quello Universale, Viene approvato
da noi Anchora; state sano.

di Fiorenza Il di 21 di Luglio 1570.

A tergo: Al Mag(nifi)co M(esse)r Mario Tolosano Cancelliere
          d'Arezzo

q(uest)o è posta nel Lib(r)o delle delib(erazio) ni di
n(ostra Cancellaria segnata A.A. 2 272 in publico Palazzo

4.   17 October 1570

Excerpt from the record on the deliberation on the site of
the Loggia by the Rectors of the Misericordia.   FDL, no.
1484, _Deliberazioni_ _dal_ _1564_ _al_ _1571_, BB 85, fol. 311.

*

Electio et deputatio loci et situs opti ad faciendum fabricas fructibus Mariotti de Cofaniis.

. . . elegerunt pro loco et sito apto opportuno ad faciendas
fabricas.   Et situ qui est a via saxonis usque; ad viam
Sileis, et a latere quod edificia incipiant cu(m) uno
eoru(m) conrnu, et capite a via Saxonis et a pilastro
ib(i) in quo est pieta imagine Glorissimae Verginis Maria,
et proseguitur versus cornu, et capite edificia et fabrica
sint ibi olim erat apothici carnis venali et vulgari . . .
et modello pr(a)es(t)ati Georgii de Vasariis . . .

5.   5 August 1572

Letter from Vasari in Florence to the Deputies for the
construction of the Loggia in Arezzo.   FDL, 1485, Deliberazioni, 1571-1573, BB 86, fol. 287v.

*

    Molto Magnifici Signori deputati osservandissimi

Le Signorie Vostre si saranno di me molto maravigliati
che io non habbi prima che ora risposto alla lettera
de' XVIIII del passato, le quale non mi trov' in
Fiorenza ma alla Vernia con il Serenissimo Gran Duca,
quale mi condisse per suo servito alla fortificatione
del Sasso di Simone et doppo fatto quanto occoreva mi
licentio' né ho hauto primo che hora commod di rispond-
ere alle Signorie Vostre.   La quale mi é stata molto grata
per vedere il gran contento ch hanno preso della resolutione fatto da loro Altezze sopra la muraglia et come
si sonno degnate farmi loro principale architettore.
Del ché le ringratio, avertandole che dalla fede et
amore non sarano mai defraudate, che cosi ho facto con
chi ha hauto di me bisogno, et tanto più far lo debo
per la mia patria et per li mia cittadini.   Ho inteso
tutti li loro desiderii et maxime di vedere alli giorno
loro tal cosa nata, però ho dato a fare il modello, et sub-
ito practico con un bonissimo capomaestro lo mandarò.
Et forse allora, se no sarò molto occupato, verrò costi.
Intanto scrivo a messer Nerozzo Albergotti che si fac-
cino le provisioni et si incamini quanto fa bisogno.   Et
hora che sono in Fiorenza attendero a questa cosa con
tutto il mio potere.   Però le Signorie Vostre si riposino
sopra di me, et farò cosa che, oltre restarà ogni homo
contento, anco monstratò che la vurtù çhe Dio mi ha data,
ho il meglio salvato per eseguirlo in mia patria, come ho
facto in ogni occasione che misi è porta.   Et secondo che
si potrà spendere, si faccia che piu tosto ne sia d'avanzo
che ne manchi, come aboccandoci insieme intenderanno.   Et
con questo fine mi li offero et raccomando.   Di Fiorenza,
il di 5 di Agosto 1572.

Di Vostre Signorie amorevolissimo

               il Cavalier Giorgio Vasari

A tergo:
Alli Molto Signori osservandissimi, li signori deputati
sopra la frabrica (sic) del Monte di Pietade Aretino

6. 11 August 1572

Letter from the rectors of the Misericordia in Arezzo to
Giorgio Vasari. FDL, 1485, <u>Deliberazioni</u>, 1571-1573, BB 86,
fol 288-288v.

*

      Molto Magnifico Signore Cavalieri

Receverimo la lettera di Vostra Signoria a noi gratissima,
intendo havere acceptato il carico che si li (é) dato, et
ci provettiamo molto della amorevolleza, diligentia et
virtù sua. Desideramo et la preghiamo che quanto prima
possendo, la si conferisca finn (sic) qui, accio che sul
luogo istesso la ne dimostrà quello et quanto come da
prima si possi et si deve fare per il buon principio della
fabrica nostra, acciò che non si dessi mano a fare cosa
che non servissi et bisognassi poi con qualche danno dell'
utile et dello honore disfarla, ma sì ingominci (sic) con
buon principio, et cosi più facilamente cresca et habbi
con il tempo il suo felice et desiderato fine. Et intanto
la indugerà a venire, sarà contenta essere dinanzi al
Magistro della Parte per ottenere licentia da quello
di possere cavare et pigliare li sassi delli fragmenti
et delle reliquie della muraglia dell antiqua et desolata
rocca per servirci di essi sassi nella nostra fabrica li
quali sono vicine (sic). Certificando il Magistrato che
non ne succede danno alcuno, anzi servitio alla rocca che
è oggi in piedi, perciò che detti fraggamenti (sic) di
detta muraglia vecchia sonno certo modo trinciea et volgono
la offese, et levandosi tali fragmenti di detti muri vechi,
la detta rocca nova rimane di ogni turno libera et più
expedita.

Apresso, occorendo, sicome Vostra Ecelenza (sic=Signoria)
sa, ampliare et allargare l'orto del Signore Cemmissario
della banda di sopra, per renderli tanto quanto della
banda di sotto se li torrà nel fare il sito delle loggie,
bisognarà serrare certa via che camina dal canto di sopra del detto orto del Signore Commissario et infra esso
orto et li campi ch ha qui vi detto Magistrato, et retir-
ando et riducendo detta via in quel luogo dove sonno hora
detti fraggamenti (sic) della muraglia vecchia et dove si
caveranno detti sassa (sic). Inperò Vostra Signoria pro-
curarà di operare di ottenare et haver licentia dalli
prefati Capitani di Parte ancora di questo, cioè di muttare
detta via nel modo sudetto. Inoltre li piacera di adomandare

dal detto Magistrato licentia di far portare il tereno, quale si caverà a' piedi dell'orto del Signore Commissario et dal fondamente delle logge che qui faranno col condurlo et ispargenderllo sopra li campi et terre pure delli detti Signoria Capitani di Parte, posti dentro al procinto della rovinate desolata rocca, in certe basse che vi sonno, dove non sara impedimento alla rocha nova che oggi e in piedi, né sarà danno alli campi detti, dove esso terreno si spargerà, per essere detto terreno buono et acto a fructaré et a condire essi campi, si come la Signoria Vostra è benissimo informata et potrà al Magistrato exporlo. Di che la preghiamo adunque, aspettando del tutto buono et expedita resolutione. Ete bene valete.

Di Arezzo, il di XI (Agosto 1572)

Di Vostra Signoria Magnifica

                          Affectionatissimi li deputati sopra
                          la fabrica della Confraternit di
                          Santa Maria di Misericordia della
                          Cita di Arezzo.

A tergo:
A molto Magnifico et nostro osservandissimo il Signore Cavalier messer Giorgio Vasari

7.   13 August 1572

Letter from Vasari in Florence to the Deputies for the
construction of the Loggia in Arezzo.   FDL, 1485, Deliberazioni, 1571-1573, BB 86, fol. 288v.-289.

*

Molti Magnifici Signori deputati miei osservandissimi

Poiché mi si porta occasione che Francesco Menichi, capomaestro di loro Altezze alla Parte, vien costi per loro
occurentie con ordine di havervi a dimorare qualche giorno,
non ho volutoto (sic) mandare in benefitio della fabrica
seco a lungo discorere et ordinarli in questo principio
quanto occorre, et di quello m'e parso più a proposito
et oportuno que ne ho segnato cosa per cosa per lo apunto
in uno suo libretto.   Vostre Signorie adunque li daranno
quella fede che alla persona mia, al quale ho comesso che
dia ordine di far levare il tereno et fare li fondamenti,
et che li porti un luogo più commodo che sia possible per
la spesa.   Intanto si farà il modello, et lui adivisarà di
mano in mano, et cosi farò io, acciò si faccia quanto
occore.   Però Vostre Signorie stiano di buonissimo animo,
che io non mancarò, sicome ho promesso, haver l'ochio a
tutto sicome costi fossi presentialmente.   Per hora non
occore che costi venglia, il che si farà in tempo più oportuno.   Et con questi fine mi vi offero et raccomando.   Di
Fiorenza, il di 13 di Agosto 1572.

Di Vostre Signorie Magnificie

Il Cavalieri Giorgio Vasari

A tergo:
Alli Molto Magnifici Signori deputati della fabrica del
Monte di Pieta di Arezzo, miei osservandissimi.

8. 30 August 1972

Letter from the Deputies for the construction of the Loggia
in Arezzo to Giorgio Vasari in Florence. Attached to it is
a request to Cosimo I to reuse the stones of the recently
destroyed Rocca in the construction of the Loggia. FDL,
1485, Deliberazioni, 1571-1573, BB 86, fol. 289v-290.

*

L'introclusa è la suplica che si è facta a sua Altezza per
ottenere quanto in essa et conforme a quello che per lettere
habiamo insiemi tracato. La piacerà adunque quanto prima
presentarla et procurare di ottenere benigno riscripto.
Con che facciamo fine, et nostor Signore Dio la sonservi
sana. Di Arezzo, il di 30 3i Agosto 1572. Di Vostra
Signoria Magnifica

Affectionatissimi mi deputati sopra la fabrica
delle loggie

A tergo: Al Molto Magnifico Signore Cavalieri messer
Giorgi Vasari

*

Serenissimo Gran Duca

Li deputati della fabrica delle loggie che con partici
patione di Vostra Altezza si sonno designate fare nella
cita di Arezzo per il servito della Fraternita della Miser-
cordia et del Monte della Pietà di quella cità, hutuilmente
suplicano l'Altezza Vostra si degni concederli gratia di
poter far portare il tereno quale si caverà nel fondare et
fare dette loggie, sopra li campi et terre delli Signori
Capitani di Parte posti dentro al procinto della antiqua
et desolata rocca, in certe basse che vi sono, dove detto
tereno non sarà di impedimento alcuno alla rocca nova
che oggi è in piedi, né sarà di danno alli detti campi dove
egli si spargerà, per essere detto tereno che qui si
porta buono et atto a fructare et a condire essi campi,
et dall'altra banda di grandissimo grovamento et risparmio
di spesa a detta fabrica, essendo detto luogo et detti
campi doce si desidera il tereno, molto vicino et propinquo
al luogo dive si hanno a fare et cavare li fondamenti per

detta fabrica. Suplicano ancora detti deputati Vostra
Altezza di degni cencederli gratis di possere cavare et
pigliare alcuni sassi de' fragmenti della muraglia di essa
antiqua et desolata rocca, per servitio della fabrica
d'esse loggie, di che non si vede danno alcuno alla rocca
nova, anzi a quello commodo, perciò che detti fragmenti
della muraglia vecchia fanno certo modo trincea et tolgono
la offese, et lavandosi tali fragmenti di detti muri vecchi,
la detta rocca nova rimarrà di ogni intorno più libera et
più spedita. Et dall'altra banda detti sassi saranno di
molto risparmio di spesa in detta opera et fabrica delle
loggie, per essere a quella molto propinqui et vicini. Il
che riceveranno per grazia singularissima da Vostra Altezza
Serenissima, alle quale pregono perfecta felicta et contento.

9. 6 September 1572

Letter from Vasari in Florence to the Deputies for the
construction of the Loggia in Arezzo. FDL, 1485, <u>Delibera</u>-
<u>zioni</u>, <u>1571-1573</u>, BB 86, fol. 290.

*

       Molti Magnifici Signori deputati
       Signori miei osservandissimi

Come le Signorie Vostre veder potranno, il Serenissimo
Gran Duca ha segnata la suplica che me si è mandata
per informatione al Signore Commissario, quale è stato
benigno amatore del vero et del giustitia, ché cognos-
ciuto p'utile, benefitio et commod si de' campi, loro
altezze, come della nuova muraglia, non mancarà giusto il
suo potere di non fare un referto che si capissi in sua
Signoria ne sarete senza altro compiaciuti. Però le
Signorie Vostre gli potranno raccomandare, presentandogne
il negotio con quella prontezza di animo che possono,
facendole toccar con mano come il tutto sta, et rimesso
in quel bell'animo et giuditio sarete con la gratia di
Dio compiaciuti. Dicendo ancora, che quando Sua Signoria
hara facto l'informatione, se le Signorie Vostre si deg-
naranno rimandarla la racomandarò al Signore Gratino,
acciò nel leggerla, se vi fosse alcuno ostaculo, possa,
informato da me, rimoverlo con destrezza et modestia
della mente di sua Altezza, acciò siate di questo compiaciuti sicome lo desiderlo. Et con questo fine, piegan-
doli da Dio ogni felicità et contento, me li offero et
racomando. Di Fiorenza, li VI di Septembre 1572.

Di Vostre Signorie Molto Magnifiche

               amorevolissimo

               il Cavalier Giorgio Vasari

A tergo:
Alli Molto Magnifici et Signori miei osservandissimi
li Signori deputati della fabrica del Monte della Pieta
di Arezzo

10. 18 October 1572

Payment documents for the wooden model of the Loggia
designed by Vasari. FDL, no. 1703, <u>Libro</u> <u>della</u> <u>nova</u>
<u>fabrica</u>.

5 left

Lutio di Guasparri di contro di dare adi 18 di 8bre y 70
cotanti da Ant(oni)o cam(erlingh)o in qu(esto)....y 70.0.0

5 right

Lutio di Guasparri punino di avere adi 18 di 8bre y 80 p(er)
il modello di legni mandato da Firenze dal Cavaliere Giorgio
Vasari nel modo sano a fare le case et loggie di d(et)ta
fabrica in qu(esto) ....y 70.0.0

6 left

Spesi minuti di d(et)ta fabrica dieno dare adi 18 di 8bre
y 70 p(er) il modello a conto Lutio punino cred(ito) re
....y 70.0.0

4 right

Antonio di Mariotto Nardi di avere adi 18 di 8bre y 70
cotanti a Lutio di Guasparri punino deb(ito)re ...y 70.0.0

15 November 1572

6 left

Et adi detto a Lando di Bastiano p(er) vettura il modello
porto da Fiorenza pag(a) to Antonio Nardo cam(erlingh)o
....7 2.0.0

N.B. y = lire

11. 17 October 1573

Record of a letter, now lost, from the Rectors of the
Misericordia of Arezzo to Vasari. FDL 1485, Deliberazioni
1571-1573, BB 86, fol 275v.

*

Die 17 mensis octobris 1573

Congregati supra scripti domini rectoresin eorum solito
auditorio, servatis servandis, una cum quatour viris adiunctis et deputatis a publico et generale consilio super
facbrica porticorum, et obtento partito per omnes fabas
nigras, deliberaverunt et declaraverunt literas ad dominum Georgium de Vasaris mitendo et includendo quandam
notulam preciorum solitorum dari et solvi pro pluribus
fabricis et muris factis et constructis in civitate
Aretii a diversis personis particularibus et publicis
societatibus, universitatibus et collegis ad effectum
ut visa huius modi notula, facilius possit et melius arbi-
trare, laudare et indicare salarium et mercedem sive pret-
ium persolvendum magistro Alfonso Castelli pro fabrica
porticorum et appotecarum et pro muris per eum fabricatis
et constructis, fabricandis et construndis in ivitate
Aretii pro dicta fraternitate, iuxta autoritatem et
facultatem, dictamatque atributatam dicto Georgio, et
exortando eundem dominum Georgium quatenus in faciendo
dictum arbitrium, arbitramentum et laudum et declarationem
dicte mercedis et salari, et super dicta mercede et salario
comendatam habeat dictam fraternitatem et civitatem seu
universitatem dicte civitatis, et prout in dictis literis
latius apparet, ad quas relatio heabeatur omno meliori modo.

In margin: litere ad dominum Equitem Georgium de Vasaris
             Fabrica

12.　26 January 1575

Deliberation of the location for the Dogana of Arezzo, ASA,
<u>Deliberazioni</u> <u>del</u> <u>Magistro</u> <u>dei</u> <u>Priori</u> <u>e</u> <u>del</u> <u>Consiglio</u>
<u>Generale</u>, no. 27, 1571-1575, fol. 181 recto.

*

. . . Che la Dogana et casa pro uso della communita di
Arezzo debba farsi et fabricarsi a somma (del)la Piazza
Grande, et debba la detta Dogana principarsi et fondarsi
dalla testa del muro della casa della Fraternità dove di
presente habita Signor Vicentio Torri, notaio aretino, cioè,
dove sono le scalette et entrata di essa casa, et la casa
per uso del Cancelliere della città debba fabricarsi sopra
detta Dogana, et con detta fabrica si debba seguiri verso
il cante del Monte del Pietà; et questo essero per luogo
et situ di essa Dogana et casa ancora piu secondo che dal
capo maestro della fabrica che di presente si fa quando
sara nel luogo con detti Signori Deputati passa et sara
giudicati che meglio convegna a risegga. Con il parete
et disegno del quale si debbino poi ordinarsi, et distribursi
le stanze che convenghino et siano necessarie a detta Dogana
et casa.

in margin:　Deliberatio et Declaratio Loci et Situ pro
　　　　　　 Dogana et Domo Civitatis in Nova Fabrica
　　　　　　 Fraternitatis

13. 20 July 1579

An itemized list of stonework completed to date includes
mention of "9 botteghe sotto le Loggie fino alla ferrata
della Dogana."

FDL, no. 1487, Deliberazioni, 1577-1579, fol. 239

14. 14 March 1583

Payments for the modello for the repetitive houses. FDL,
no. 1703, Libro della nova fabrica.

45 left

Et adi 14 marzo 1582 y centocinquantuni cotanti a M(aestr)o
Alfonso di Santi Castelli capo m(aestr)o et altri p(er)
conto de la lui fatto nel modo hanno da farsi le case chi
vanno dalla Dogana in la stimato in Fiorenza et in Arezzo
in tutto y 151 et pag(at)o da Nicola Francesci nostro
cam(erlingh)o ....y 151.0.0

166 right

Et adi detto li cotanti a spese fatte in Fiorenza
....y 151.0.0

155 right

Et adi 3 di Marzo y sette et tre et quattro cotanti a Andrea
di Luca p(er) aver portato da Fiorenza il modello fatto da
M(aestr)o Alfonso nel modo ch(e han)no da esser le case de la
fabrica p(er) l'avenire........................y   7.3.4

N.B. y = lire

15. 17 March 1590

Payment to ironworkers for work on "cateno del ultimo pilastro".

FDL, no. 1720, Libro della fabrica, 1591, 25 left.

16. 29 February 1591

Rectors of the Misericordia to the Nove Conservatori del Dominio in Florence. FDL, no. 177, Registro delle Lettere, CC 3, fol. 119 verso.

. . . apresso hanno comperate buon numero di case vecchie et si sono tornate p(er) edificare dove elle erano gran quantità di detta nova fabrica. Et in dette case erano gran quantita di tetti coperti ed lastri còme si vede la tavolatura fattone le quali lastre ne hanno servito in questo novo edificio quale e tutto coperto col tegole é coppi di terra cotta et ne si trove del detto ritratto di lastre le quale sono stato la cura . . .

17. 9 March 1591

Notice of work on the last bottega. FDL, no. 1720, Libro della fabrica, 1591.

55 left

Et adi detto a Maestro Annibale di Rosado et a Paolo suo figlio per piu opere et tempo messe per avere fatto due imposte alla ultimo porto delle bottege in capo alla Loggia...y. 8.0.0

18. 20 April 1591

Payment to "Sano da Bastiano Bertacchi fiorentino al presente capo maestro de la fabrica". The last payment to Alfonso Parigi is made on 13 April 1591.

Libro della Fabrica, FDL no. 1720, 1591, 38 left.

19. 26 June 1593

Letter from the Rectors of the Misericordia in Arezzo to
Donato dell'Antilla in Florence. FDL, no. 177, Registro
delle Lettere, CC 3, fol. 148.

Mentions that "in brevi tempo il salone della nova fabrica
sara finito di coperto".

20. 7 February 1596

Payment to Sano da Bastiano for work on Loggia "per piu e
molti capi di lavori di mura".

FDL, no. 1720, Libro della Fabrica, 1591, fol. 28 left.

NOTES

NOTES TO INTRODUCTION

[1]P. Barocchi, Vasari pittore, Milan, 1964, is the standard monograph with full bibliography. Cf. also S. J. Freedberg, Painting in Italy, 1500-1600, Baltimore and Harmondsworth, 1970, 305-314.

[2]G. Spini, "Architettura e politica nel principato mediceo," Rivista storica italiana, LXXXIII, 1971, 792-845, particularly 796-798. This study had been reprinted in somewhat altered form as the introduction to G. Spini (comp.), Architettura e politica da Cosimo I a Ferdinando I, Florence, 1976. See my review in JSAH, XXXVII, 1978, 205-206.

[3]A. Palladio, I quattro libri dell' architettura, Venice, 1570, 1.

[4]This subject (with a new chronology for the dates of Vasari's consultations) will be considered in a forthcoming article by H. Millon and C. Smyth.

[5]R. Wittkower, Gothic vs. Classic, New York, 1974, 30.

[6]M. Bassi, Dispareri in materia d'architettura e prospettiva, Brescia, 1572, 47-49.

[7]F. Baglione, Le vite de' pittori, scultori, architetti, ed intagliatori, dal pontificato di Gregorio XIII fino a tempi di papa Urbano VIII nel 1642, Rome, 1642, 11-14.

[8]F. Milizia, Memorie degli architetti antichi e moderni. Venice, 1785, II, 29-31.

[9]J. Burckhardt, Der Cicerone, Basel, 1855, 343-345.

[10]A. Ricci, Storia dell' architettura in Italia, Modena, 1857-1859, III, 250.

[11]A. Grandjean de Montigny and A. Famin, Architecture toscane, Paris, 1815.

[12]H. Steegman and H. von Geymuller, Die Architecture der Renaissance in Toscana, Munich, 1885-1904, IV, iv. 1-7.

[13]K. Frey, Der literarisches Nachlass Giorgio Vasari's vol. I, Munich, 1923, hereafter cited as Frey, I. K. Frey, Der literarisches Nachlass Giorgio Vasari's, vol. II, Munich, 1930, hereafter cited as Frey, II. H. Frey, Neue Briefe, Burg b.M., 1940, hereafter cited as Frey, III.

[14]U. Dorini, "Come sorse la Fabbrica degli Uffizi," Rivista degli archivi toscani, V, 1933, 1-40.

[15]D. Viviani-Fiorini, "La constuzione delle Loggie Varariane di Arezzo," le Vasari, xi, 1940, 109-117, and XII, 39-46, hereafter cited as Viviani-Fiorini, 1940; Dr. Viviani-Fiorini, "La Badia di Arezzo e G. Vasari," Il Vasari, xii, 1941, 74-83.

[16]A. Venturi, Storia dell' arte italiana, Milan, 1938-1940, XI, ii, 385-454, hereafter cited as Venturi, 1938-1940.

[17]P. Barocchi, "Il Vasari architetto," Atti della Accademia Pontaniana (Naples), VI, 1956-1957, 113-136, hereafter cited as Barocchi, 1956-1957.

[18]R. Zürcher, Stilprobleme der italieneschen Baukunst des Cinquecento, Basel, 1947, 38.

[19]W. Hager, "Zu Raumstruktur des Manierismus," Festschrift Martin Wakernagel, Cologne, 1958, 112-140.

[20]L. Berti, "L'architettura manieristica a Firenze e in Toscana," Bolletino del Centro Internazionale di Studi di Architettura Andrea Palladio, IX, 1967, 211-218.

[21]E. Panofsky, "The First Page of Vasari's Libro," Meaning in the Visual Arts, New York, 1955, 169-235.

[22]U. Procacci, "L'architettura nel Aretino: il medio e il tardo Rinascimento, Atti del XII Congresso di Storia dell' Architettura (Arezzo, 1961), Rome, 1969, 123-152.

[23]J. Lessmann, _Studien zu einer Baumonographie der Uffizien Giorgio Vasari's in Florenz_, Ph.D., Bonn, 1975, hereafter cited as Lessman, 1975.

[24]E. Cochrane, _Florence in the Forgotten Centuries_, Chicago, 1973, hereafter cited as Cochrane, 1975. For Spini, see note 2.

[25]First observed by Ackerman, 1970, 291.

NOTES TO CHAPTER I

[1]Vasari's own account of the commission is appended
to the Life of Bramante (IV, 165-167). The modern biblio-
graphy on the cupola is: J. Durm, "Santa Maria dell'
Umilità. Grosskonstructionen der italienischen Renaissance,"
Zeitschrift fur Bauwesen, 1902, 13-14; Venturi, 1938-1940.
XI, ii, 443-447; Barocci, 1956-1957, 125; U. Procacci,
"L'architettura nell aretino, Atti del XII Congresso di
Storia di architettura, Arezzo, 1961 (Rome, 1969), 124;
Lessmann, 1975, 177-178; Fossi, 1973, 83-136; Heydenreich-
Lotz, 1974, 395, n. 11; Fossi, 1977, 127-142; M. Bussioni,
"La chiesa della Madonna dell' Umilità," Ventura Vitoni e
il Rinascimento a Pistoia, Pistoia, 1977, 39-44.

[2]Lessmann, 1975, Ibid.

[3]Barocchi, 1956-1957, Ibid.

[4]This was first published by P. Sanpaolesi, "Ventura
Vitoni, architetto pistoiese," Palladio, III, 1939, 248-
266. The documentary evidence on Vitoni's career has been
collected by F. Quintiero, "Regesto e documenti," Ventura
Vitoni e il Rinascimento a Pistoia, 65-82.

After Giuliano departed for France, Antonio da
Sangallo the Elder and Antonio del Pollaiolo were consulted
on the design. Sangallo merely re-measured the modello,
perhaps foretelling the irregularities which would trouble
Vasari (see note 25). Bussioni has asserted that Pollaiolo's
visit merely involved the decoration of the church.

[5]Fossi, 1973, 85-6.

[6]IV, 166.

[7]L. Dami, "Ventura Vitoni," Bolletino storico
pistoiese, XVI, 1914, 1-40.

[8]A Chiti, Il santuario della Madonna dell' Umilità
in Pistoia, Pistoia, 1952, 34. Chiti asserts that during
a visit to Pistoia in 1555 to inspect the new fortifications,

Cosimo I was impressed by the beauty of the unfinished structure, and thus he ordered Vasari to complete it. Neither
Cosimo's reaction nor his visit are substantiated by any
documentary evidence. His interest and patronage, however,
are borne out by his correspondence with Vasari on the
cupola. See Appendix I: Vasari's contribution.

[9]The contract for the lantern between Vasari and
Andrea di Matteo, scarpellino, has been published (IV, 167,
n.1; L. Bargiacchi, Tempio e opere della Madonna dell'
Umilità in Pistoia, Pistoia, 1890, 34). The correct date
should be 25 January 1568 (see Appendix I: Vasari's Contribution).

[10]Fossi, 1973, 85.

[11]First noticed in Frey, I, 675. See also Appendix I:
Document 3.

[12]The church was subjected to a close analysis during
its restauration. The pertinent dimensions and drawings are
found in M. Baldi, G. Bragioni, C. Vannochi, Basilica della
Madonna dell Umilità, Instituto di Restauro, Facolta di
architettura, Florence, Archivo, 34-65, 1965, n.p.

[13]Fossi, 1973, 87-89. The extent of the work is described as "500 scudi in assurare la cupola e scudi 1000 a
fortificare da basso e dare fine al mattonato."

[14]Ibid.

[15]Fossi, 1973, 109. See also note 22.

[16]Ibid., 113.

[17]Ibid., 131. The deputies deliberated "del disordine
de dua peli esistenti nella cupola di dentro."

[18]Ibid., 94. This was by no means a novel device. In
his first Venetian commission, Jacopo Sansovino used iron
chains, among other things, to repair the main cupola of St.
Mark's (VII, 500). A similar proposal for "the wiring-up of
an existing structure" was proposed by Francesco di Giorgio
for the Tiburio of Milan Cathedral, and this project has been
studied most recently by F. Fergusson, "Leonardo da Vinci and
the tiburio of Milan Cathedral," Architectura, VII, 1977, 175-
192. Vasari never mentioned this project in the Lives.

[19]See Appendix I: Document 3.

[20]Fossi, 1973, 110-111.

[21]Ibid., 29-30.

[22]Ibid., 110.

[23]Lafri's Memoriale has been reprinted twice: IV, 169-174; and as an appendix to L. Bargiacchi, Tempio e opere, 1890.   Although the two tests do not always agree, there is no difference in their content.   The original manuscript is lost.   Lafri's architectural career was limited to only a very few buildings: he designed the choir for the Duomo and the choir stalls for San Francesco in his native city (Theime-Becker, XII 215; also "Il seicento pistoiese" in F. Gurrieri et al., Architettura ed interventi territoriale nella Toscana granducale, Florence, 1972).   The problem of making a Renaissance addition to a Gothic structure was faced by Bramante, Francesco di Giorgio, and Leonardo da Vinci in their proposals for the tiburio of Milan Cathedral. This involved conformity with both Gothic ornament and structure, and Bramante's remarks have been recently reviewed by Fergusson, "Leonardo da Vinci and the tiburio of Milan Cathedral," 190-191.   Although Vasari faced the difficult question of conformità in Pistoia, his structural difficulties were less urgent since he could (and did) continue the base into his double shell dome.

[24]The solution which Lafri proposed attempted to redistribute the weight of the cupola.   It was also highly impractical.   The lantern would have been demolished, and then 14 braccia of the extrados would have been ripped away. The bricks would have then been used as fill for the windows, the stairs, and 4 braccia of the void between the shells. The exterior shell would have been remade in wood, and the exterior ribs would have been covered in lead.   In place of the lantern, Lafri proposed to build a small, wooden-roofed structure which was supported by modillions (IV, 373).

[25]Dimensions of the interior faces of the octagon (clockwise, starting with the choir (high altar)):   8.39 m., 8.40 m., 8.38 m., 8.37 m., 8.91 m., 8.48 m., 8.48 m., 8.53 m.   The source of this problem is the wider dimension which Vitoni chose for the opening between the vestibule and the octagon.   It is not certain whether this was a mathematical error in laying out the foundations for the octagon or a constraint imposed by the property lines of the site.   The

latter is a distinct possibility. The sacristy at the rear
of the church was not built until 1655 (A. Chiti, Il
santuario della Madonna dell' Umiltà, Pistoia, 1952, 58).

[26]G. Poleni, Memorie istoriche della Gran Cupola del
Tempio Vaticano, Padua, 1748, 390.

[27]Baldi et al., "Condizioni geologiche," Basilica
della Madonna dell' Umiltà, 1965.

[28]Poleni, Memorie istoriche, 1748, 101-104. This was
based on Allesandro Cecchini's belief that the slight outward billowing of the Florentine dome was caused not by its
own weight but by the weakness of the foundations.

[29]Baldi et al., "Conclusioni," Basilica della Madonna
dell' Umiltà, 1965.

[30]The only theorist who approaches dome design from
a technical point of view is Filarete (A. Averlino, il
Filarete, Tratatto di architettura, ed. A. M. Finioli and
L. Grassi, Milan, 1972, I, 202-204). His description of
the cupola for the Duomo of Sforzinda is, however, rather
problematic. He is concerned only with the dimensions of
the double-shell dome, for he fails to give a clear account
of the principles with which they were derived (obviously
rule of thumb). Furthermore his octagonal dome is placed
over a square crossing, thus necessitating the use of
squinches. Given the large amount of masonry to be supported on comparatively slender piers, it is doubtful if
his solution would have ever stood up. This may be one of
the reasons why Vasari thought Filarete's treatise was
silly (II, 457).

[31]cf. Mainstone, Developments in Structural Form,
London, 1975, 283. The first scientific analysis was T.
LeSeur, F. Lacquier, R. Boscovitch, Parere di tre matte-
matici sopra i danni, che si sono trovati nella cupola di
San Pietro, Rome, 1743. It is quoted at length by R. di
Stefano, La Cupola di San Pietro, Naples, 1963, passim;
also in Poleni, Memorie istoriche della Gran Cupola del
Tempio Vaticano, Padua, 1748.

[32]Ackerman, 1970, 210; di Stefano, La cupola di San
Pietro, 1963, 141.

[33]R. Baldacci-R. DeMaestri, "Premesa per una analisi statica delle strutture portanti la Basilica di S. Maria di Carignano," Galeazzo Alessi e l'architettura del Cinquecento, Genoa, 1975, 327-332. The central cupola of Alessi's church shows cracking throughout its entire structure. The greatest number of cracks are distributed radially from oculus of the double shell dome, and they continue throughout the tambour and the supporting piers. The causes are threefold: settling of foundations, thermal variation, and the excessive weight of the cupola relative to the tambour.

[34]Although many words have been written on the history of the design of the dome of St. Peter's, the only modern discussions of its structure are di Stefano, La cupola di San Pietro, Naples, 1963, and H. Saalman, Michelangelo and Santa Maria del Fiore and St. Peter's," Art Bulletin, LVII, 1975, 374-409. Professor Saalman has suggested that di Stefano should be utilized with utmost caution.

[35]These points have been asserted by R. Mainstone, Developments in Structural Form, 126. See also R. Mainstone, "Brunelleschi's Dome of Santa Maria del Fiore and Some Related Structures," Transactions of the Newcomen Society for the History of Engineering and Technology, XLII, 1969-1970. They were recently repeated by R. Mainstone, "Brunelleschi's Dome," Architectural Review, CLXII, 157-166.

[36]This is clearly shown by Sanmicheli's Madonna della Campagna outside of Verona. Its dome spans more than 17 meters over a circular drum, and it is constructed with a tapering single shell covered by a built up wood extrados in the Venetian tradition. After having seen the wooden model in 1566, Vasari characterized it as bellisima but he also indicated that the bad judgment of the deputies had maimed the design (VI, 355).

[37]Vasari is unequivocal on this subject: "E per non esser egli (Vitoni) molto sperto in cose cosi grande, non considerò al peso della tribuna che potesse star sicura, avendo egli nella grosseza di quella muraglia fatto nel primo ordine delle finestre e nel secondo dove son le altre, un andito che camina attorno; deve egli venne a indebolir le mura, che sendo quello edifizio di basso senza spalle, era pericoloso voltarla, e massime negli angoli delle cantonate dove aveva pignere il peso della volta di detta tribuna" (IV, 166).

[38]M. Trachtenberg, The Campanile of Florence Cathedral, New York, 1979, 24-25.

[39]There is no evidence indicating precisely how Vitoni hoped to vault the Madonna dell' Umilita. Since he had constructed a double shell base, it is possible that he planned a double shell dome in the manner of either Florence Cathedral or the Baptistry. Lafri's statement that Vasari did not follow Vitoni's design should be taken with a grain of salt, since the single shell, Pantheon-like domes proposed by Chiti and Bargiachi (F. Quintiero, "Madonna dell' Umilita; evoluzione del linguaggio," Ventura Vitoni e il Rinascimento a Pistoia, Pistoia, 1977, 45-54), require a substantial amount of masonry to transfer a single shell dome to a double shell base. Quintiero's drawings are problematical since the third story is shown solid in section, while in fact it contains a walkway connecting the bifora windows.

[40]According to Mainstone, the stone chains counteracted the dome's tendency to burst apart, while the spinapesce provided a stronger bond for the brick coursing of both domes (Mainstone, "Brunelleschi's Dome," 166). These expedients were rendered unnecessary by the shorter distance which Vasari's dome had to span.

[41]Cf. G. Giovannoni, "Tra la cupola di Bramante e quella di Michelangelo," Saggi sul l'architettura del Rinascimento, Milan, 1936, 143-176.

[42]H. Saalman, "Michelangelo and Santa Maria del Fiore" 398, has proposed that the Lille drawing should be dated later than the customary 1547-1549 (Ackerman, 1970, 333) since Michelangelo's model of that date probably did not include consideration for the design of the dome.

[43]One critic has called this aspect "protobaroque" (Fossi, 1973, 86). This may be a reaction to how the forms of the lantern appear to explode from a central core--certainly the most activated design in Vasari's ouevre--but its brittle forms and reliance on Michelangelo make it a clear statement of Vasari and his own time.

[44]Heydenreich-Lotz, 1974, 395, n. 11. On a letter to Vasari dated 1 July 1557, Michelangelo sketched the coffering for the Chapel of the King of France in St. Peters (illustrated in Frey, I, 481-485). In character and design, it repeats the same idea used in San Giovanni dei Fiorentini, though the shape of the vault is more complex. Cf. F. Hartt, Michelangelo Drawings, New York, 1970, 353, nos. 511 & 512.

[45]Although there is no concrete evidence that Vasari had visited such monuments, his aid Battista Naldini was one of the many artists who inscribed his name on the walls of the Domus Aurea. Cf. R. Dacos, "Grafitti de la Domus Aurea," Bulletin de l'Institut Belge a Rome, XXXVIII, 1967, 172.

[46]R. Dacos, La découverte de la Domus Aurea et al formation des grotesques a la Renaissance, London and Leiden, 1969, 172. Both Vasari (I, 193-194) and Serlio (IV, xi, p. lxx) insist upon the liberty of the artist, thus justifying grotesques by their overture to fantasy and creation.

[47]Vasari's experiments in the style of ancient fresco decorations are confined to works of the 1540's. The most prominent examples are the decorations in San Michele in Bosco, Bologna (1540; Barocchi, 1964, plates 8-11) and for his ceiling decoration God Blessing The Seeds of Abraham in his own house in Arezzo (1548; Barocchi: 1964, plate XVI). One of the strongest influences on Vasari's early painting style was Raphael (S. G. Freedberg, Painting in Italy, 1500-1600, Harmondsworth & Baltimore, 1970, 306) and its grotesquerie and cartouches are derived from the Vatican Logge. This subject is rarely discussed in the literature on Vasari's paintings. Cf. P. Barocchi, "Il valore dell' antico nella storiografia vasariana, le mondo antico nel Rinascimento," Atti del V Convegno Internazionale di Studi sal Rinascimento, Florence, 1958, 217-236.

[48]J. Schulz, "Pinturrichio and the Survival of Antiquity," Journal of the Warburg and Courtald Institutes, XXV, 1962, 35-55.

[49]The problematic history of this commission which included Vasari, Ammannati, and possibly Michelangelo is outlined by J. Pope-Hennesey, Italian High Renaissance and Baroque Sculpture, London, 1970, 376-377.

[50]Cf. Howard, 1975, 23. A similar pattern is also found in the main reading room of the Library. Vasari, however, could not have seen this until his second trip to Venice in 1566.

[51]W. Wolters, Plastische Deckendekoration des Cinquecento in Venedig und im Veneto, Berlin, 1968, 15.

[52]Cf. W. Lotz, "Italienische Plätze des 16
Jahrhunderts," Jahrbuch der Max-Planck Gesellschaft, 1968,
41-60. The relationship to ancient libraries is stressed
by Howard, 1975, 26.

[53]The Capella dei Principi has been badly treated by
historians. This is evident in R. Wittkower, Art and
Architecture in Italy, 1600-1750 (The Pelican History of
Art, 16), Third rev. ed., Harmondsworth and Baltimore, 1973,
129. The best and most complete study is in L. Berti, Il
principe del studiolo, Florence, 1968, 198-209. A dissertation covering all aspects of its history will be completed
by Mr. Andrew Morrogh for the Courtald Institute, London.

[54]The attribution of the Temple of Victory to
Ammannati dates from the beginning of the Twentieth Century
and is not supported by any documentary evidence. To the
contrary, circumstantial evidence connects Vasari with the
commission. The basic idea for the octagonal plan must have
been Vasari's. A letter of 4 June 1569 from the Archbishop
of Arezzo informs Vasari that the foundations are made and
that the work is proceeding swiftly (U. Procacci, "L'Architettura nel Aretino," 1969, 124). In a very circuitous way,
Fossi has affirmed the attribution to Vasari by citing similarities with the Madonna dell' Umilità. This is wrong
since Ammannati began his work in Pistoia three years after
the completion of the Temple of Victory (Fossi, 1967, 99-
101).

[55]Though exposed brick facing rarely appears in Tuscan
architecture, Vasari was not the first designer to use it.
It was probably suggested by the Palazzo Grifoni (Fossi,
1967, 61-66) which in turn reflects Roman examples like the
Palazzo Farnese.

[56]In June, 1566, Vasari toured the Marches. After
having seen Ravenna and Rimini, he ordered sketches of the
Tomb of Theodoric from Naldini. Frey assumes that this is
related to the vaulting of the Madonna dell' Umilità, but
it is important to remember that the cupola of the tomb is
made out of a monolithic piece of stone (Frey, II, 245).

[57]S. Giovanni in Oleo was built in 1509 by Antonio
da Sangallo the Younger on the site where the Evangelist
suffered the trial of the boiling oil. The dedication and
history of the tempietto at Isola Bisentina remain unknown
(S. Sindig-Larsen, "Some Functional and Iconographic Aspects
of the Centralized Church in the Renaissance," Acta, II, 203-
252).

[58]This was first mentioned by Procacci, "L'Architetture nel Aretino," 1969, 123-124.

[59]The polygonal form was a recurrent theme in numerous designs for the Capella dei Principi (Berti, Il principe del studiolo, 1968, 198-209; I. M. Botto, Mostra di disegni di Bernardo Buontalenti, Florence, 1968, 91-115).

[60]L. & H. Ettlinger, Botticelli, New York, 1977. R. Lightbrown, Sandro Botticelli, Berkeley and Los Angeles, 1978, Vol. I, Life and Work, 130-133, and Vol. II, Complete Catalogue, 94. The painting is in the Fogg Art Museum, Harvard University.

[61]See G. Fanelli, Firenze. Architetture e città, Florence, 1973, vol. 2, figs. 615-620. The execution and attribution of these scenes has never been resolved. The most recent discussion of this thorny problem is by E. Pillsbury, "The Sala Grande Drawings by Vasari. Some Documents and New Attributions," Master Drawings, XIV, 1976, 127-146.

[62]The vertical exaggeration of elements did not preclude an attempt by Vasari to correctly locate them relative to each other. (J. Pinto, "Origins and Development of the Ichnographic City Plan," JSAH, XXXV, 1974, 44).

[63]This might not have been the case if an urban renewal plan of 1960 destroyed the buildings adjacent to the Madonna dell' Umilità. At that time a large plaza was proposed for the East side of the church, mistakenly portraying the Madonna as a free-standing temple in the Albertian sense (La Nazione, 30 December 1960).

[64]"Ma, nel vero, Ventura merita che sene faccia memoria, perche quella opera e la piu notabile cosa moderna, che sia in quella citta." (IV, 167).

[65]K. W. Forster, "Metaphors of Rule," Mitteilungen des Kunsthistoriches Institut in Florenz, XV, 1971, 90, fig. 28. The sign of Capricorn over the city of Florence: "DEL DUCA COSIMO DE' MEDICI: Questo Signor, mezzo tra pace e guerra (come porta del caprio l'influenza), dichiara a ogun' chi' il fato et la prudenza, fan' che l'huom regni longamente in terra."

NOTES TO CHAPTER II

[1]A. Mabellini, Le rime di Benvenuto Cellini, Torino, 1896, 113.

[2]J. Ackerman, "The Gesu and Contemporary Church Architecture," Baroque Art: The Jesuit Contribution, New York, 1972, 15-27.

[3]M. Hall, "The Tramezzo in Santa Croce Reconstructed," Art Bulletin, LVI, 1974, 325-334; ____, "The Ponte in Santa Maria Novella," Journal of the Warburg and Courtald Institutes XXXVII, 1974, 157-173.

[4]Some documentary evidence has been collected by D. Viviani Fiorini, 1941, 74-82; P. Laspeyres, Die Kirchen der Renaissance in Mittel-Italien, Berlin, 1882, 24; C. Stegmann and H. von Geymuller, Die Architektur der Renaissance in Toscana, IX, Munich, 1885-1904, ch. 4, p. 2; P. Frankl, Principles of Architectural History (trans. J. O'Gorman), Cambridge, 1968, 24, 31; Heydenreich-Lotz, 1974, 365, n. 14; Lessmann, 1975, 178-179. The history of the Badia before Vasari's activity is covered in M. Salmi, "Ricerche intorno all Badia di SS. Flora e Lucilla ad Arezzo," L'Arte, XV, 1912, 281-293; M. T. Bartoli, "La Badia delle SS. Flora e Lucilla in Arezzo," Studi e documenti di architettura, VI, 1976, 27-38; D. Taddei, "gli antecedenti stilistici della Badia delle SS. Flora e Lucilla," Studi e documenti di architettura, VI, 1976, 39-48.

[5]See Appendix II: Document D.

[6]The altar now in the Badia once stood in the Capella Vasari, the high altar of the Pieve in Arezzo which Vasari had remodeled in the 1550's. It was transferred to the Badia in 1865 when the Pieve was fancifully restored to the Gothic style (C. Isermeyer, "Il Vasari e il restauro delle chiese mediovale," Studi Vasariani, Florence, 1952, 231; ____, "Die Capella Vasari und die Hochaltar in der Pieve in Arezzo," Eine Gabe der Freunde fur C. G. Heise, Berlin, 1950, 137-153.

[7]See note 31.

[8]C. Smyth, Mannerism and Maniera, Locust Valley, 1962, 10-12.

[9]J. Burckhardt, Der Cicerone, Leipzig, 1874, I, 356. This represents a change from the original edition where the church was merely "gracious" (Basel, 1855, 345).

[10]G. Penco, Storia del monachesimo in Italia, Rome, 1961, 338. Five monasteries had already joined the order before it was formally approved by Martin V in 1419. Earlier, Gregory XII had given the monks the right to elect their own abbot. This was central to the growth of the order in spiritual and material terms. In the Later Middle Ages Popes and rulers with papal privileges bestowed abbeys to a secular prelate or lay magistrate who occupied the Abbots lodgings and enjoyed the revenues of the position while delegating authority to the prior.

[11]T. Leccisotti, "La congregazione benedettina di S. Giustina e la riforma della chiesa al secolo XV," Archivio della R. Deputazione Romana per la storia patria, LXVII, 1941, 460. Most of the bulls issued by Eugene IV, a Venetian, helped the Congregation gain power by returning to the Abbot rights and privileges which had been ceded to princes and bishops.

[12]Penco, Storia, 342.

[13]A list of all monasteries belonging to the Cassinese Congregation (including dates of incorporation) can be found in P. Smitz, Geschichte des Benediktinerordens, Zurich, 1960, III, 177.

[14]C. Isermeyer, "Le chiese di Palladio in rapporto al culto," Bolletino del Centro Internazionale di Studi D'Architettura, X, 1968, 42-57. The capitolo generale was held almost every year under a president and four visitors elected at the time of the meeting. The body of delegates was composed of the abbots of the various monasteries, who themselves were elected for three or four terms. The capitoli for the years 1424-1504 have been published (T. Leccisotti, Congregationis S. Iustinae de Padua O. S. B. ordinationes capitolorum generalium, pars I (1424-1474), Montecassino, 1939; pars II (1475-1504), Montecassino, 1970.

[15]T. Leccisotti, "Sull' organizazione della congregazione 'De Unita'," Benedictina, II, 1948, 238-243. Benedictine scholars never have reached a consensus on the ultimate effect of the centralized organization. Leccisotti emphasizes the democratic aspects of the constitution, while others (notably Cuthbert Butler, Benedictine Monasticism, London; 1919, 254) emphasize its oligarchical aspects.

[16]G. Penco, Storia dell' monachesimo in Italia nell' epoca moderna, Rome, 1968, 278-284.

[17]T. Leccisotti, "Le condizioni economiche dei monasteri Cassinese di Toscana alla meta del '600," Studi in onore di Amintore Fanfani, V, 1962, 289-312.

[18]Penco, Storia, 1968, 278-284.

[19]Recorded in the Libro della Fabrica, ACV, filza 58.

[20]Isermeyer, "Le chiese di Palladio," 45.

[21]1475: Quod nullus prelatorum mutet fabricas per alios inceptas, nisi autoritate capituli generalis, vel saltem visitorem et cum magno consiglio.

1490: Conclusum est pro edificis erigendis in omnibus nostri congregationis monasteris, et in specie pro Tiburtine civitate, Ravenna, Ferrarie, et Magguzani, faciendis prius dessigna fiant quibus diligentissima consideratis, postem fiant modelli ad arbitrium tamen patrio presidentis et visitorum, adiunctis duobus aliis prelatis nostre congregationis.

(Leccisotti, Congregationis . . . ordinationes capitulorum, II, 1970, 3, 58).

[22]P. Pirri, Giovanni Tristano e, primordi della architettura gesuitica, Rome, 1955.

[23]Ackerman, "Gesu," 27.

[24]H. Jedin, "La politica concilare di Cosimo I,"
Rivista Storica Italiana, LXII, 1950, 343-373 & 477-496;
Cochrane, 1974, 60-62.

[25]Jedin, "La politica," 492.

[26]A. d'Addario, Aspetti della controriforma a Firenze,
Roma, 1972, 124-131.

[27]N. Rodolico, "Cosimo I e il consiglio di Trento,"
Archivio Storico Italiano, CXXII, 1964, 5-9.

[28]S. Pietro: A. Ghidiglia Quintavalle, S. Pietro in
Modena, Modena, 1965; S. Giovanni Evangelista: M. Salmi,
"Bernardo Zaccagni e l'architettura del Rinascimento in
Parma," Bolletino d'Arte, XII, 1918, 81-166; Praglia:
Heydenreich-Lotz, 1974, 94; S. Sepolcro: J. Ganz, Alessio
Tramello, Fraunfeld, 1968, 37-52.

[29]Heydenreich-Lotz, 1974, 118; B. Zevi, Biagio
Rosetti, architetto ferrarese, Torino, 1960, 309-314; Zevi
explained S. Benedetto as a derivation from Brunelleschi's
Santo Spirito in Florence. There is some question to
Rosetti's role--he was listed only as a stimatore for the
houses which were to be demolished for the construction of
the church. The building suffered heavy damage in World
War II and was rebuilt.

[30]This was first stated by Steegman and Geymuller
(note 4). The churches of San Francesco in Carpi and S.
Sepolcro in Piacenza were also connected to this type
(Heydenreich-Lotz, 1974, 365, n. 4).

[31]Most recently by P. Taddei, "gli anticedenti stilistici della Badia delle SS. Flora e Lucilla" Studi e documenti, VI, 1976, 39-48, which also restates the filiation
of the Badia with San Salvatore in Venice. The plan of the
Venetian church contains several features also found in
Arezzo but with two exceptions: the addition of a third
domed bay, and the employment of narrow barrel vaults between the domed bays. Burckhardt (Cicerone, I, 356) first
made the connection between the two churches. Lotz's statement that San Salvatore and San Sepolcro belonged also to
the Cassinese Congregation is incorrect (Heydenreich-Lotz,
1974, 317). San Salvatore was Augustinian (G. Lorenzetti,
Venezia e suo estuario, Rome, 1956, 386) while San Sepolcro
was affiliated with the Benedictines from Monteoliveto (J.
Ganz, Alessio Tramello, 37). For these reasons it is

unlikely that Vasari used San Salvatore as a direct means of inspiration, and he also failed to mention it in the Lives.

[32]G. Fiocco et al., La Basilica di Santa Giustina: arte e storia, Castelfranco Veneto, 1970, 145-147.

[33]Isermeyer, "Le chiese di Palladio," passim.

[34]In Arezzo, the cloister was built from a design by Giuliano da Maiano (?) sometime after 1489 (Salmi, "Ricerche," 292). At Santa Giustina, the reconstruction of the cloister was begun under the patronage of Barbo in 1415 (G. Fiocco et al., La Basilica, 111.)

[35]Penco, Storia, 1968, 276.

[36]G. Cattin, "Tradizioni e innovatrici nella normative e nella practica liturgico musicale della Congragazione Cassinese," Benedictina, XIX, 1970, 259, n. 26.

[37]Ibid., 295-96.

[38]Penco, Storia, 1968, 38. Among them were Don Paolo di Ferrara, don Placidio Falcano, and Don Arcangelo da Lonato. This was less evident in other orders. The Jesuits did not use music in their services, and the Carthusians were openly hostile to music. The Camaldolesi still used the Gregorian chant. Isermeyer ("Le chiese di Palladio," 45) has noted that the very same orders continued to follow the old practice of placing the choir in front of the main altar.

[39]Isermeyer, "Le chiese di Palladio," 45; Hall, "The Ponte in Santa Maria Novella," 172.

[40]R. Wittkower, Architectural Principles in the Age of Humanism, London, 1952, 156-157; Howard, 1975, 67.

[41]K. G. Fellerer, "Church Music and the Council of Trent," Musical Quarterly, XXXIX, 1953, 576-597. The Council's reaction to the problem of Church music was similar to its decrees on the visual arts. Although it did not deal with style and practice, it moulded fundamental attitudes on the role of music in the Church. On 10 September 1562 it ruled that music must serve to uplift the faithful,

that it must be intelligible, and that secular forms were
to be avoided. The demand for intelligibility caused a
transformation of the plainchant. In current opinion, the
reforms effected by the Council were modest. (F. Ghigi,
"Italy 1300-1600," Music from the Middle Ages to the Renaissance (ed. F. Sternfeld), London, 1973, 244-249).

[42]V. Scamozzi, L' idea dell' architettura universale,
Venice, 1615, II, 326.

[43]F. di Giorgio Martini, Tratatti di architettura,
ingegneria, e arte militari (ed. C. Maltese- L. Maltese-
Degrassi), Milan, 1967, I, 40 (Ill. f. 11, tav. 17).

[44]Lessmann, 1975, 174. This is discussed further in
Chapter V of this study.

[45]The copy which Vasari refers to is the Codex Magli-
abechiano II. I. 141 in BNCF, and its subject is fortifications and military machinery. It is likely that Vasari
could have consulted one of the other treatises by di
Giorgio now in the Laurentian Library (Ashburnham 361) or
Turin (Biblioteca Reale, Salluziano 148) which show the
illustration under discussion.

[46]F. Graf Wolf Metternich, "Der Entwurf Fra Giocondos
fur Sankt Peter," Festschrift Kurt Bauch, Munich, 1957, 155-
170.

[47]Ibid., 158. The cellular aspect of the plan is explained as an attempt to isolate religious functions: choir-
chair for the Bishop of Rome, ambulatory for the display of
relics, and nave ambulatory for lesser saints.

[48]F. Graf Wolf Metternich, Die Erbaung der Peters-
kirche zu Rom im 16 Jahrhunderts (Römische Forschungen der
Biblioteca Hertziana, XX), Vienna-Munich, I, 35; L.
Ragghianti-Collobi, Il libro de' disegni del Vasari,
Florence, 1974, 124. The drawing comes from the volume
acquired by J. P. Mariette in the 18th Century. For the
history of the collection, see O. Kurz, "Giorgio Vasari's
Libro de' Disegni," Old Master Drawings, XII, June 1937, 1-
7. An inscription on the plan (opinione e dignio di fra
Jocondo), possibly by Sangallo the Younger, certifies its
authenticity. Instead of publishing a photo of UA 6,
Ragghianti confuses the issue by illustrating UA 254 instead.
This drawing is connected to fra Giocondo in the older literature (Metternich, Erbaung, 28). The drawing has been

re-cut, for the remnants of a border can be seen on the
upper part of the sheet. Geymuller (Die ursprünglichen
Entwürfe für St. Peter, Vienna and Paris, 1875, 262-269)
that the plan is echoed in some drawings by Sangallo the
Younger (UA 252, UA 254), but no other scholars have taken
a stand on this question. The relevance of the latter
drawings for Vasari's scheme is limited; their naves do
not adapt themselves to the kind of double transept used
by Vasari.

[49] Metternich, Der Entwürf Fra Giocondos," 167.

[50] H. Wurm, Der Palazzo Massimi alle Colonne, Berlin,
1965, 199-200. Peruzzi took up the theme of the syncopated
nave for one of his schemes for St. Peter's (UA 16;
Metternich, Erbauung, fig. 100). Screen facades are used
for side chapels in both vaulted and domed bays. The T-
shaped piers often used by Peruzzi (UA 451, UA 16) are not
unlike those used by Vasari in the Badia. However,
Peruzzi's details are more geometric in character due to
their overlapping modular design.

[51] Cf. Heydenreich-Lotz, 1974, plate 194.

[52] Shown in UA 339, UA 342, (Wurm, Der Palazzo Massimi,
pls. 29, 37, 45a, UA 1575.

[53] Frey, II, 239, 241.

[54] The contract for the Badia's stonecutting reads:
"Il detto zoccolo et la base et colonne et capitello alte
braccia sette e tre quarti et la sua grosseza a piedi di
diamatro largha una braccia et a sommo oncie circa dieci
puo vere misure p(er) cosa respettivamente secondo il
disegno dato ot darsi dal prefato m. Giorgio." Viviani-
Fiorini, 1941, 78.

[55] S. Serlio, Il quarto libro di Sebastiano Serlio,
first issued Venice, 1537. In the Lives (V, 431) Vasari
says that Serlio was the author of two books on architecture in which were, among other things, "trenta porta
rustiche e venti delicate." The portals refer to the
Sixth, or Extraordinary Book, first published at Lyon in
1551 and in Italy in 1557. Vasari must have done some
sloppy editing for the second edition. In the 1550 edition, Vasari spoke of Serlio's Third and Fourth books which
were the result of the labors of Peruzzi (Vasari-Ricci, III,

172). At the time of writing the first edition of the
Lives, Vasari probably did not know of the French publications of Books I, II, & V which were not published in
Italian until 1551 (W. Dinsmoor, "The Literary Remains of
Sebastiano Serlio," Art Bulletin, XXIV, 1942, 74). By
the time of the writing of the second edition, Vasari certainly must have been acquainted with all of Serlio's books.
In fact, he easily could have purchased a copy of the 1566
collected edition of Books I-V and the Extraordinary Book
when he visited Venice that very same year.

[56] This was possibly not desired by Vasari. In a
letter of 16 December 1566, Borghini tells the Abbot that
the stonecutters might have taken some liberties in the
execution of the work for the church. See Appendix II:
Chronology of Construction.

[57] In form Vasari's Serliana is closer to Palladio's
Basilica in Vicenza (begun ca. 1550) than to Giulio Romano.
Given an adequate allowance for some slightly different
details and a change in material, the comparison is still
striking. Although Vasari admired the Basilica for its
Doric columns (VII, 527), he probably saw it only in 1566,
after he had submitted the modello for the church.

[58] Biblioteca Ricciardiana, Edizioni Rari, 120; p. 47.
"Mia viddi al modello suo, schizai questo come più ragione
d' architettura." Ammannati's words are indicative of the
changes which he proposed to Vasari's design. The Serliana
would have replaced the trabeation on the ground floor, and
it would have been set between double piers, thus giving
the composition an effect of plasticity in comparison to
Vasari's usual stark planarity. He also adds Michelangelesque
consoles to the intermediary zone and closes the upper story.
(E. Vodoz, "Studien zum architektonischen Werke Bartolomeo
Ammannatis," Mitteilungen des Kunsthistoriches Institut in
Florenz, II-III, 1941, 67; B. Ammannati, La città: appunti
per un tratatto, (ed. M. Fossi), Rome, 1970, 348.

[59] Vasari's Ricordanze were completed after his death
by his nephew Marcantonio. In the entry for 1573, Marcantonio writes "il disegno della chiesa di Santa Flora et
Lucilla de' monaci neri, di Arezzo, sua patria" (Frey, II,
886).

[60] Vodoz, "Studien," 120, describes the plan as a
reminiscence of the Badia.

[61]San Biagio exactly repeats the parti of the Badia;
the only difference is the use of paired arches where
Vasari employed the Serliana. Any architectural filiation
to either the Badia or San Salvatore on Venice is difficult
due to the problematical history of the church. (R. Sassi,
Le chiese di Fabriano, Fabriano, 1961; R. Facchini, Memorie
storiche della chiesa di San Biagio e Romualdo di Fabriano,
Fabriano, 1925). Its construction was begun in 1537, and
it was finished by 1579. The name of the architect is not
known. In 1741, a major earthquake destroyed the church,
and plans for its reconstruction were drawn by Francesco
Nicoletti. At this point the design was subjected to a
liturgical review, and the result was that the first church
was too long and too narrow. Nicoletti's design, in comparison, had too many chapels which were directly accessible
to the public. One contemporary source says that the church
was rebuilt according to the older design (Facchini, Memoria
storiche, 46).

[62]For the importance of variants on the syncopated
plan to 17th and 18th Century Architecture, see R. Pommer,
18th Century Architecture in the Piedmont: The Open Air
Structures of Juvarra, Alfieri, and Vittone, New York,
1967, 79.

[63]Cf. R. Krautheimer, Early Christian and Byzantine
Architecture, Baltimore and Harmondsworth, 1965, 287-290.
The Veneto-Byzantine sources for the Fra Giocondo plan are
discussed by Metternich, "Der Entwürf Fra Giocondos," 164.

[64]E. Panofsky, "The First Page of Vasari's Libro,"
Meaning in the Visual Arts, New York, 1955, 214.

[65]Ibid., 222.

[66]They were the Badie at Florence, Bonsalazzo, Arezzo,
Poggibonsi, Veruccia di Pisa, Castello, and Settimo. This
was first mentioned in the Cronica of G. Villani, (ed. G.
Ridolfi), Florence, 1923, IV, ii.

[67]This was the Badia at Settimo, which recieved its
name from the fact that it was the seventh and last of the
Badia to be built (cf. M. Salmi, L'architettura romanica
in Toscana, Milan, 1928, 33). It had a three aisled plan
terminated by a semicircular apse. A similar plan was used
for the first Florentine Badia which was later superseded
by Arnolfo di Cambio's church (cf. U. Middledorf - W. Paatz,

"Die Gothische Badia zu Florenz," Mitteilungen des Kunsthistoriches Institut in Florenz, III, 492-517; W. Paatz,
Die Kirchen von Florenz, Frankfurt, 1955, I, 264-318).
The renovation carried out in 1627 by Matteo Segaloni has
never been studied. While his unimaginative design perhaps deserves its lack of scholarly attention, its two main
features--the use of a Greek cross plan and the employment
of a Serliana to screen the choir from the church--are to
be found in Vasari's church. The Florentine Badia also
belonged to the Cassinese Congregation.

[68]Panofsky, "Vasari's Libro," 213.

[69]A. Legrenzi, Vicenzo Borghini, Udine, 1919; G.
Falena, "Vicenzo Borghini," Dizionario biografico degli
Italiani, Rome, 1970, XII, 680-689.

[70]L. Ginori Conti, L'apparato per le nozze di
Francesco de' Medici e Giovanna di Austria, Florence, 1934.

[71]E. Pillsbury, "Drawings by Vicenzo Borghini for
the Apparato in Florence in 1565," Master Drawings, V,
1967, 281-283.

[72]E. Pillsbury, "Borghini as Draftsman," Yale Art
Gallery Bulletin, XXIV, 1973, 3-11.

[73]Viviani-Fiorini, 1941, 79; Gaye, II, 202.

[74]Frey, II, 182; E. Pillsbury, "The Temporary Facade
on the Palazzo Ricasoli," Report and Studies in the History
of Art, 1969, 80.

[75]M. Hall, "The Ponte in Santa Maria Novella," 158.

[76]V. Borghini, Discorsi, Florence, 1585, I, 145.
"Della forma di esso Tempio non essendo propriamente al
servizio di nostro culto."

[77]Ibid., 432, 439.

NOTES TO CHAPTER III

[1]Charles Dickens, Pictures From Italy, ed. D. Paroissien, New York, 1973, 240.

[2]F. Braudel, Capitalism and Material Life (trans. M. Kochan), London, 1973, 405.

[3]This is to be found in almost every guidebook to Florence, whether old or new. While Braudel uses the term "gallery" to describe the Florentine structure, it is both misleading and incorrect, for its application is generally limited to spaces within residential buildings reserved for the display of art. Cf. N. Pevsner, A History of Building Types, Princeton, 1976, 112. Also W. Prinz, Die Entstehung der Galerie in Frankreich und Italien, Berlin, 1970, 62-66. Neither recognizes the parallel phenomenon exemplified by the Corridoio.

[4]Jodoco del Badia, 1902, 3-11. This is essential since it contains numerous widely scattered archival references. Also Venturi, 1938-1940: XI, ii, 420-426; Barocchi, 1956-1957, 127-128; Lessmann, 1975, 175-177. The significance of the Corridoio for modern designers has been noted by M. Dennis, "The Uffizi: Museum as Urban Design," forthcoming in Perspecta: The Yale Architectural Journal, Vol. XVI.

[5]Frey, III, 181-183.

[6]D. Heikamp, "Zur Geschicte der Uffizientribuna und der Kunstschränke in Florenz un Deitschland," Zeitschrift für Kunstgeschicte, XXVI, 1963, 193-268; Lessmann, 1975, 102-111.

[7]The present link from the grotto to the Pitti probably dates from the 17th Century additions built to the palace. It does not appear in Buonsignori's reliable map of 1584. To be correct, the Corridoio linked (as implied in the contract) the Palazzo Vecchio and the gardens adjacent to the Pitti Palace. For the Grotto, see D. Heikamp, "La grotta grande del Giardino dei Boboli," Antichita viva, N. 4, 27-43.

252

[8]L. Ginori-Conti, L'apparato per la Nozze di Francesco de' Medici e Giovanna di Austria, Florence, 1935.

[9]A. M. Nagler, Theatre Festivals of the Medici, New Haven, 1964, 14.

[10]Cochrane, 1973, 91.

[11]Vasari's Ricordo of 1 August 1565, Frey II, 878.

[12]D. Mellini, Descrizione della entrata de la Serenissima Regina Giovanna d'Austria, et dell' apparato fatto in Firenze nella venuta et per le feliccisme nozze di Sua Altezza et dell' Illustrissimo e Eccelentissimo S. Don Francesco de' Medici, Florence, 1565. Quoted in del Badia, 1902, 3.

[13]VII, 703-704. "Come si e fatto il gran corridore, che attraversando il fiume va dal Palazzo ducale al Palazzo e giardino de' Pitti; il quale corridore fu condotto in cinque mesi con mio ordine e disegno, ancor che sia opera da pensare che non potessi condursi in cinque anni. Oltre ch anco fu mia cura far rifare, per il stesso nozze. . . ."

[14]Nagler, Theatre Festivals, 14.

[15]Lessmann, 1975, 88-89. In 1565 the Uffizi was far from finished. At this time the users of the Corridoio went across the piano nobile of the Uffizi to the house of Trayano Boba for access to the North Arm of the Arno riverbank. The stair which now descends from the second floor of the Uffizi cannot have been built before 1600, according to Lessmann. This connection is shown in H. van Cleve's view of Florence, Rome, Gabinetto dei Disegni e Stampe, 2287. Also illustrated in Fanelli, 1973, II, fig. 605.

[16]del Badia, 1902, 4.

[17]Aeneid, II, 453-457, trans. W. F. Jackson Knight, Harmondsworth and Baltimore, 1958.

[18]W. L. MacDonald, The Architecture of the Roman Empire, vol. I, An Introductory Study, New Haven, 1965, 21-25.

[19] Suetonius, _Nero_, XXXI, trans. J. C. Rolfe. (Loeb Classical Library, 38) Cambridge and London, 1965, II, 134-139.

[20] Suetonius, _Caligula_, XXII.

[21] _Ibid_.

[22] Suetonius, _Nero_, XXXI.

[23] N. Rubinstein, "Vasari's Painting of the _Foundation of Florence_ in the Palazzo Vecchio," _Essays in the History of Architecture Presented to Rudolf Wittkower_, London and New York, 1967, 69.

[24] _Ibid_. It is also shown on Del Massaio's topographical map of Florentine churches of 1470 (Fanelli, 1973, II, fig. 388).

[25] Cochrane, 1973, 63-65.

[26] del Badia, 1902, 9. With the exception of the Boba house behind the Uffizi, the only houses which Cosimo had to acquire were located near the via dei Bardi at the South End of the Ponte Vecchio. Payments were made to the Paganelli and Ricci families in 1567 and 1576 (two years after Cosimo's death!) respectively.

[27] Cochrane, 1973, 79-80; Frey, I., 266.

[28] Alberti, _De re aedificatoria_, V, ii. _L'architettura_, (trans. C. Bartoli), Florence, 1550, 125. There is no significant difference between the Latin and the Italian texts on this matter.

[29] _Ibid_.

[30] Filarete, _Tratatto di architettura_ (trans. J. Spencer, Yale Publications in the History of Art, XVI), I, 164. Spencer suggests that Filarete's drawing derives from descriptions of Ancient fortified bridges.

[31] C. Mango, _The Brazen House. A Study of the Imperial Palace of Constantine_ (Arkeologisk-kunsthistorike Medelelsen, Bind 4, Nr. 4), Copenhagen, 1959, 87-92.

[32]Ibid.

[33]J. Buchkremer, "Die Karolingische Porticus der Aachener Pfalz," Bonner Jahrbucher, CIL, 1949, 212-238.

[34]Moriz Dreger, Baugeschicte des K. K. Hofburg in Wien (Ost. Kunttopgraphie, XIV) Wien, 1914, 104, 126, figs. 73a & 96. The passage to the church went across the top of the walls of the palace complex along the Herrengasse. It was destroyed along with other buildings in the 18th Century to create a square in front of Fischer von Erlach's Library. At the end of the 16th Century another raised passage was built to connect the Hofburg with the Palace of the Archprince (begun 1575), but it was destroyed in 1661 for the construction of the Leopoldtrakt (Fig. 73).

[35]The most studied example is the Palatine Chapel in Monreale. Cf. E. Kitzinger, I mosaici di Monreale, Palermo, 1960, 24. Mr. Richard Tuttle has informed me that a passageway built in the 17th Century connected Palazzo Ducale with the Duomo in Mantua.

[36]G. Zaretti, "Il passeto del Vaticano," L'illustrazione vaticana, IV, 1933, 841-843; E. Ponti, "Il corridore," Capitolium, 1934, 243-256.

[37]VI, 449-450. According to Vasari, Bramante delegated the responsibility for the passetto to Antonio, who received a salary of ten scudi monthly. Little came of it due to the death of Julius II. Cf. G. Giovannoni, Antonio da Sangallo, Rome, 1959, I, 41 & 183.

[38]Ackerman, 1964, 113-114.

[39]B. Zevi, Biagio Rosetti, architetto ferrarese, Turin, 1960, 350, 493. The via coperta was begun in 1471 for Duke Ercole D'Este by Pietro Benvenuto degli Ordini, and Rosetti added another story at the end of the Quattrocento. A diary from that period refers to it at the "via secreta."

[40]A number of overhead passageways were built in Sabbioneta. A document of 27 March 1753 (ASM, Arch. Mag. Com. Nuovo, busta 139, fasc. 9) calls for repairs to a pasetto between the Palazzo Ducale and the Church of the Incoranata. Other passageways to the Castello, the Armeria, and the theater were then ready for demolition. This was brought to my attention by Prof. Kurt Forster.

[41]A two story, arched structure connected the Castello
(now the Palazzo Madama) with the Corte. It is shown in a
1572 view by Giovanni Creigher (A. Peyrot, Torino nei Secoli,
Turin, 1965, nos. 9-10). It was built on the wall system of
the city, facing both town and countryside. When the addition to the city built by Carlo Emmanuele isolated the
Castello, the "galleria" remained. Cf. also A. Peyrot-
V. Viale, Immagini di Torino nei secoli, Turin, 1969, n. 15.

[42]P. Rotondi, The Ducal Palace of Urbino, London, 1969,
49 & 97.

[43]Lecture by C. L. Frommel, Fogg Art Museum, Cambridge,
Massachusetts, Fall 1976. Cf. J. Ackerman, The Cortile
del Belvedere, Rome, 1954, 192.

[44]Ackerman, 1970, 193-194; Frommel, 1973, II, 111, n. 62.

[45]J. Hess, "Die päpstliche Villa bei Aracoeli,"
Miscellanea Biblioteca Hertziana, 1961, 239. A drawing in
the Uffizi (UA 576: 262 mm. X 1040 mm., pen with ink wash
contains the inscription on the reverse "corridoio di s
marco" (Fig. 77). The remainder of the inscription, in a
16th Century hand, is difficult to read, and it is attributed (for no reason) to Peruzzi. It may represent an
idealized scheme for the passageway, for the structure as
built sat at an oblique angle to the San Marco courtyard,
and began its course as an extension to a room in the palace
(not as an independent structure shown in the drawing). The
spacing of the arches does not correspond to the street
pattern shown in older maps of Rome. It was destroyed for
the construction of the monument to Victor Emmanuel.

[46]Ackerman, 1964, 143. It is not improbable that this
project could have stirred the imagination of Cosimo I. Although our knowledge of it comes from a single letter, the
writer is the Florentine Ambassador in Rome, Gianfigliazzi,
reporting to Cosimo. The letter is now in the Florentine
Archives (ASF, Mediceo, 3284). Cf. R. Ancel, "Le palais
du vatican," Revue Benedictine, XXV, 1908, 70.

[47]L. Hautecouer, Histoire du Louvre. Le chateau. Le
Palais. Le musee, Paris, n.d., 22. The exact relationship
between the Corridoio and the passageway connecting the Louvre
with the Tuileries has never been clarified, and it is still
uncertain which came first. In 1563, the French crown purchased land near the Tuileries. On 9 March 1565, a letter
written by Catherine de' Medici proposed a linkage between

the two palaces, and on the same day, Charles IX gave
orders for its construction. This is almost exactly contemporaneous with the construction of the Corridoio, which
began on 19 March 1565. The first stone for the Parisan
project was laid on 11 July 1566, but it was not realized
until the reign of Henri IV.

[48]Venturi, 1938-1940, XI, ii, 426.

[49]This was proposed by Lessmann, 1975, 433, n. 760.
"Se la citta (tutta) in piena fusse divisa da alcuno fiume,
(allora) apresso alle ripe sue o lite so si debba ordinare
piazze overo ample strade con portici continuati, et ap-
presso (di) altri belli palazzi ornati." Francesco di
Giorgio, Tratatto di architettura, (ed. C. Maltese and C.
Maltese-DeGrassi), Milan, 1967, II, 366.

[50]Frey, III, 182.

[51]Barocchi, 1956-1957, 128.

[52]See Appendix III: Chronology. del Badia, 1902, 9,
believes that the vaults were walled up as a response to
crimes which were committed under the arches of the North
Arm.

[53]See Appendix III: Chronology.

[54]Frey, III, 100.

[55]Alberti, De re aedificatoria, II, ii & vi. The
privacy prescribed by Alberti was meant to keep neighbors
from seeing, hearing, or interrupting the daily life of
others. He goes on to say that wise princes have placed
themselves out of the way of troublesome commoners.

[56]This is visible on some of the early views and maps
of Florence (Buonsignori), and it is confirmed by Bellotto's
18th Century View of the Arno (Cambridge: Fitzwilliam Museum
Fanelli, 1973, II, fig. 752).

[57]Lessmann, 1975, 453, n. 759.

[58]E. Nash, Pictorial Dictionary of Ancient Rome,
London, 1968, II, 785 & 790.

[59]W. Braunfels, _Mittelalteriche Stadtbaukunst in der Toskana_, Berlin, 1953, 113-115.

[60]II, 380; G. Carocci, "Breve notizie sopra alcuni antichi edifici," _Bulletino dell' Associazione per la difesa della Firenze antica_, II, 1901, 41-42.

[61]M. Bucci, _I palazzi di Firenze. Quartiere di Santa Croce_, Florence, 1971, 97-105. Although both palaces lack a full documentation of their construction, it is likely that both were constructed in the 16th Century. The Cecchi-Serristori is often attributed to Baccio d' Agnolo, and its design repeats elements from Bramante's Belvedere. It is likely that the present facade was the result of a major renovation of an existing structure, since the rustication at street level is more Quattrocentesque in character. On the other hand, the facade of the Palazzo dell' Antella probably dates from the second half of the 16th Century. Its structure includes fragments of buildings dating back to the 14th Century, and a disc in its lower zone bears the date 1561. Bucci has asserted that Giulio Parigi's responsibilities as "construttore" in 1619-20 were limited to the coordination of artists working on exterior fresco decoration, thus providing a _terminus ante quem_ for its construction.

[62]Del Massaio, topographical view (Fanelli, 1974, II, fig. 388).

[63]Compare Fanelli, 1973, II, fig. 365.

[64]F. Bocchi, _La belleza della città di Firenze_ (amp. G. Cinelli), Florence, 1677, 112-113. By the 17th Century, the Corridoio had become a Renaissance equivalent to a modern cross town expressway. Cinelli notes that it accommodated small carriages holding two people each, all pulled by hand between the palaces. The statements on the Corridor by Baldinucci are not credible (Baldinucci, _Notizie dei Professori di Disegno_, Florence, 1846, II, 498).

[65]D. Mellini, _Ricordi intorno ai costumi, azioni, e governo del Ser. ma. Gran Duca Cosimo I_ (ed. D. Moreni), Florence, 1820, 32-33; quoted in del Badia, 1902, 9.

[66]Mellini, _Ricordi_, 111; quoted in del Badia, 1902, 8.

[67]S. Sinding-Larsen, "A Tale of Two Cities," _Acta_, VI, 1976, 178.

[68]_Ibid._ The Volta dei Peruzzi is a single arch spanning a street and connecting two palaces in the family complex. The Volta dei Girolami consists of a number of Medieval houses acquired by the family of that name and held by them until the end of the 18th Century (L. Ginori-Lisci, _I palazzi di Firenze_, Florence, 1972, II, 597). The actual date of construction for either _volta_ cannot be ascertained.

NOTES TO CHAPTER IV

[1] Frey, II, 523, n. 6. This was brought to my attention by Johanna Lessmann. The courtly entourage left Florence on 30 July, and Vasari was with them for the entire length of the journey. In Venice, Cosimo Bartoli hinted at the existence of the project by referring to "della belleza ordinata di fare alla patria vostra (Vasari's Arezzo) in Frey, II, 536. The only other studies of the Loggia are Viviani-Fiorini, 1941-1942; R. Ramagli, "Le Logge Vasariane," Studi e documenti di architettura, VI, 1976, 87-102.

[2] See Appendix IV: Document I.

[3] The condition of the site is described as "il luogho dove erano le becarie, quali di presente si trovano rovinate" in the Supplica of the Rectors of the Misericordia to Francesco on 20 October 1570 (Frey, II, 539).

[4] Frey, II, 540.

[5] The order of La Casa Pia di Santa Maria di Misericordia was founded in 1264 to perform works of spiritual and corporal mercy under the protection of the Blessed Virgin. (G. Rondinelli, Relazione sopra lo stato antico e moderno di Arezzo (1583), Arezzo 1755, 44). Its work took care of the social needs of the city. It was a religious brotherhood in name only, for the rectors of the Misericordia were chosen every four months by the priors of the city. In 1363, property was purchased on the Piazza Grande for the construction of their offices. The Misericordia functions to this day, but its historical archive which includes a list of all Baptisms in the city is now in the possession of the Fraternita dei Laici, an organization founded in the 19th Century to care for the city cemetery and some agricultural holdings.

[6] A. Angelucci, Memorie per servire di guida al foresterio in Arezzo, Florence, 1809, 102.

[7]M. Salmi, Civiltà artistica nella terra aretina, Novara, 1971, 102, 129; G. Severini, L'architettura militare di Guiliano da Sangallo, Pisa, 1970, 37-42.

[8]Various rebellions occurred in 1409, 1431, 1502, and 1529. This bit of campanilismo is stressed in the only modern history of Arezzo (M. Falciai, Storia di Arezzo, 1928, 185).

[9]Falciai, Storia, 214, quotes Gregorio Sinigardi's diary that on 21 October 1561 the demolition of the Duomo Vecchio was begun with "gran disturbo alla citta a vedere disfare si bello et santo Duomo dove erano molto cose belli, santi, et notabile." The plan of the church is recorded by Giorgio Vasari il Giovane (UA 4788).

[10]Falciai, Storia, 215.

[11]The painting was commissioned in 1478 by the rectors of the Misericordia (III, 215), thus explaining the prominent position of their own palace in the background of the painting. Cf. U. Pasqui, Bartolommeo della Gatta, monaco camaldolese, pittore, ed architetto, Arezzo, 1926, 14-16.

[12]M. Becker, "The Florentine Territorial State and Civic Humanism in the Early Renaissance," Florentine Studies: Politics and Society in Renaissance Florence, London, 1968, 109-134.

[13]R. Burr Litchfield, "Office Holding in Florence after the Republic," Renaissance Studies in Honor of Hans Baron, Florence, 1971, 533.

[14]E. Fasano-Guerini, Lo stato mediceo di Cosimo I, Florence, 1973, 58-59, 94.

[15]A. Anzilotti, La constituzione interna dello Stato Florentino sotto Il Duca Cosimo I de' Medici, Florence, 1910, 71.

[16]The need for rental houses was mentioned in July, 1570 when the rectors petitioned the Priors of the city for permission to build a structure which would be useful to both the city and the confraternity (Appendix IV: Document 2). The construction of the Loggia began on 27 January 1573 (Viviani-Fiorini, 1941-1942, 115) while the location of the Dogana was not debated until 26 January 1575 (Appendix IV: Doc. 12).

[17]See note 5.

[18]B. Pullan, Rich and Poor in Renaissance Venice, Oxford, 1971, 584.

[19]The offices for the Monte were most certainly located at the Western end of the Loggia on the upper floor. Unfortunately, nothing of the original layout survives. In the 18th Century this space was transformed into a theater, and later it was changed again to house the Tribunal Court for Arezzo, a function which it performs to this day. Cf. R. Ramagli, "Le Logge," 95-96.

[20]W. Lotz "Italienische Plätze des 16. Jahrhunderts," Jahrbuch der Max-Planck Gesellschaft, 1968, 41-60.

[21]C. Krinsky, Introduction to Cesariano's de Architectura, (Como, 1521), Munich, 1969.

[22]Lotz, Italienische Plätze," 58.

[23]In 1557, Vasari made some internal renovations to the Palazzo del Parte Guelfa, then seat of the Florentine Monte di Pietà. A balcony was also constructed at the North-east corner of the structure (II, 380). Cf. also G. Carocci, "Breve notizie sopra alcuni antichi edfici," Bulletino dell' Associazione per la difesa della Firenze antica, II, 1901, 41-42.

[24]G. Chierici, Il palazzo Italiano dal secolo XI al secolo XIX, Milan, 1952, I, 130.

[25]Ibid., 135.

[26]Howard, 1975, 48-49.

[27]C. Coleschi, Storia della città di San Sepolcro, Città di Castello, 1886, 153-154. Prince Ferdinand I de' Medici also provided financial assistance for the project. Cf. also Salmi, Civilità artistica, 143.

The building requirements of a Monte di Pietà were not specific to preclude the use of other traditional architectural forms. Very often, a converted palace served the needs of the organization, as was the case for the Monte di Pietà in Rome during the Cinquecento. It did not receive a next structure built to its needs until the beginning of the Seicento. Outside of office space, the only special requirement which a Monte presented was the inclusion of a

chapel in the new building. For Rome, see M. Tosi, Il
sacro Monte di Pietà e le sue amministrazioni, Rome, 1937;
H. Hibbard, Carlo Maderno and Roman Architecture, London,
1971, 218-220. For Naples, see A. Blunt, Neapolitan Baroque
and Rococo Architecture, London, 1975, 45-46.

[28]Rondinelli, Relazione, 96.

[29]J. Paul, Die mittelalticher Kommunalpalaste in
Italien, Diss., Freiburg im Breisgau, 1973; ____, Der
Palazzo Vecchio in Florenz: Ursprung und Bedeutung seiner
Form, Florence, 1969.

[30]C. Krinsky, Introduction to Cesariano's De architectura, passim.

[31]C. Westfall, In This Most Perfect Paradise:
Alberti, Nicholas V, and the Invention of Conscious Urban
Planning in Rome, 1447-1455, University Park, 1974, 99.

[32]Cochrane, 1973, 56-66.

[33]The history of the office of Procurator of St.
Mark's is conveniently summarized in Howard, 1975, 8-10.

[34]Ibid., 11.

[35]Ibid.

[36]Ibid., 25; W. Timofiewitsch, "Zwei Zeichungen
Vicenzo Scamozzis fur die ausaufteilung der Libreria Sanso-
vinos," Mitteilungen des Kunsthistoriches Institut in
Florenz, X, 1961-1963, 209-212.

[37]Lessmann, 1975, 165. In her excellent dissertation
on the Uffizi, Johanna Lessmann devotes an entire chapter
to the history of the administrative office building in Italy
(verwaltungbaues). While much of the same material covered
in her study has been used in this chapter, her focus and
conclusions are somewhat different. In her study, the Uffizi
is presented as an amalgam of three distinct building types
--the communal palace, the row house, and the porticoed
street. In each case, the history of the building type is
traced back to its ancestors in Antiquity or the Middle Ages.
Though this provides an almost complete list of office structures built in Italy during the Renaissance, it fails to make
several important distinctions in form and function. First,
no attempt is made to distinquish buildings which contain

administrative agencies from those which house the entire
governmental structure for a town. Second, no recognition
is given to the fact that most of the projects housing administrative agencies date from the end of the Quattrocento
or the Cinquecento, thus avoiding discussion of the important fact that the construction of the new buildings is related to the development of the regional state in Italy.
A notable omission from her list of projects is reconstruction of the Rialto in Venice. To be sure, the row house
and the porticoed street were important for the formulation
for the Uffizi, but in size and function the communal palace
would surely belong to another category of building. In
addition, no discussion is given on buildings like the Loggia
which contained important administrative offices but which
were primarily rental, income-producing structures. While
Lessmann's study avoids some important questions in the
interpretation of this building type, her discussion of the
material is certainly more insightful and sophisticated than
the recent analysis of the problem by one of the most eminent
scholars in the field of Architectural History (N. Pevsner,
A History of Building Types, Princeton, 1976, 26-28).

[38]R. Cessi- A. Alberti, Rialto. L'isola - il ponte -
il mercato, Bologna, 1934, 36.

[39]Ibid., 44, and Doc. IV, 315.

[40]Ibid., 63.

[41]Howard, 1975, 47-61.

[42]Ibid.

[43]G. Giovannoni, "L'urbanistica italiana nel Rinascimento," Saggi sulla architettura del Rinascimento, Rome,
1935, 286-288.

[44]M. Rosci, "Il Palazzo dei Giureconsulti e l'urbanistica del Cinquecento a Milano," Galeazzo Alessi e
l'architettura del Cinquecento, Genoa, 1975, 493-501. The
Giureconsulti were a private college of nobles who were involved with governmental administration. Like the Misericordia, its origins were in the Middle Ages, but it wielded
its greatest power in local affairs duirng the Cinquecento.

[45]L. B. Alberti, De re aedficatoria (G. Orlandi ed.)
V, iii, 375.

[46]Cessi-Alberti, Rialto, 99. The purpose of the
project was, in the words of a contemporary observer, Marino
Sanudi, "per crescar betteghe et meiorar di fitto la
Signoria."

[47]Ibid., 36. On 12 March 1573, the butchers of Arezzo
petitioned to the city for aid on account of the "gran penuria
di bestiami di macello rispetto alla mala condizioni di tempo"
which resulted in "loro poveria." ASA, Deliberazioni del
Magistro dei Priori e del Consiglio Generale, 1571-1575,
entry for 12 March 1572 (1573).

[48]Rosci, "Palazzo dei Giureconsulti," 494.

[49]C. Frommel, Der Römische Palastbau der Hochrenais-
sance, Tubingen, 1973, II, 331-332.

[50]Howard, 1975, 55-61.

[51]Palladio's unfinished Loggia del Capitanato in
Vicenza was begun in 1571, but years later severe compro-
mises altered its design. (J. Ackerman, Palladio,
Harmondsworth and Baltimore, 1966, 118-123). Bay by bay
construction of loggia-like buildings was not unusual; a
drawing of the Palazzo dei Giureconsulti indicates the unfinished state which Vasari might have seen in Milan during
1566 (Rosci, "Palazzo dei Giureconsulti," fig. 387). In
Tuscany, the Servite Loggia on the Piazza Santissima
Anunziata in Florence was begun in 1516, but it was not completed until the following century (J. del Badia, La loggia
a destra nella Piazza Ssma. Anunziata," Arte e Storia, 1886,
I, 82-83).

[52]Marcia B. Hall, "The Operation of Vasari's Workshop
and the Designs for Santa Maria Novella and Santa Croce,"
Burlington Magazine, CXV, 1973, 207.

[53]Alfonso Parigi the Elder is one of the most ubiqui-
tous yet mysterious figures in Late Cinquecento Architecture
in Florence. Almost nothing is known of his architectural
training except that it could not have been hurt by his
marriage to Ammannati's sister (Thieme-Becker, XXIV, 223).
In the early 1570's he was involved in the construction of
the residences for the Florentine magistracies on the West
arm of the Uffizi (Lessmann, 1975, 96-98), but his most important contribution to the history of Florentine architecture is his Taccuino, a notebook recording his architectural

activity (BNCF, Ms. Palat. 853). The Taccuino records
only part of his contribution to the Loggia which lasted
until his death in 1590. Some of the entries are published (F. Gurrieri, "Il Taccuino del Parigi e loro atti-
vita alla corte granducale, Florence, 1972, 47-50). In
many documents he is referred to as "Alfonso di Santi
Castelli," but weekly payments refer to him as "Parigi."
He is certainly the same architect mentioned in a letter
of 3 July 1573 (Frey, II, 797).

[54]F. Baldinucci, Notizie de' professori del disegno,
Florence, 1773, XVI, 182-188.

[55]The design for the Dogana was ordered from the capo
maestro in 1575 (Appendix IV: Doc. 12), and Parigi was
paid for the design of the houses in 1582 (Appendix IV:
Doc. 14).

[56]Frey, II, 735.

[57]Letter of 11 August 1572 (Appendix IV: Doc. 6).
Also letter of 30 August 1572 (Appendix IV: Doc. 8)

[58]Frey, II, 691.

[59]Frey, II, 735.

[60]Frey, II, 738.

[61]Frey, II, 814-815.

[62]J. Ackerman, "Architectural Practice in the Italian
Renaissance," Journal of the Society of Architectural Historians, XIII, 1954, 8.

[63]F. Malaguzzi Valeri, L'architettura in Bologna nel
Rinascimento, Rocca S. Casciano, 1899, 194; M. Walcher-
Cassoti, Il Vignola, Trieste, 1960, 140.

[64]Lotz, "Italienische Plätze," 58.

[65]C. Smyth, "The Sunken Courts of the Villa Imperiale
in Pesaro," Essays in Memory of Karl Lehmann, Locust Valley,
1964, 310-311.

[66] VI, 326; Smyth, "Sunken Courts," 310.

[67] VI, 325-326. In addition, Ammannati knew Genga and had worked in Urbino, and Raffaellino del Colle, one of Vasari's primary assistants, had worked on the decorations inside the Villa Imperiale (Smyth, "Sunken Courts," 311).

[68] W. Lotz, "Architecture in the Later 16th Century," College Art Journal, XVII, 1958, 85-95.

[69] Cf. FDL, 599, Pigioni, 1574-1596. An idea of the amount of inflation in Tuscany is given by the rent rolls for the property owned by the Misericordia. For instance, a shop under the Loggia which rented for y 22 every three months in 1578 had risen to y 42 in 1595.

[70] P. Tomei, Le case in serie nell' edilizia romana dal '400 al '700," Palladio, II, 1938, 83-92; E. Trincanato, Venezia minore, Venice, 1958; B. Zevi, Biagio Rosetti.

[71] L. Ginori, I palazzi di Firenze, Florence, 1972, I, 138.

[72] C. Elam, "Lorenzo de' Medici and the Urban Development of Renaissance Florence," Art History, I, 1978, 45-60, partic. 49-51. During 1477-1478, the property was acquired from various landholders by Lorenzo de' Medici who intended to build houses there.

[73] Instituto di Restauro dei Munumenti- Facolta di architettura, Firenze, Firenze: Studi e richerche sul centro antico, I, Pisa, 1974, 87; A. Andreucci, Chiesa dalla Nunziata, Florence, 1858, 178.

[74] Elam, "Lorenzo de' Medici," 50-51. Cf. also I. del Badia, "La loggia a destra nella Piazza SSma. Annunziata," Arte e storia, I, 1886, 82-83. The houses were constructed by the Servite order as an investment in real estate. It was begun in 1516, but it was not completed until the following century. The Servite Loggia may have been the most elegant row house project in 16th Century Florence, but the largest and most extensive project of this kind has never been fully investigated. During this period the entire Prato Ognissanti was developed as a residential square. Its designer is unknown, and the only secure date for the project

is 1589 when the South range appears on the Buonsignori
map of Florence.

[75]UA 7868 verso and UA 7869. Pen and ink freehand
with grey wash over ruled pencil. Original dimensions are
unobtainable; the drawings were cut at a later date to be
bound in a sketchbook which is attributed to Antonio da
Sangallo the Elder and Francesco da Sangallo. In style,
the drawing accords with others attributed to Francesco.
According to del Badia, Francesco worked on the Servite
Loggia in the mid 1550's as architect for the completion
of the third and fourth houses of the Servite Loggia.
These drawings were brought to my attention by Caroline
Elam. Allowing for modifications and renovations to the
interior of the Servite houses, the plans closely resemble
the existing building in their dimensions, room layout, and
location of circulation (Istituto di Restauro dei Monumenti,
Facoltà di Architettura, Florence, Firenze: Studi e ricerche
sul centro antico, Pisa, 1974, I, plates LVI-LIX). The
significant differences are the window arrangement on the
mezzanine and the addition of a third window on the piano
nobile. The latter difference would have created an un-
satisfactory relationship with the arcades on the ground
floor. While this drawing might represent an earlier
scheme or be a design for an altogether different project,
it is more likely that it is an incorrect copy of a drawing for the Servite houses.

[76]Elam, "Lorenzo de' Medici," 54-58.

[77]UA 980. Cf. G. Giovannoni, Antonio da Sangallo il
Giovane, Rome, 1959, 43-44.

[78]Sangallo's Casa del Pozzo in Rome is the best example
of the application of a differentiated plan to a small palace
on a narrow site (Frommel, 1973, II, 175-179). For an example of cellular plan row houses in Quattrocento Tuscany,
cf. F. Formichi, "Le dodici case nuove di Pienza," Studi e
documenti di architettura, VII, 1978, 117-128.

[79]FDL, 600, Pigioni dal 1574 al 1596, HH 2, fol. 90.

[80]A. del Vita, Guida di Arezzo, Arezzo, 1953, 38.
This fact is also recorded by a plaque on the facade of the
Loggia.

[81]Quoted in Fanelli, 1973, I, 373. At the Rialto in
Venice, a small wooden and marble loggia was erected to keep

the nobles separate from others who transacted business in the area (Howard, 1975, 49).

[82]M. Villani, _Cronica_, Florence, 1846, VII, 41.

[83]For Barocci's difficulties in executing this commission, see E. Pillsbury and L. Richards, _The Graphic Art of Federigo Barocci_, New Haven, 1978, 58-59.

NOTES TO CHAPTER V

[1]Vasari's collection of drawings has been recon-
structed by L. Ragghianti-Collobi, Il libro de' disegni del
Vasari, 2 vols., Florence, 1974. It is an elaboration and
extension of the reconstruction proposed by O. Kurz,
"Giorgio Vasari's Libro de' disegni," Old Master Drawings,
XII, 1938, 1-15 & 32-44. The question of the influence of
the drawings in the collection on Vasari's architectural
designs has already been touched upon in Chapter II.
Another possibility concerns UA 136, a plan for Bramante's
Palazzo dei Tribunali in Rome which shows the remains of
one of Vasari's characteristic borders along its upper edge.
The Palazzo dei Tribunali, which was supposed to house the
papal Curia, is composed of four duplex house units within
the structure of the palace plan, and its combination of
domestically scaled rooms connected by private staircases
could have easily suggested the plans of the Magistracy
offices (cf. Frommel, 1973, III, fig. 176a). A more elaborate version of the Tribunali plan was drawn by Giorgio
Vasari the Younger as an ideal version of the Uffizi (cf.
Lessmann, 1975, 48-49) for illustration in his La città
ideale.

[2]S. Serlio, Il terzo libro, ed. Venice, 1619, 64
verso.

[3]W. Lotz, "Palladio e ;'architettura del suo tempo,"
Mostra del Palladio, Vicenza, 1973, 30.

[4]J. Ackerman, Palladio, Baltimore and Harmondsworth,
1967, 22.

[5]The style of Vignola's later buildings has been
aptly characterized by J. Coolidge, "Vignola, and the Little
Domes of St. Peter's," Marsyas, II, 67-68.

[6]S. J. Freedberg, Painting in Italy, 1500-1600,
Baltimore and Harmondsworth, 1971, 286.

[7]This subject has never been studied systematically.
The only study (inadequate) is V. Fasolo, "L'architettura

nella opera pittorica di Giorgio Vasari," Atti del XII Congresso di Storia dell' Architettura, Arezzo, 1961 (Rome, 1969), 215-238.

[8]Like the Badia, the church of San Pietro was under the jurisdiction of the Cassinese Congregation. In 1566, Vasari traveled through North Italy and visited San Benedetto al Po with the Abbot of Perugia.

[9]The preparatory drawing for the painting can be dated ca. 1565-1567, according to Borghini's invenzione for the theme. Cf. C. Monbeig-Goguel, Vasari et son temps (Inventaire general des dessins italiens, I), Paris, 1972, 175.

[10]E. Panofsky, "The First Page of Vasari's Libro," Meaning in the Visual Arts, New York, 1955, 214.

[11]Cf. Lessmann, 1975, 171. Though the tomb was not set up in San Pietro in Vincoli until 1544, the architecture of the lower part has been completed in 1513-1514.

[12]The thorny history of the Del Monte tomb has never been clearly elucidated. The best discussion is J. Pope-Hennesey, Italian High Renaissance and Baroque Sculpture, London, 1963, II, 75-76. A preliminary drawing by Vasari in the Louvre presents a more elaborated scheme with different sarcophagi which recall the Medici tombs in the New Sacristy in San Lorenzo. Cf. C. Monbeig-Goguel, Vasari et son temps, 154-155. The drawing itself (Inventaire 2198) is notable for its polychromatic design with yellow, red, and green marble indicated in colored chalk.

[13]J. Coolidge, "The Villa Giulia: A Study of Central Italian Architecture in the Mid-Sixteenth Century," Art Bulletin, XXV, 1943, 193.

[14]Lessmann, 1975, passim. This was first stated by W. Lotz, "Mannerism in Architecture: Changing Aspects," Acts of the XX International Congress of the History of Art, Princeton, 1963, II, 244.

[15]Ackerman, 1970, 291.

[16]The same conclusion is reached by Lessmann, 1975, 191, using additonal examples which this writer believes

to be extraneous. Furthermore, Lessmann's discussion
sources for architectural composition, thus failing to
put them into any larger context of Vasari's architectural style in general.

[17]H. Wurm, Der Palazzo Massimo alle Colonne, Berlin,
1965, 21.

[18]Lessmann, 1975, 187.

[19]G. Algeri, "Alessi in Umbria," Galeazzo Alessi e
l'architettura del cinquecento, Genoa, 1975, 193-194.

[20]Fossi, 1967, 149-155.

[21]Ibid., 93-98.

[22]Ibid., 149-154.

[23]Cochrane, 1973, 121.

[24]Ibid.

[25]Though this structure has not been certified as a
"Vasari" in documents, the attribution is almost universally accepted. Cf. Barocchi, 1956-1957, 128.

[26]A. Mancini, Cortona nel medioevo, Florence, 1897,
329; A. del Vita, "Un opera d'architettura poco nota," Il
Vasari, IV, 1931, 178-188.

[27]Lessmann, 1975, 171.

[28]The only study is M. Labo, "Il Vasari come critico
dell' architettura," Studi vasariani, Florence, 1952, 67-72.

[29]Ackerman, 1970, 37.

[30]S. Serlio, Il terzo libro, 69 recto.

[31]Cf. M. Rosenfeld, "Sebastiano Serlio's Late Style in
the Avery Library version of the 6th Book," JSAH, XXVIII,
1969, 171; Barocchi, 1956-1957, 114, connects the two architects by their common interest in "empirismo."

[32]BNCF, Cod. magl. X, 100; reprinted almost completely in L. Ginori-Conti, L'apparato per le nozze di Francesco de' Medici e di Giovanna di Austria, Florence, 1936.

[33]W. Dinsmoor, "The Literary Remains of Sebastino Serlio," Art Bulletin, XXIV, 1942, 77.

[34]Barocchi, 1956-1957, 113-114, states that Alberti is immediately recognizable among the various components of "la cultura vasariana." Barocchi is correct only to the extent that Alberti's theory reappears often in Vasari's Introduction to the Lives; she fails to note Vasari's sharp criticisms of Alberti's buildings.

[35]A fair evaluation of Vasari's criticisms on Antionio da Sangallo the Younger is C. Wilkinson, "The New Professionalism in the Renaissance," The Architect: Chapters in the History of the Profession, ed. S. Kostof, New York, 1977, 124-160.

[36]Ackerman, 1970, 290.

[37]Freedberg, Painting in Italy, 288.

BIBLIOGRAPHIC NOTE

All works cited in the text are documented in the
Notes, and they constitute a working bibliography of the
buildings under consideration in this study. A full
bibliography on Vasari's architecture was made unnecessary
by the publication of Jacopo Barozzi Il Vignola e gli
architetti del Cinquecento: repertorio bibliografico,
Vignola, 1974. This useful book contains full bibliog-
raphies on all major architects in 16th Century Italy,
and the entry on Vasari is both complete and up to date
on the modern literature. Any bibliography on Vasari's
architecture would duplicate the entries found in the
repertorio, and all readers are directed to that work
for further information. Much of the same information is
also found in the bibliography of Lessmann, 1975. All
major studies are discussed in the introduction to this
thesis.

LIST OF ILLUSTRATIONS

SGF   Gabinetto Fotografico, Soprintendeze
alle Gallerie, Florence

SMA   Soprintendeze ai Monumenti e Gallerie,
Arezzo

SMF   Soprintendenze ai Monumenti, Florence

All other photographs which are not credited are by
the author. In some cases, despite all efforts, it
has been impossible to determine or contact copy-
right holders.

<u>Figure</u>

Figure

Figure

105. Florence: Gianfigliazzi house (Ginori-Conti, *I palazzi di Firenze*).

106. S. Buonsignori. Map of Florence, 1584, detail (SGF).

107. Florence: Via de' Servi row palaces (*Firenze: Centro storico antico*).

108. A. Sangallo the Elder, Florence: Servite Loggia

109. F. Sangallo (?) Florence: Servite Loggia, plan for row house (UA 7868, SGF).

110. A. Sangallo the Younger. Rome: Row house, plan (UA 980, SGF).

111. A. Parigi. Arezzo: Loggia, reconstructed plan of typical row house unit (drawing by Lee Jablin).

112. F. Barocci, Madonna del Popolo, ca. 1575. Florence, Uffizi (SGF).

113. Arezzo: Loggia, Facade from steps of Misericordia's palace.

114. Florence: Uffizi, view towards Palazzo Vecchio.

115. Florence: Uffizi, facade (Lessmann, 1975).

116. Vignola. Bologna: Portico dei Banchi, detail.

117. Vasari. *Saint Benedict and the Angels*. Perugia, San Benedetto.

118. Vasari, *The Incredulity of Thomas*. Florence, Santa Croce (SGF).

119. Arezzo: Duomo, organ loft (Alinari-Editorial Photocolor Archives).

120. B. Peruzzi. Rome: Palazzo Massimo, sketch for facade (UA 128, SGF).

121. G. Alessi. Perugia: S. Maria del Popolo.

122. Sangallo workshop. Vatican: Belvedere, elevation of eastern corridors of lower court (SGF).

ILLUSTRATIONS

Fig. 1

Fig. 3

Fig. 2

Fig. 4

Fig. 5

Fig. 6

Fig. 7

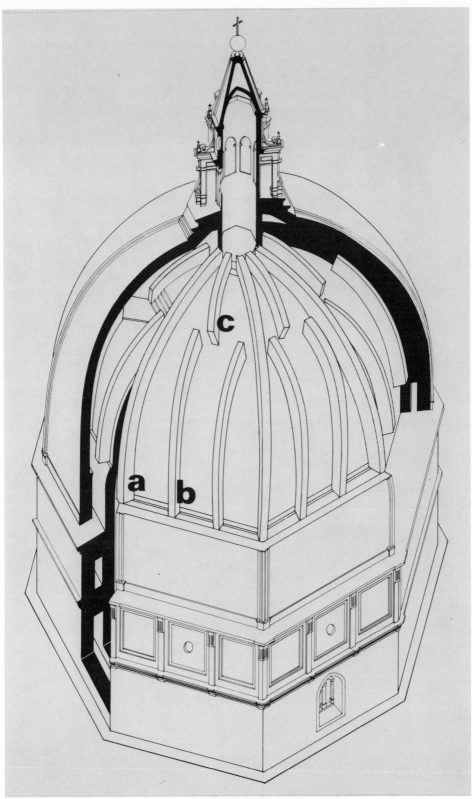

Fig. 8

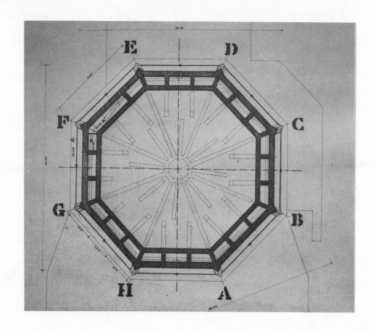

Fig. 9

Fig. 10

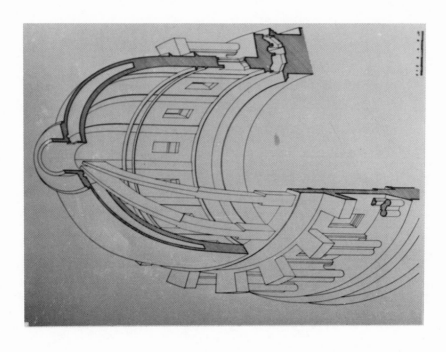

Fig. 12

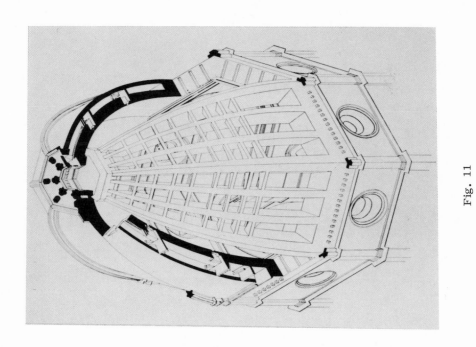

Fig. 11

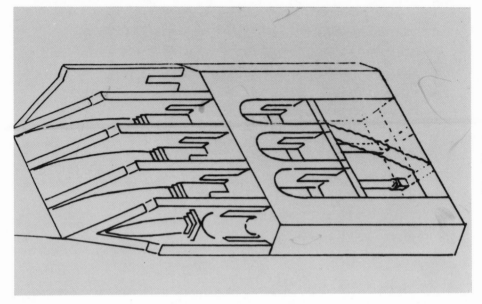

Fig. 14

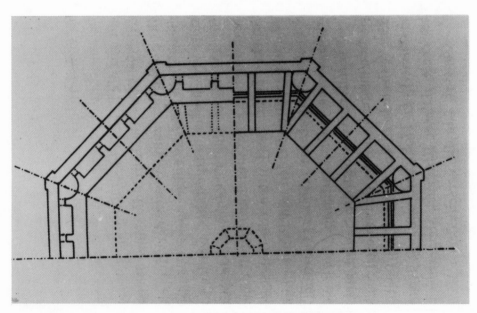

Fig. 13

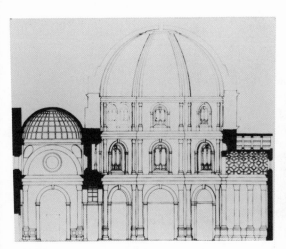

Fig. 15

Fig. 16

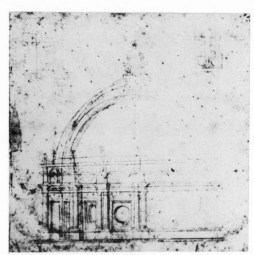

Fig. 17

Fig. 18

Fig. 19

Fig. 20

Fig. 21

Fig. 22

Fig. 23

Fig. 24

Fig. 25

Fig. 26

Fig. 27

Fig. 28

Fig. 29

Fig. 30

Fig. 31

Fig. 32

Fig. 33

Fig. 34

Fig. 35

Fig. 36

Fig. 37

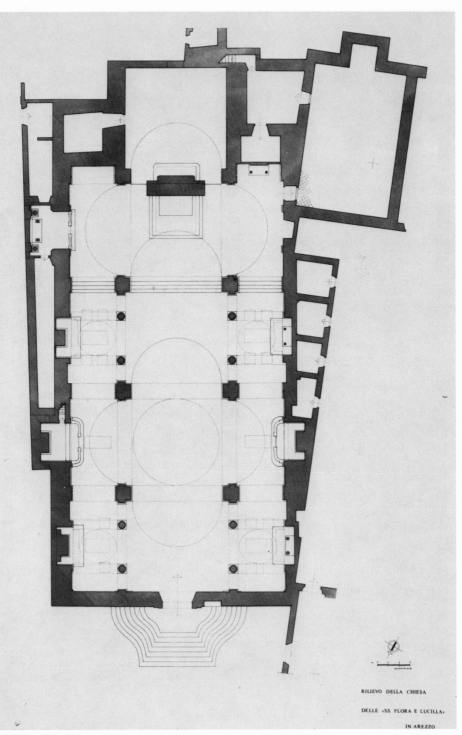

RILIEVO DELLA CHIESA

DELLE «S.S. FLORA E LUCILLA»

IN AREZZO

Fig. 38

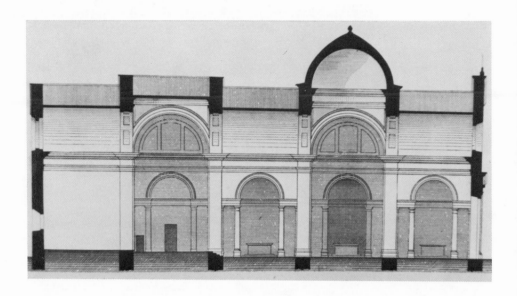

Fig. 39

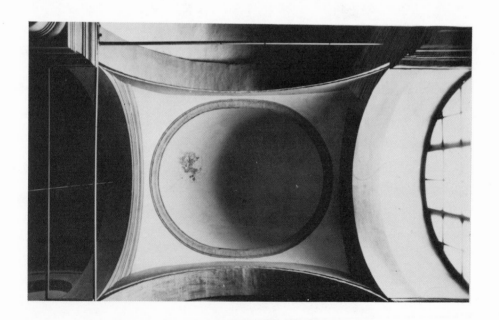

Fig. 40

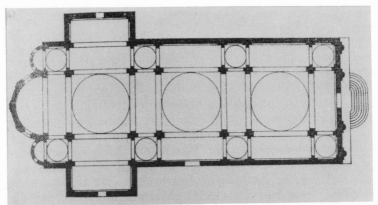

Fig. 41

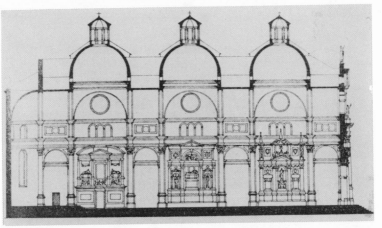

Fig. 42

Fig. 43

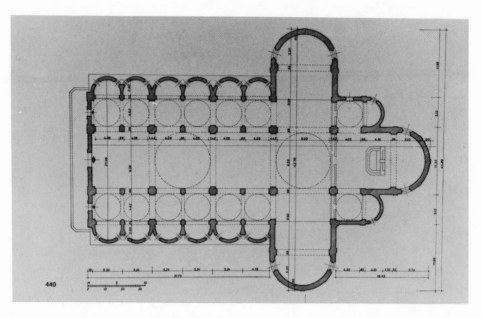

Fig. 44

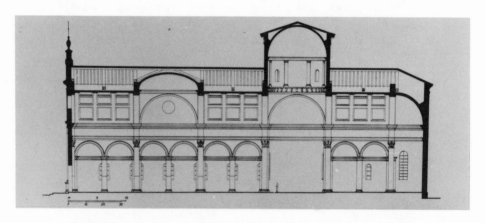

Fig. 45

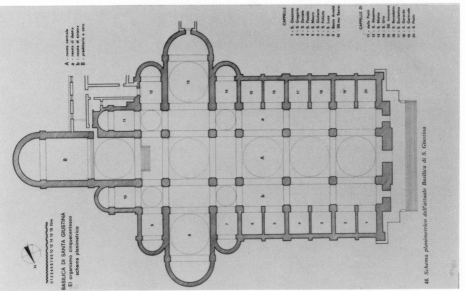

BASILICA DI SANTA GIUSTINA
El organismo cinquecentesco
schema planimetrico

A · navata centrale
a · navata di destra
b · navata di sinistra
B · presbiterio e coro

CAPPELLE
1 - S. Giacomo
2 - S. Gregorio
3 - S. Daniele
4 - S. Paolo
5 - S. Mauro
6 - S. Giuliano
7 - S. Urbano
8 - S. Luca
9 - Beato Arnaldo
10 - SS.mo Sacra

CAPPELLE DI
11 - delle Porte
12 - S. Massimo
13 - S. Urio
14 - S. Felicita
15 - SS. Innocenti
16 - S. Benedetto
17 - S. Gerardo
18 - S. Gertrude
19 - S. Carmelo
20 - S. Pietro

48. Schema planimetrico dell'attuale Basilica di S. Giustina

Fig. 46

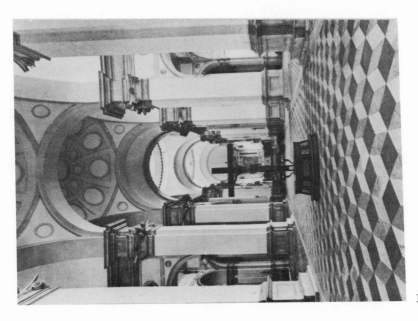

Fig. 47

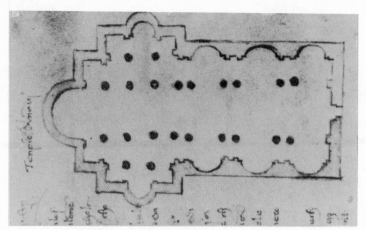

Fig. 48

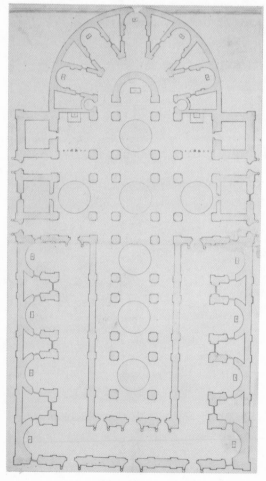

Fig. 49

Fig. 50

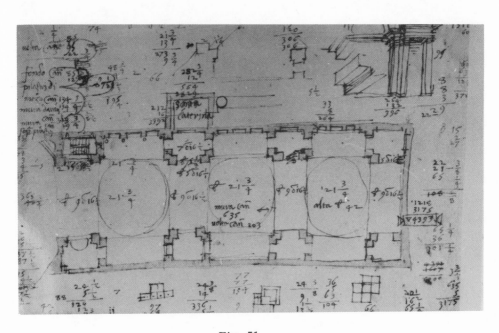

Fig. 51

Fig. 52

Fig. 53

Fig. 54

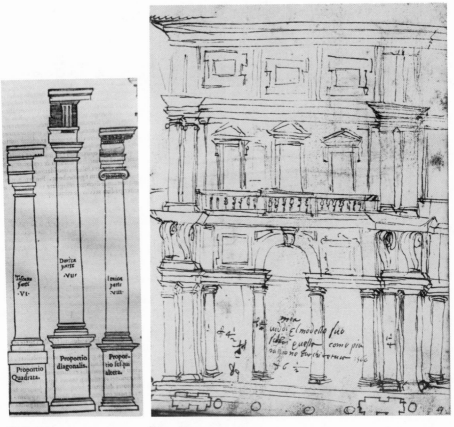

Fig. 55   Fig. 56

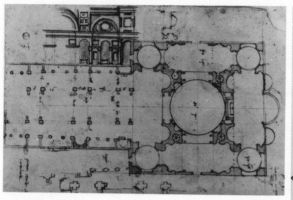

Fig. 57

Fig. 58

Fig. 59

Fig. 60 (fold-out)

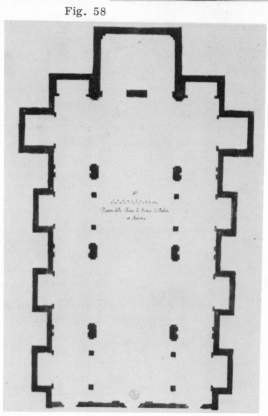

Fig. 61

Fig. 62

Fig. 63

Fig. 64

Fig. 65

Fig. 66

Fig. 67

Fig. 68

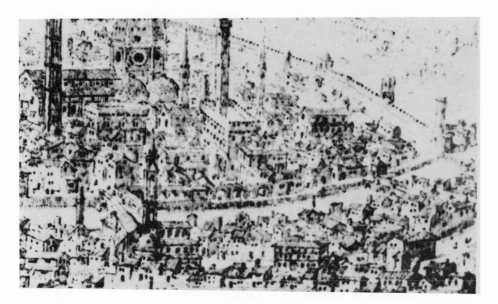

Fig. 69

Fig. 70

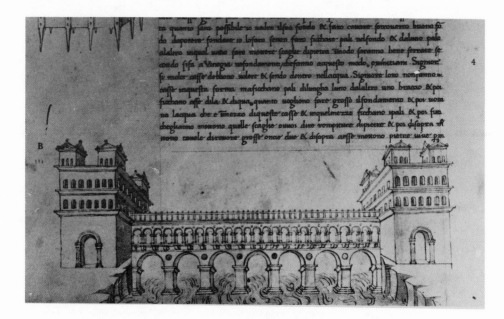

Fig. 71

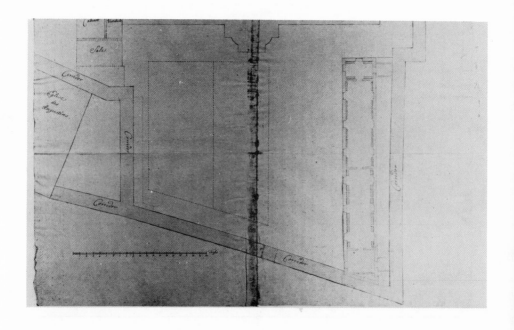

Fig. 72

Fig. 73

Fig. 74

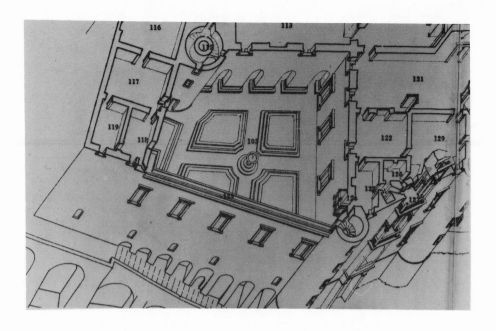

Fig. 75

Fig. 76

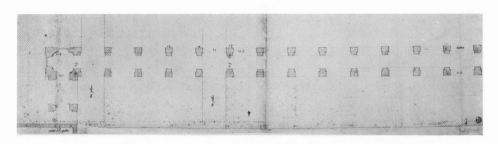

Fig. 77

Fig. 78

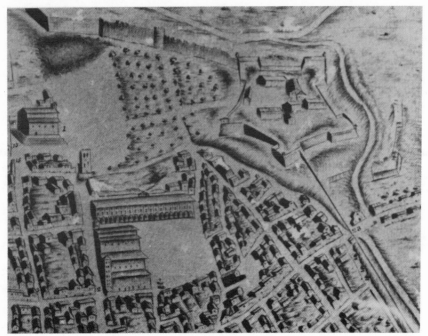

Fig. 79

Fig. 80

Fig. 81

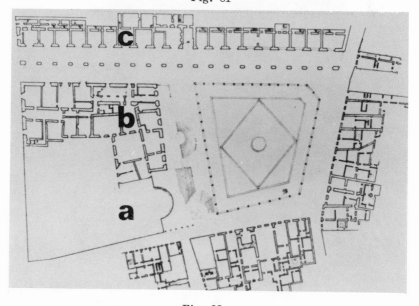

Fig. 82

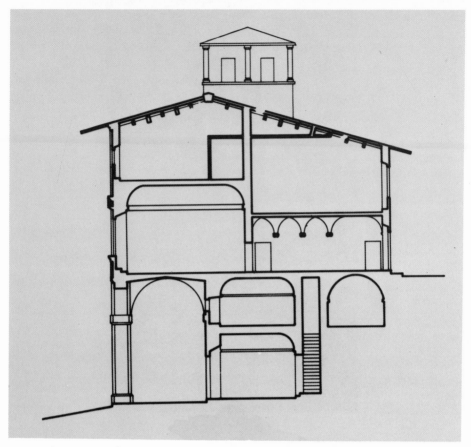

Fig. 83

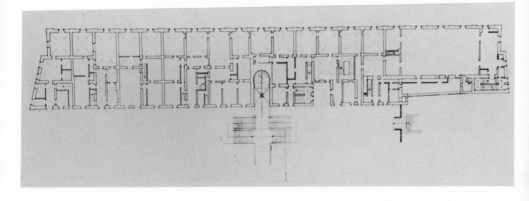

Fig. 84

Fig. 85

Fig. 86

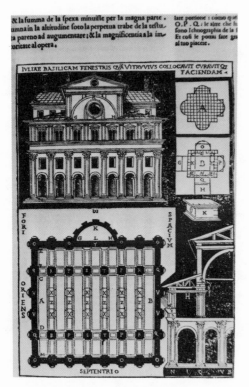

Fig. 87

Fig. 88

Fig. 89

Fig. 90

Fig. 91

Fig. 92

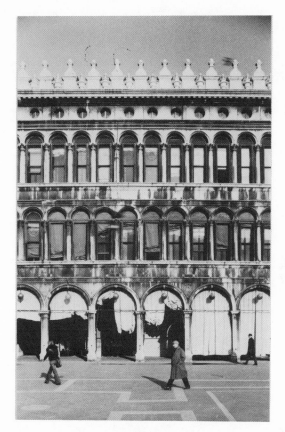

Fig. 93

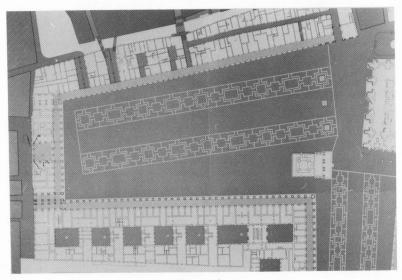

Fig. 94

Fig. 95

Fig. 96

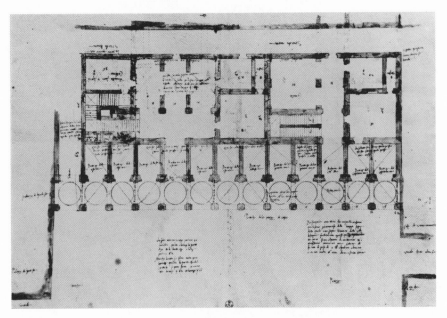

Fig. 97

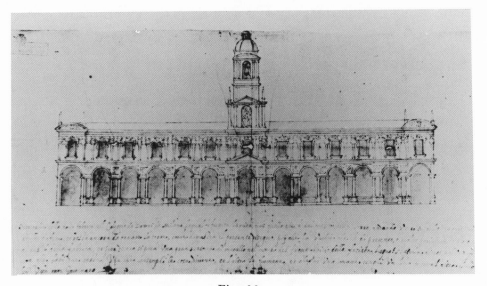

Fig. 98

Fig. 99

Fig. 100

Fig. 101

Fig. 102

Fig. 103

Fig. 104

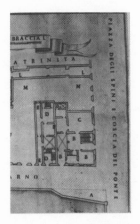

Fig. 105

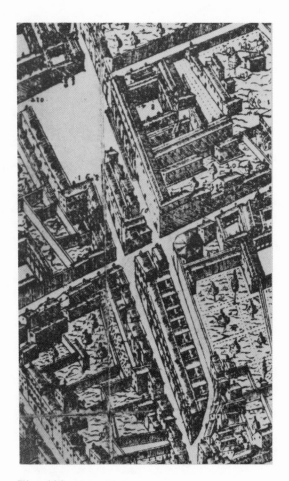

Fig. 106

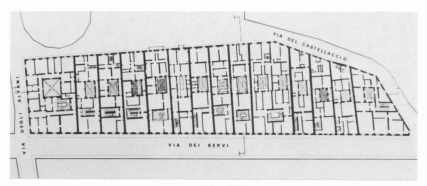

Fig. 107

Fig. 108

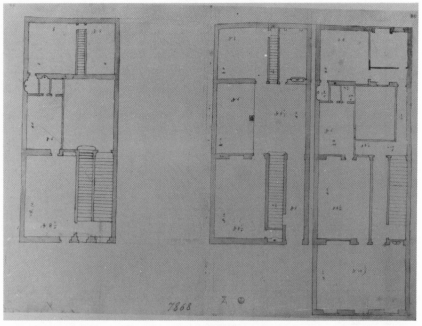

Fig. 109

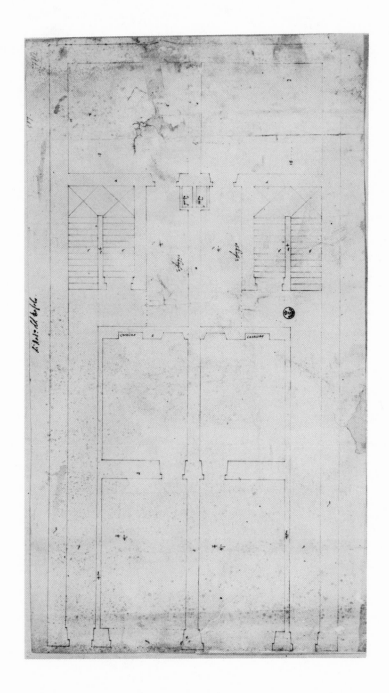

Fig. 110

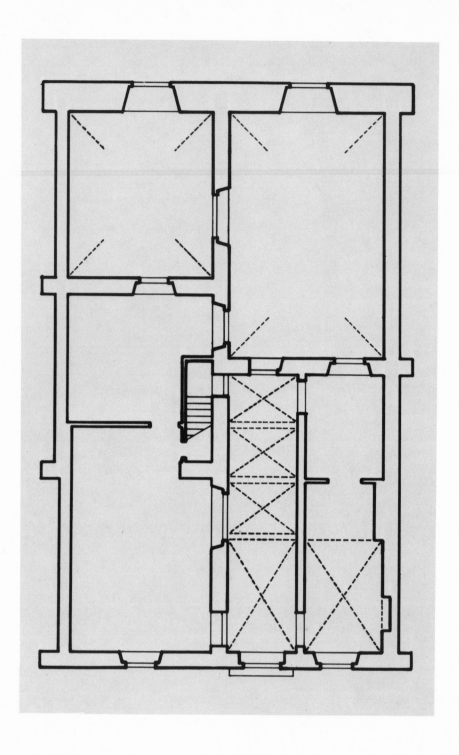

Fig. 111

Fig. 112

Fig. 113

Fig. 114

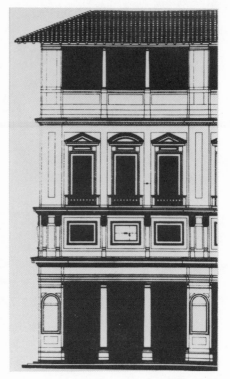

Fig. 115

Fig. 116

Fig. 117

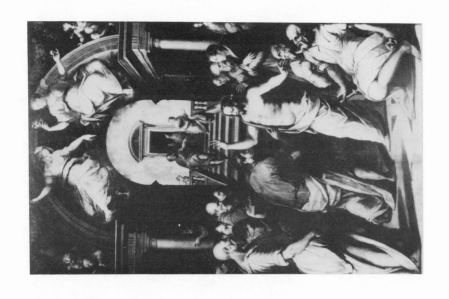

Fig. 118

Fig. 119

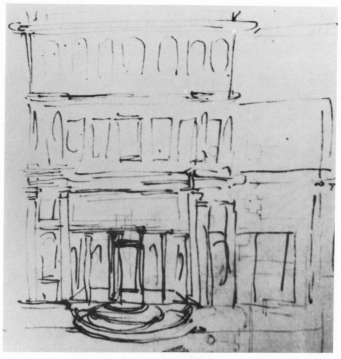

Fig. 120

Fig. 121

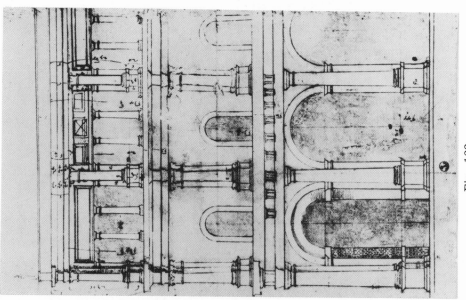

Fig. 122

Fig. 123

Fig. 124

Fig. 125

Fig. 126

Fig. 127

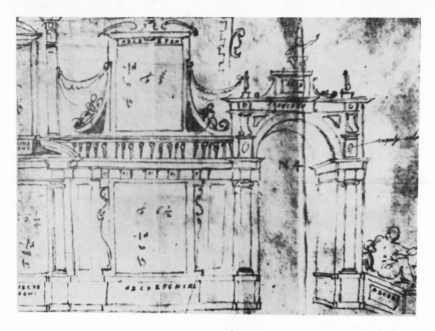

Fig. 128

Fig. 129

Fig. 130

Fig. 131

Fig. 132

Fig. 133

Fig. 134